MY LIFE AS A LONG SHOT

MY LIFE
AS A
LONG SHOT

From Cuba to Rye

VIVIEN GOODMAN MALLOY

Printed in the United States of America.

Designed by Susan Turner

Cover photo by Kathy Landman
Frontispiece: Vivien Matacena, Cuba, 1932

ISBN: 978-1-951568-05-4
Library of Congress Control Number: 2020904544

SMALL
BATCH
BOOKS

493 SOUTH PLEASANT STREET
AMHERST, MASSACHUSETTS 01002
413.230.3943
SMALLBATCHBOOKS.COM

I OWE THE STORY OF MY LIFE TO MY MOTHER. SHE WAS BEAUTIFUL, inside and out. Her soul shone through her eyes and in her touch. She had the softest skin. She was wise and warm and funny. She was a true raconteur, and we all loved listening.

She was the anchor in my life, the one who was always there. I felt it was she and I against the world, facing the uncertain future, until she found her love and her happiness with Andy Goodman. I came along for the ride, and wasn't I the lucky one? When Daddy proposed to Mommy, he said, "Would Vivi like me as a father?" 'Nuff said . . . the die was cast. I was part of the package that Mommy brought to the enterprise. She was the hub of the great big wheel of our family—all the Cubans, all the Goodmans, adoring family and friends galore. It was she who threw open her heart and her arms to us all.

I quote her. I tell her stories. She is so much of who I am. Thank you for my life, Mommy. I hope I made you proud. I certainly tried. *Te mando besitos.*

—VGM,
Rye, New York
Spring 2020

CONTENTS

Nena Mañach as an infant, Madrid, Spain, 1909.

NENA'S STORY

My mother was born in Tembleque, Spain, in the region of Castilla, about an hour outside of Madrid. Her roots and heritage, however, lie in the family's hometown of Ares, in Galicia. An autonomous community in Spain's northwest corner, with rolling green hills that stretch to a rocky coast of swirling fogs and mists, Galicia, often described as "green Spain," is more like Vermont or the British Isles than the Mediterranean shores. It has, in fact, a culture with strong Celtic influences. *Galegos* (Galicians) play the *gaita* (bagpipe), dance jigs, and wear kilts at celebrations and festivals.

My mother's full name was Maria Consuelo Candida Francisca Catarina de Siena Robato y Mañach, but everyone always called her "Nena," which comes from the Galician word for "little girl." Even when she was in her late eighties, Mommy could still sing a Galician lullaby that her father had sung to her.

Nena was born prematurely in April 1909. Not only was she premature . . . she was completely unexpected. My grandmother, Consuelo Robato y Mañach, was due to give birth at the end of

May or early June in 1909, but she went into labor early, at the end of April, while the family was at their vacation home in Tembleque, Spain. A midwife attended my grandmother—my abuelita—and she gave birth to a big, beautiful boy who, sadly, was born with the umbilical cord wrapped around his neck and died at birth. After the stillborn delivery, Abuelita kept complaining of pain. The midwife told her it was just the afterbirth, but it wasn't. It was my mother.

In those days, before ultrasounds, twins were usually a surprise. My mother told me that at birth she was unfinished—she was born with no hair or fingernails and was only as big as a broiler chicken (about three pounds), so tiny that the midwife thought she, too, would die. The midwife put my mother down in between her own breasts to keep her warm and then put a basket lined with wine bottles wrapped in flannel by the fire to warm. She put my mother in this simple incubator and turned her attention back to Abuelita. In spite of her small size, the baby started crying. She lived!

When Nena was born, her father, Eugene, was thrilled to finally have a daughter. He had three older sons—Eugene, Jorge, and Manuel—and had just lost Nena's twin brother in childbirth. In his joy, he threw a baptismal party for her, inviting the whole town of Tembleque.

In 1909, Tembleque was a quiet farming town, but at one time it had been a thriving, riverside commercial stop. However, when the river dried up, so did all of the town's business. There's still the bridge, as well as a lovely Gothic church, but no river.

Tembleque's most famous native son was my uncle Jorge Mañach, Nena's older brother. He became a great statesman, a university professor in Cuba, Puerto Rico, and the United States, as well as an author. He wrote a definitive biography of the Cuban national hero and poet José Martí. A plaque bearing Jorge's portrait and listing his achievements marks the home where he lived in Tembleque.

The first time Nena went back to Tembleque, she told me that the old women who saw her walking down the main street of town went running into the church to pray because they thought she was

Tembleque, Spain, birthplace of Nena.

Harry and Vivien at the door of the church where Nena was
baptized, Tembleque, Spain, 1997.

the ghost of her mother coming back. People said my mother bore a
striking resemblance to Abuelita, but I could never see it. I found
Mommy, with her soft features, to be much more beautiful.

My mother lived in Spain only briefly. When she was very young,
my grandfather decided to move the family to a little island called
Cuba. He had heard of great opportunities there for lawyers, as there
were plenty of rich sugar plantation owners in need of legal services.

In later years, Mommy used to say that sugar was a crop that led to laziness and lack of ambition. You'd plant it, harvest it, get sugar and rum from the stalks, and use the stalks for fuel and feed for the oxen. Then you just sat around for six months until the next crop.

Grandfather Eugene immigrated to Cuba with his family and built a thriving legal firm in Havana. He also became a civic leader among the many Galician émigrés to Cuba and was very instrumental in preserving and celebrating Galician culture in Cuba. The Galician Center in Cuba (Centro Lorico), now named the Gran Teatro de La Habana, was constructed between 1908 and 1915 and was financed by Galician immigrants, who envisioned a place where they could gather to celebrate their heritage through song, poetry, and dance. In recognition of Eugene's involvement, a statue was erected in his honor when the center was completed.

Sadly, Grandfather Eugene died suddenly while making a speech, when Nena was only five years old. He was in his forties or fifties. He was brought home on a stretcher, and the men bearing him told my grandmother that he had fainted. Mommy later told me that Abuelita lifted the white sheet covering her husband, saw his face, and said, "No, he's dead. I know he's dead."

The Galician Center (Centro Lorico) in Havana, Cuba (now the Teatro de La Habana).

Although he died when she was quite young, Nena remembered her father very well. Eugene really spoiled his youngest child and only daughter. One day at lunch, when my grandfather was ladling out soup as he did every day, my mother said that she didn't like the soup and wanted alphabet soup. My grandfather said to my grandmother, "You heard her—give the child what she wants." An indulgent father to his daughter, to be sure.

In contrast, Abuelita had always been very stern with Nena. I think Abuelita was trying to prepare my mother for the uncertainties of life, which Abuelita knew well, but I also feel that there may have been a rivalry for Eugene's attention. Abuelita may have resented Nena for being the center of his affections.

My mother recalls that on the day of Eugene's death, she was riding her tricycle on the patio when her mother came up to her and told her that her father had died. Abuelita said that from that moment forward, things would be different. From then on, she would have to do what her mother told her, no questions asked.

It was in this time of tragedy that Abuelita, then in her thirties, demonstrated her prodigious strength of character. Suddenly the head of a household with three teenage sons and a young daughter, she navigated moving her grieving family forward.

Education had always been the family mantra, and Uncle Jorge, a brilliant scholar, had been accepted at Harvard University. Within months of Eugene's death, Abuelita had made arrangements to move the family to Cambridge, Massachusetts, where Jorge would attend Harvard, his brothers would attend Boston Latin School, and Nena would attend Sacred Heart Academy.

They adjusted to life in Cambridge, but it wasn't easy for Abuelita and her children. With all the boys in school, the family lived off the monthly insurance checks from Grandfather Eugene's life insurance policy. Each month, when the check came, Abuelita would take the subway downtown with my mother and Manuel, the youngest but strongest son. They would buy food supplies for the month, always including a peck of potatoes, which, at ten to fifteen pounds, Manuel would have to carry.

The three of them shopped for clothes at Filene's Basement. Abuelita, ever practical, would buy Nena's clothes a size or two larger than needed, so they would last. On one shopping trip, Nena, stylish even as a child, saw a coat with a fur collar and cuffs (probably rabbit). Although she wanted that coat badly, Abuelita bought a scratchy woolen brown one—a size or two too large—as well as a pair of large shoes that she would stuff with tissue in the toes until my mother grew into them.

Abuelita was a fanatic about cleanliness. Mommy would quote her mother years later, saying, "Soap doesn't cost much. It doesn't matter if you are poor, you can always be clean." Mommy told me once that she came into the house and there was Abuelita, on her hands and knees, scrubbing the floor to show the maids how it was done. She ended up cleaning the entire floor.

When the family had been living in Cuba, they would bring maids over from Spain. Much like the young women who came from Ireland and England to America to work as maids, young women from Spain came to Cuba. Many of these young women had long, fancy names, but to Abuelita they were all "Maria." In Europe, these "Marias" were used to bathing once a week. Well, that wouldn't do in tropical Cuba—Abuelita made them all bathe twice a day.

While the family was in Cambridge, a very wealthy doctor—a member of the Cushing family—began courting my grandmother. Their attachment got very serious, so Abuelita wrote to her two sisters, Cuca and Edelmira, asking them to come to America to meet him. Even though she was a widow raising four children, she wanted their opinion.

Once her sisters arrived in Cambridge, a date was set for them to meet Abuelita's suitor. At the appointed hour, the whole family was awaiting the doctor's arrival for tea in the front parlor. Mommy told me that she was going crazy, trying to sit still and wait while dressed up in starchy petticoats. Her brothers were also dolled up in their suits.

The coach drove up, and the doctor's maid was ushered into the parlor. She said, "Mrs. Mañach, I'm very sorry to tell you that Dr. Cushing has died." Apparently, he'd had a heart attack.

Abuelita thanked the maid and sent her sympathy to the family. Then, she turned to her two sisters and said, "That's it! It wasn't meant to be. I will never marry again. Eugene was my only love. So let's have some brandy."

Like so many difficulties before this, Abuelita handled this latest twist of fate with clear-eyed strength. Her family had no money—the boys were on scholarship. Marriage to Dr. Cushing would have meant a lovely, comfortable life for all of them forever. Abuelita rose to meet the challenge of an uncertain future with fortitude, and my mother took this all in.

In spite of their budget struggles, Abuelita was generous to all around her. When she got her monthly insurance check, she would use some of the funds to host a Sunday open house for Spanish-speaking foreign students. She would cook up *ropa vieja*—Cuban meat stew—along with black beans and rice. Everyone was welcome to come and have a good meal.

After the boys graduated from high school and college, Abuelita and her children returned to Cuba to be with the rest of their family. Nena was twelve years old when the family returned to Havana, and she lived there through her teen years and into her early twenties.

Back in Havana, Nena was enrolled in Sacred Heart boarding school. She was a handful from her first day there and loved to test the rules. One story I always enjoyed involved Mommy's dorm mate, a real Goody Two-Shoes. One year, Nena wanted to wear the pale blue sash of Saint Mary for the May Day celebration. She worked very hard, was very good, and did everything right—which was not her nature—but Goody Two-Shoes got the blue sash.

Nena just couldn't let this pass. At the school, they had chamber pots underneath their beds, and Nena put boric acid in her rival's potty, so when she went to the bathroom in the middle of the night, bubbles and smoke erupted. The petrified girl started screaming, and the nuns raced to comfort her. Nena just giggled in her bed, enjoying her little taste of revenge.

All the girls at school were required to go into the garden to meditate—not Mommy's strong point. Bored, she would walk around the garden, pick ripe mangoes, and hide them in her bloomers and blouse for a secret snack later. Of course, the nuns saw her and she always got into trouble.

Although habitually on the wrong side of the nuns, Nena, to her amazement, was picked one day to bring tea to the Mother Superior's parlor, where she was entertaining a guest. The tea tray was huge, with a full silver tea service, dishes, and goodness knows what else. She carried it carefully down the halls and got to Mother Superior's front parlor, only to find the door shut.

She tried to subtly hit the door with her hip, but in spite of her care, everything on the tray rattled. When she finally got the Mother Superior's attention and the door was opened, she saw that the guest was a very handsome young man. Nena couldn't take her eyes off of him. The guest was actually the Mother Superior's nephew Titi, who would become a great family friend. To this day, I always remember Mommy's advice, "Never look at the tray or full glass you're carrying—just keep looking straight ahead and you won't spill a drop!"

All the students at Sacred Heart had to go to confession every week. One day in chapel, before confession, Nena whispered to somebody that the priest reminded her of a meatball. A nun overheard her and insisted that she confess what she had said to the priest. Mommy told me that when she went into the confessional she said, "Bless me, Father, for I have sinned. It has been one week since my last confession, and I have to confess that I called you a meatball." The priest opened the door of the confessional and ran out, laughing. Mommy told me that when the nun asked him if all was well, he told her that Mommy had gotten it right—that he did look like a meatball.

These stories say so much about Mommy—she was *simpática*. Everybody was drawn to her, not just because she was beautiful, but also for her fun-loving spirit and generous nature. She was a reflection of the sunny Cuban culture. She said that living in Cuba at that time was like living in paradise—beautiful weather and surroundings and wonderful people. Cuba was different from most places then; it was very precious. She always told me that in Cuba, you didn't have to have a lot of money, as long as you were *simpática*. That, and being from a good family, would get you invited to all the good parties.

In 1928, when Nena was eighteen, Calvin Coolidge, then president of the United States, visited Cuba. Because she spoke English so well, Nena's school selected her to greet the president on his arrival in Havana. "Welcome to our island of Cuba, Mr. President," she said, as she handed him a bouquet of flowers. When he asked her where she learned to speak such beautiful English, she told him, "In Cambridge, Massachusetts."

She was seated next to the president at a luncheon given in his honor at the home of a wealthy sugar plantation owner with a large extended family. At one point, the president looked down the long table of guests and asked her if everyone was related. Indeed, they were.

Nena was tall for her generation, with beautiful skin and features, a good figure, and lovely legs. She was very *presumida*—not vain, but particular about looking good and dressing well. She had natural style and great taste. She used to say, just walking down the streets of Paris, you could see the salesgirls or the office staff wearing simple black dresses enhanced by a lovely scarf or a pin. Simple, but they had style—and so did Nena.

She took great care of her appearance, even if she was just going to the beach. She wore white dresses and always put on makeup. She would enhance her moles by dipping the blunt end of a hatpin in mascara and darkening them into "beauty spots." As a child, I loved watching her at her dressing table. To this day, I could tell you every move: lipstick, powder, rouge, and her signature moles.

If she was going to a big party, she would pick out a dress from the pages of *Vogue Paris* or some other fashion magazine and bring it to Tia Cuca, Abuelita's sister. Tia Cuca, a masterful seamstress, would whip up a perfect replica of the dress for my mother.

Nena used to say that in Cuba, all you needed was somebody with a guitar and a couple of people and you had a party. She played the guitar a little herself, and she was also a wonderful dancer and loved to dance. She played tennis a little, and even rode polo ponies when her friends invited her. But these pursuits were not passions; they were more like adventures.

When she moved to New York, I think she realized that people tended to be more serious about their pursuits. Later on in life, she became a golf nut. At dinner every night, we'd have to listen to a hole-by-hole description of her round that day at the Westchester Country Club. Daddy would just roll his eyes in amusement. But regardless of her newfound passion for golf, my mother didn't believe in raising a sweat. She couldn't understand why people would run and jog, remarking, "I have never seen a jogger smiling."

She was a good eater and loved simple food, particularly Cuban food. Even though her married life was grand, complete with cooks and staff, she'd ask to be served what they were eating in the kitchen. In the city, she'd have her chauffeur park so he could buy hot dogs from the Sabrett vendors on the street—one for her and one for him.

Although she loved to eat, she did not cook much. Abuelita had discouraged Nena from cooking when she was a young girl in Cuba. Her family, though not wealthy, could afford a maid and a cook, and Abuelita didn't want Nena in the kitchen. But whenever my mother had the chance to cook, she certainly had fun with it. As we were growing up in Rye, Mommy was famous for her "tilted cakes." No matter what she did, all of her cakes turned out lopsided. She bought a new stove and had the kitchen floor calibrated, but somehow her cakes were still "tilted." Delicious, lopsided, and always good for a laugh.

That was Mommy, especially as a young woman in Cuba—she enjoyed everything about life. "Don't be so serious," she'd say. "There's time to be serious, but not now. Before you know it, you won't be able to travel or have fun. So just enjoy."

NENA'S FIRST MARRIAGE

My biological father, Rafaele "Lello" Matacena, was Italian and the eldest son and heir of a prominent family from Naples. He was an accomplished pianist—a child prodigy—and wanted to be a conductor, but his father insisted he pursue an engineering degree. After Lello graduated from the University of Padua with a degree in civil engineering, his father sent him all over the world to tour the sites of important engineering projects. He was supposed to join the family engineering firm after his world tour.

One of the stops on this grand tour was a visit to Cuba, where one of Lello's uncles, Orestes Ferrara, was an important lawyer,

Rafaele "Lello" Matacena. *"To my Nenaella. Lello, Miami, 9 Nov., '31."*

journalist, and statesman who later served as ambassador to the United States. It was on this trip to Havana, when he was touring the site of a tunnel that was to be built under the harbor, that he met and fell in love with Nena. She was invited to a dinner party at his uncle's home, and Lello was seated next to her. The story that my mother told me of their meeting is etched in my memory. She said that during the meal, he turned to her and said, "Senorita, you are so beautiful, but so sad." That opening led to Nena's telling him the cause of her *tristezza*. She had been dating a man whom her family did not approve of, and she was not allowed to communicate with him. She wanted to write him, and Lello offered to take the message. Ultimately, she fell in love with the messenger.

She was in love with Lello, but she told me that he was very possessive and jealous of her. He did not want to share her with the group she went around with, which included her cousins as well as friends. He wanted her eyes just on him. Abuelita was scared of him in a way. Scared for Mommy.

After their courtship, they went to New York City, where Nena's brother Jorge and his wife, Margot, lived while Jorge was teaching at Columbia University. Lello and Nena were married in Saint Patrick's Cathedral in 1932. Nena adored her brother and asked Jorge and Margot to be witnesses to the marriage ceremony, and they signed the wedding certificate.

Shortly after the wedding, Nena and Lello parted for what both thought would be a short time. Nena boarded a train for Miami and then went back to Cuba, and Lello sailed back to Italy to smooth things over with his Neapolitan family. His mother had warned him that if he married this girl from Cuba, she would take a knife and kill herself. As the oldest son in his family, Lello was expected to marry a very wealthy girl that his parents had chosen, the daughter of friends. Marriage to Nena, an unknown girl from Cuba, would wreck all their plans. Not surprisingly, when Lello got back to Italy, he faced a very irate mother and father.

I believe that Lello had the best of intentions when he left for

Italy. He had to go back and smooth things over, because if Nena had gone to Naples as his new bride, it would have been horrible for her. The last time they saw each other was at the train station in Manhattan. Lello had a bunch of violets, and he tore the bunch in half, giving one half to my mother and keeping the other half for himself, saying, "Before these are withered, we will meet again."

Lello promised to send for Nena when things calmed down, but in the end, it didn't work out, and my father was never able to smooth things over with his family. There was hell to pay with his parents, and he was threatened with disinheritance and the loss of his position in his father's engineering firm.

Lello's mother, my grandmother Filomena Matacena, was an extremely strong woman. Her family, the Salsis, were a very wealthy, "old money" family, but her husband Gennaro's family, the Matacenas, had worked for their fortune, founding a civil engineering firm in Naples. Between both families, they had plenty of money and a beautiful home, but Gennaro loved to gamble. According to family lore, one day after lunch, he left in his coach, complete with horses and footmen, and several hours later, he returned home walking. He had gambled everything away.

After the confrontation with his parents, Lello went to Paris and tried to make it on his own as a civil engineer, but he fell into a deep depression. He then returned to Italy and rejoined the family's engineering firm. Although he wrote letters to Nena and wanted to find a way to be together, they were never reunited.

Nena was also depressed and unhappy, of course, but like her mother before her, she had to be strong. She was twenty-three and expecting a child. When my mother's family discovered that she was pregnant, and with Lello back in Italy, her brothers wanted her to get an abortion. She refused. I never dared to ask her how she or Abuelita felt about it.

My uncle Jorge wrote to Gennaro, telling him that Nena was pregnant and demanding that the Matacena family provide some support.

Nena and Lello in Cuba, 1931.

My grandfather responded, by letter, saying that they weren't going to do anything, that it was Lello's concern.

Nena accepted this news. She didn't go to Italy on her own; she was too scared. She was very young, and she knew that she would be there without family to comfort her, and with a mother-in-law who would have been a terror.

Some people said that Lello abandoned my pregnant mother, but I refuse to believe that it was that simple. I feel that he was trapped by his life's circumstances, that he loved my mother but didn't know a way out. I guess he was weak, but I forgive him.

AFTER LELLO LEFT

I know my mother was very dismayed when Lello didn't return; everyone was. To be abandoned by the man she loved! The whole thing was a scandal. Even though my mother came from a very good family—and in Cuba, that was what counted—they didn't have very much money, so she had to go to work. With her background, she was able to get highly desirable positions. She became secretary to the president of Cuba and, later, social secretary to the president's wife.

After my birth, on August 14, 1932, we lived with Abuelita in her house in the El Vedado section of Havana, a lovely upper middle class neighborhood. Our home was built in the typical Spanish style: one floor, white limestone, with a tile roof. The main entry had a tall, wrought iron gate that opened to two paths bordered by greenery, which then led to the first patio. This first patio was open to the sky and had a covered walkway with many rooms off of it, all of which had high ceilings and ceiling fans. The second patio—the "*tras* patio," as my mother called it—was surrounded by the bedrooms, dining room, kitchen, and servant quarters.

Since my mother had to go to work, Abuelita stepped in to care for me. My uncles, who lived nearby, adored me and often

Nena holding Vivien, Havana, Cuba, 1932.

Abuelita and Vivien, age three, in their El Vedado home in Havana.

argued over who would take me to the park. After our visits to the park, with its lake and ducks, we would often go to El Carmelo, an ice-cream shop a few blocks from our house. My favorite ice-cream dish was *helado tostado*, or toasted ice cream. It was made with any flavor ice cream and a marshmallow topping, which was quickly broiled and then served at the table all brown and toasty.

Abuelita's sisters, my great-aunts, also lived in Havana. Edelmira was the wealthiest, and she lived in a grand mansion. She had many children, many nannies, and few worries. Abuelita was the second wealthiest and was strong, smart, and wise. The third sister, Tia Cuca, was a beauty with a heart of gold. Mommy adored her.

Along with the help of my nanny, Tata, Abuelita essentially raised me during my early years. She treated me with much affection and I loved her dearly, but she was tough—her nickname was The Colonel. She called the shots, including her determination that, although born a lefty, I become right-handed. My mother told me later that Abuelita would tie my left hand to the high chair to force me to use my right.

Even though she was firm and strict, Abuelita was also loving and so much fun, with a wonderful sense of humor. I remember sitting on a stool in the bathroom, listening to her and watching while she bathed. She'd make a joke when you least expected it. One time, I was sitting at her feet on our porch as she fanned herself gracefully with the little heart-shaped fan she always carried. (All the women in Cuba carried fans; it was very Spanish—a way to stay cooler and to enhance their hand gestures.) I asked her, "What's for dinner?"

"Fly soup," she replied, without missing a beat. "There are so many flies around here, I've made you fly soup for dinner." And I believed her.

Another funny story I remember has to do with my love for plants and flowers, which showed itself early on this lush island. Almost every day, a flower vendor walked by our house. When I was about three, I would stand in the front garden behind the wrought iron gate and call to the vendor, *"Psst, psst! Flores! Florero!"* I ordered sweetheart roses and baby's breath (my favorite combination) and brought them inside and put them in a vase on the dining room table.

No one knew who had ordered the flowers at first. Then, at the end of the month, Mommy got a bill from the florist. She asked him who had ordered all of these flowers, and he said, *"La senorita."* Me! I learned all about a charge account early in life. To this day, I have a strong affinity for flowers and am a passionate gardener, maybe from my Italian ancestry.

We lived next door to a family with several children. I played with them and frequently shared a glass of milk or two with them at their house. I began to refuse to drink the milk at home, saying that the neighbors' milk tasted better! I didn't realize that my mother was ordering my milk from Miami since she didn't trust the quality of Cuban milk. Unbeknownst to me, she would bring my milk to

Nena and her cousins in Varadero, Cuba. Left to right: Elsie, Carmela, Nena, Puchie, and Clara.

the neighbors' house so I would drink it there. She told me that those neighbors kept a photo of me on their piano.

My mother was wonderful and kindhearted, but she did not know how to handle the crises that come with raising small children. My abuelita was more experienced and would often come to the rescue. Once, when I rocked back too far in my high chair, I fell backward and Mommy fainted. Abuelita handled my spill. Another time, I was choking on a candy and Mommy didn't know what to do. A neighbor turned me upside down and shook me until I coughed it up.

In spite of her failed marriage and an infant to support, Mommy was still the belle of the ball in Cuba. If you were young and pretty like she was, you got invited everywhere. Initially, Mommy declined all of the invitations to luncheons, dinners, and parties and instead came straight home from work. But Abuelita urged her to socialize. "You're young. Go out!" she'd tell her.

Cuba drew many young Americans to its shores, not only to visit its gorgeous beaches, but also to enjoy the wonderful music and beautiful people. One of these young Americans, named Mendel—the scion of his family's specialty store—sailed his yacht down to Cuba to visit friends. Sailing with him was another scion of a family-owned luxury retailer, Andrew Goodman. Once they arrived in Cuba, Mendel invited several guests, including my mother, to join him for a luncheon and swimming party on the boat. It was at that party that my mother met Andy, the heir to the Bergdorf Goodman department store in Manhattan and one of New York's most eligible bachelors.

I heard in later years that my mother wore a beautiful white bathing suit on that day that showed off her gorgeous legs, and Andy was entranced immediately. Mommy told me that she noticed him, too. He was very handsome, and very well-spoken. When she first saw him, he was talking to somebody and describing a hat. His gestures were, at that moment, somewhat effeminate. Mommy couldn't hear the conversation, but from what she saw of his gestures she thought he was gay. What a shame, she thought, such a nice, handsome young man.

This misunderstanding was quickly corrected, and he called her after the yachting party and asked her to dinner. But when the evening of their dinner date arrived, she forgot. She was tired and had gotten ready for bed after dinner. Abuelita asked her if she had any plans. "No, nothing," Mommy said. Andy thought she stood him up. It's a miracle they got together at all. Once this second misunderstanding was rectified, their long-distance romance began.

Andy went back to New York, calling Mommy from time to time or sending her telegrams. In those days there was no voice mail, so they needed to coordinate when they would talk on the phone. On one such occasion, my mother wasn't home at the appointed hour, and Andy was upset. When they spoke again, she explained that there had been a hurricane and she was forced to stay overnight at a friend's. Andy was still doubtful until he saw an article about the hurricane in *The New York Times*. That was the proof he needed. For Andy Goodman, it didn't happen unless it was printed in *The Times*.

Their courtship, though not long, was complicated. I was at least two when they began dating. Andy had a sister, Ann, who would visit Havana regularly. I remember Ann taking me to the park to feed the ducks.

Once Mommy and Andy realized that their romance was getting serious, they decided that my mother should move to New York so that they could see each other more often. But because Mommy's relationship with Andy was secret at this time—she couldn't let it be known that she was dating the son of the president of Bergdorf Goodman—I stayed in Cuba with Abuelita.

Andy got Mommy a job at a couturier as a fashion model manager. She would sit at a desk in the stockroom and coordinate the models showing clothes to customers.

She lived in an apartment by the elevated subway train, the "El." It was so close to the tracks that the whole place would rattle and shake when the train went past. One day, Andy arrived and knelt before Mommy, intending to propose. He tried once, twice, three times, but trains roared by each time, interrupting the tender moment. Finally, he said to Mommy, "Would Vivien like me for a father?" Mommy joyously accepted.

They decided to get married in Cuba. My Goodman grandparents did not attend the wedding; bad weather prevented them from getting to Havana for the ceremony. However, they had already met Mommy, at the Kentucky Derby in May of that year.

Andy had invited Mommy to come to the Derby, but she had nothing to wear to such an event, so she went to El Escorial, a store in Havana, and bought a dress and hat. When she got off the train from Miami in Kentucky, she looked gorgeous. Andy was busy placing bets for his friends who were back in New York, so her future father-in-law picked her up at the station. Grandfather asked Mommy where she got her beautiful outfit. When she told him, he replied, "If anyone asks you, you got it at Bergdorf's!"

For me, the news of the marriage came suddenly. I was three at the time, and I remember being at a beautiful estate in Cuba with my nanny, Tata. It was a *finca,* a fancy ranch estate, outside Havana, owned by an American couple named Kaffenburg. Mommy was all dressed up, looking especially beautiful that afternoon, when she came to me and said, "You know Andy? My friend Andy? Well, we're going to get married this afternoon. You stay here and play with your toys." Then she continued, "But when we come back, your name is not going to be Vivien Matacena anymore; it's going to be Vivien Goodman. Can you say it? Vivien Goodman."

And that was it. No fussing with psychologists or counselors. Looking back, I think this was my introduction to handling the cards I was dealt; here's the next chapter of the book—let's get on with it! That was fine with me.

Before we left Cuba for New York, Mommy asked me what I wanted to bring to America, and I said the only thing I wanted was *"Mi Tata!"* Tata, my beloved nanny, was a loving and wonderful lady; huge in size and very black in skin color. Proud of her heritage, Tata would always say, *"Soy de la Nación,"* meaning "I am from Africa," and she had some tribal scars to prove it.

Tata had cared for me since the day I was born. I have a wonderful photo of the two of us on a lawn—just a tiny, white baby with red hair and green eyes, wearing a white dress, sitting on the lap of my Tata. Sadly, this cherished photo has gone missing.

She had her own brand of voodoo beliefs and always pinned a small black bead on my clothes. When Mommy once asked her why she did it, Tata told her that I was so beautiful, but so white. She explained that when she would take me out in the pram, everyone would notice me— with my red hair, green eyes, and fair skin, I stood out. Tata believed that evil spirits would take me without this protection.

Mommy didn't agree. She told Tata not to put the beads on me, but Tata paid her no mind. One day, on Tata's day off, Mommy found a bead pinned inside my diaper. No one would steal me away—even when Tata wasn't there. Mommy did not quibble with Tata over the beads after that.

As much as I loved my Tata, Mommy couldn't accommodate my

request to have her accompany us to America. She was concerned that Tata would be miserable there and didn't think the paperwork for immigration would be easy. So it became evident that there would be just one constant in my life moving forward—Mommy.

So what began with complications and misunderstandings became a love story that lasted for fifty-six years, until Daddy's death in 1993.

Two

THE EARLY YEARS

AFTER THE WEDDING, I JOINED MOMMY AND MY NEW DADDY ON their honeymoon, sailing to New York, headed for our new life together. First, we flew to Miami, my first plane ride, and I remember running up and down the aisle of the plane. From there, we boarded a ship headed for New York, a pretty long voyage in those days.

I remember boarding the ship in Daddy's arms. Just after boarding, he stood on deck, holding me in one arm and carrying my "toidy seat" (portable potty) and a wire basket of milk bottles in the other. Suddenly, the boat whistle blew, startling me. I wrapped my arms around his neck tightly and heard the milk bottles clanking together as we swayed. But Daddy didn't drop the milk or the potty or me.

I couldn't speak a word of English. When I heard Daddy coming toward the stateroom, I'd say—in Spanish—"Mommy, Mommy. Quick, quick! That man is coming. *El hombre*. Put on a dress! Cover up!"

I was clearly jealous about the turn of events. I wanted to keep Mommy for myself. In fact, from what I've been told, I was an abso-

Vivien in Rye, New York, 1935.

lute brat on the trip and very tough to please. When Mommy would show me a yellow dress, I would say, *"No me gusta, no me gusta!"* I *don't like it!* The blue one? *"No me gusta!"*

There was a little schoolroom on the ship that had old-fashioned desks with inkwells. I even misbehaved there. A little girl with long braids sat at the desk in front of me, and I dipped her braid in the inkwell.

Finally, we arrived in New York and my new Goodman grandparents, Edwin and Belle, picked us up at the pier in a beautiful car driven by a chauffeur. When we got in the car, I wanted to hear my favorite song and asked Mommy, "Where is the radio?" Back then, even the most luxurious cars didn't have radios. So from that moment on, I was known as The Duchess.

My grandparents took us to their home on the ninth floor of Bergdorf Goodman, the penthouse. The apartment spanned the entire floor of the building. We entered through a discrete, private entrance and I took my first ride up in the private elevator to their home. It was a grand apartment with high ceilings, tall windows, and a beautiful view of Central Park and Fifth Avenue.

I was taken to a huge bedroom filled with toys. It was as if FAO Schwarz had just delivered their entire inventory—every toy you can imagine, and all for me. Mommy came in a while later, as I was happily playing, and told me it was time to pick up my toys and get ready for dinner. I said to her, in Spanish of course, "No, Mommy, you see that little button? If you push it, the maid comes in and does it for you." Mommy told me later that she couldn't believe how quickly I had figured that out. No wonder the nickname "Duchess" stuck.

I got along well with my Goodman grandparents, especially with my grandfather. When I was five, he treated me to riding lessons, and seeing how much I loved horses, in later years it was he who took me to the races and introduced me to that world.

At a meeting with his architect at the Plaza Hotel, Grandpa Edwin sketched his vision of the Bergdorf Goodman building on a cocktail napkin. Later, the architect filled in the scene.

The window of FAO Schwarz toy store, New York City.

Grandpa's office was downstairs in the store, and when I was very little, I used to visit him there. I remember barely being able to see over the desktop, which came up to my chin. Grandpa loved having me visit, allowing me to stay in the office during meetings. I'll never forget a particular object he had on his desk. It was a small seal covered in real seal skin. I loved to pet it and can still almost feel its smooth, flat surface.

The three of us lived in the apartment with my grandparents for a short time, but one very strong memory of that time is Grandpa Goodman's breakfast. He would have two soft-boiled eggs every morning. Daddy said that Bertha, their cook, made the best soft-boiled eggs. It was Mommy who later found out Bertha's secret ingredient—an extra yolk mixed with butter. Of course, they were delicious. Next, Grandpa would have his toast with all the crusts cut off. He would cut his toast into tiny, postage stamp–size pieces and spread them with red currant jelly, then turn to me and ask, "Do you want a piece, Vivi?" It was so delicious, so special. I loved those breakfasts with Grandpa.

Where Grandpa was very warm and affectionate with me, Grandma was more distant. She came from a wealthy family that had made its fortune a generation earlier. She married a self-made man who was on his way to becoming a merchant prince, and the fact that her parents loaned Grandpa Goodman $10,000 to buy out his former partner was something she never let him forget. Grandpa tolerated her difficult behavior in part due to his own wandering eye.

Grandma Goodman's real name was Dorothy Lowenstein, and everyone called her Belle. Some members of the family shortened their last name to "Lownes" and she never forgave them for that. She felt it was hypocritical to pretend they weren't Jewish. The members of her German Jewish community were very proud of their social standing.

Grandma told stories of her childhood home, a beautiful town-house in a fashionable neighborhood in New York City. She described how her parents had a sewing room upstairs in their house, where seamstresses would sew every piece of clothing for the family by hand. Every day, a woman would come to their house to comb and dress her mother's hair. So Belle was used to luxury and clothes made to order. When Mommy married Daddy, Grandma Goodman was still having her silk underwear made to order at Bergdorf's.

Grandma and Grandpa had wonderful seats at the Metropolitan Opera that are still in the family. Daddy would tell me how Grandpa Goodman would arrive for a night at the opera, and instead of sitting down, he would stand up and turn around and face the audience, noting who was there and what they were wearing. Grandma told me that he would only sit once the conductor entered, and as soon as the conductor lifted his baton, Grandpa would go to sleep.

Belle was a very proud woman, and she adored Daddy. She had a daughter, Ann, who was a wonderful person and so sweet but could do nothing right in the eyes of her mother. Where Daddy was handsome and charming, Ann was quite tall, even by today's

LEFT: Ed, Belle, and Ann Goodman with young Vivien, Westchester, New York, 1930s. RIGHT: Belle, Andrew, and Ann Goodman in the penthouse above the store, c. 1950s.

standards. Though stylish, well-educated, and a favorite among friends, she could not win her mother's approval, whom she spent her life trying to please.

After living with my grandparents for a few months, Mommy and Daddy wanted a place of their own. We settled into our new apartment at 417 Park Avenue. My sister Mary Ann—we call her Minkie—was born in 1937. Minkie actually named herself. Her nanny called her a little "minx," which my sister couldn't pronounce, so she would say, "Minkie, Minkie!" My brother, Eddie, was born on September 2, 1939, the day after World War II broke out. Mommy cried, "My son will have to go to war someday."

Even though I learned English quickly and adapted to my new life in America, memories of Cuba were never far from my mind. I remembered, in particular, a pudding that I had eaten when I lived in Cuba. The smell of it is ingrained in my memory, deep and hidden. I smelled it once when I was nine or ten years old. There was

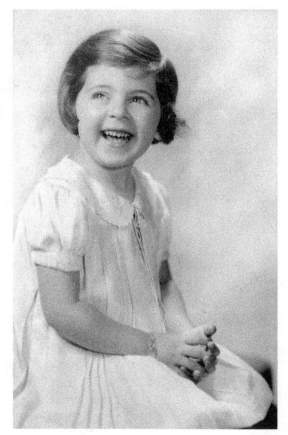

Vivien at age three.

a maid who was caring for me while my parents and siblings were in the country, suffering from whooping cough. My parents had me stay in the city with the maid to avoid catching it. We had a ball together, going to the Plaza movie theater almost every night. It must have been during this short time that she cooked this pudding, and its unique smell evoked such a strong memory in me.

They say that smell, touch, and hearing are very strong memory-builders in infants, and I bet if I could smell that pudding again today, it would bring me right back to my earliest memories in Cuba. I wish I could have bottled it to hold on to those precious memories that were slowly fading away.

Andrew and Ann Goodman and Spitz, New York City, c. 1910s. Originally named Fritz, they changed the dog's name because it was deemed too German.

After my parents' marriage, my new daddy adopted me as soon as possible. Sometime later, Lello came to New York to sue for custody. At the proceedings, Daddy was represented by a federal court judge, which must have been deeply impressive to the presiding judge. Ultimately, Lello's suit was unsuccessful, and a settlement of $16,000 was reached. Under the terms of the settlement, neither he nor his family was allowed to contact me in any way.

Andrew Goodman was a wonderful, loving father. He spoiled me just as Mommy's daddy, Eugene, had spoiled her. But I always felt that if I wasn't good, he wouldn't love me as much.

Although his family was wealthy, he was a child of the Depression and also lamented that his children "would put me in the

LEFT: Vivien, sportswoman in the making. RIGHT: Vivien the dog lover.

poorhouse." He told me once that if you couldn't pay your debts, you went there to work, and I took this seriously. I didn't want to be the reason for his ending up in the poorhouse.

SCHOOL DAYS

Mommy wanted her children to attend progressive schools, so when the time came, I was enrolled at the Walt Whitman School, located just off Fifth Avenue in a beautiful old building. My sister Minkie attended The Yard, and my brother, Eddie, attended the Urban League School. Each of these schools was considered very avant-garde and "in" at the time.

I started at Walt Whitman in kindergarten when I was about five years old. My schoolmates were the sons and daughters of the wealthy and socially prominent upper crust of New York society. I remember one afternoon I went on what is now called a "play date" with a girl from my class. Mommy dropped me off at the door, which was answered by a butler. He escorted me into the grand entry hall. It was just unbelievable. I can still see it—a huge vaulted ceiling, a staircase leading to the second floor, and marble floors. The playroom was filled with every toy a child could crave, but I focused immediately on the rocking horse. She had a big playhouse, big enough to walk into. Everything was gorgeous and over the top.

At some point, my little friend said to me, "Where does your mother buy your clothes?" I told her that we bought my dresses at Bloomingdale's, to which she replied, "Bloomingdale's? Mine come from Saks."

I remember how this comment hurt my feelings. When I told my mother about it later, she was really miffed. "That was a snobby thing to say," said Mommy. "Bloomingdale's is just fine."

I was always pretty tall for my age, and as a result was always put in the back of the line or seated in the back row. One year, I played one of the shepherds in the Christmas pageant, which was held in the main room of the school. All the parents attended, and there I was, the tallest shepherd at the end of the line holding a lantern. When we entered, I was to step apart and say my line: "Yonder there is a star. Maybe that is where the child is." I must have been six years old, but I can still remember every detail of that pageant, especially seeing my parents in the audience.

One of my schoolmates was Thomas Dewey Jr., son of the district attorney of New York, Thomas Dewey. One day Dewey Sr. came to pick up his son, who introduced us. "Dad, this is Vivien. Show her your gun." I remember Dewey Sr. perfectly. His face, his mustache, and the pinstripe suit he was wearing. He opened his jacket to reveal a leather holster and the revolver within it. Here was the dad of a friend of mine carrying a lethal weapon around all the time.

One of the things Tommy and I loved to do after school was roller-skate in the park. Years later, I must have been in my thirties, I got a call from Tommy and we caught up. Later, I told my dad Tommy had called and he said, "Why did he call? Does he want his skate key back?" I loved how Daddy always kidded me and brought me back to earth.

One thing I remember vividly from my days at Walt Whitman was the container kept on the windowsill that was filled with dirt and had a lima bean planted right at the edge, so you could see it grow. Every day, I would watch the root descend and the stem reach up until it burst through the top of the soil. I was fascinated, and I think my love of gardening was born as I watched the lima bean grow from nothing. Now, when I think of all the wonderful things in today's kindergarten classrooms, I wish I could be back in school. With so many stimulating materials, how could today's children not all be geniuses?

One time, our teacher brought the class to her farm in Pennsylvania for the weekend. It was a real farm—rustic, with an outhouse, which we all found disgusting. I don't remember animals on the farm, but I do remember our teacher showing us an asparagus patch and a rhubarb patch. I just loved being in the country and seeing how things grew naturally, untended.

A few years later, I must have been about nine years old, I came home from school and Mommy asked me, "So, how was school today?"

"I really don't think I'm learning much," I said.

"Well, what have you learned?"

"I learned that the Earth is round and that we came from apes." And that was the end of my career in progressive education!

Mommy considered a few different schools for me. First, she considered The Spence School, a very prestigious all-girls school on the Upper East Side that was and is still very hard to get into. As Mommy explained to me later, she did not pursue enrolling me at Spence because they wanted to know details about her background and how I became Andrew Goodman's daughter. She told me that they were "snobby and too nosy."

She also considered Sacred Heart, her alma mater. But between her own memories of running afoul of the nuns and its reputation as an "elite" school, she decided against it as well. That's how I ended up at Dominican Academy, which offered a traditional parochial education.

At this time, we were living at 55th Street and Park Avenue, about twelve blocks south of Dominican Academy. I walked to and

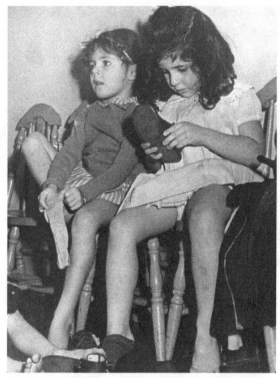

Minkie (right) and friend at The Yard.

from school every day dressed in the school uniform, which consisted of a white blouse with a Peter Pan collar and a maroon jumper.

I loved school and the nuns were fantastic. The curriculum was basic, focusing exclusively on the four "Rs": reading, writing, arithmetic, and religion. But I learned—I gobbled it up. Finally, I had the academic structure I had been missing and I thrived on it. I excelled in that learning environment and got straight As. There was no phys ed, art, or music, but we did have ballroom dancing lessons once a week. When the teacher led the class in the waltz, she would say, "Back with your right foot," and that's how I finally learned my right from my left. It so happens that my husband, Harry, was also educated by the Dominicans, at St. Augustine Academy in Larchmont, New York. Our lives were parallel in many ways unbeknownst to us until many years later.

My favorite nun was Sister Mary Raymond. She told me that God had given me the gift of faith and I should treasure it—which I always have.

She loved my father. "You don't know how lucky you are," she said. "Your father is not of our faith, but he lets your mother bring you up as a Catholic. You should be so thankful to him. He is such a wonderful man." She emphasized that over and over again. At the time, I didn't realize what a gift it was. Daddy always made sure we got to mass on time on Sundays. Years later, I complimented him on that and he said, "I did that so I could read the Sunday *New York Times* in peace."

Although she was my favorite, Sister Mary Raymond was very strict. I used to twirl my hair in my fingers while I was thinking, which Sister Mary Raymond did not approve of, so she would take an elastic band and make the piece of twirled hair stick up, calling it a "hair raid." When she was very angry, she would tuck her veil into her waist chord and run around the classroom picking out any student who was not paying attention, grab her hair, and say, "Watch out! We're going to have a hair raid in here!"

Sister Mary Raymond would give out stickers if you got a perfect score on your assignments—robins in the springtime, crosses with lilies at Easter, pilgrims for Thanksgiving. Once I missed getting a sticker on a history test because I wasn't able to identify the founder of the U.S. Navy. I only got a 90 percent and was crushed. Years later, I asked my husband, a naval officer, the same question. "John Paul Jones," he said. Of course, he knew it, and I never forgot.

Classes at Dominican Academy were small—maybe a dozen students—and it was easy to make friends. I remember three friends in particular. There was Claire Sewall, a quiet girl who had blonde hair and wore glasses. She was very smart and had beautiful handwriting. I had another friend, whose name I can't recall, whose father was the manager at the Sherry-Netherland hotel, which was just across Fifth Avenue from Bergdorf's. We both had dogs—hers an Irish setter and mine a cocker spaniel—and we used to love to take them into Central Park to play. In those days, I could go anywhere in New York City alone or with a friend, so after school my friend and I would run with our dogs up and down the mall, making them jump the arms of the benches until dusk. I would dress my dog, Spanky, in doll's clothes and he put up with it, though he never was housebroken.

The friend I remember most from Dominican Academy was Alexandra Plaissay, whose family was of Greek descent. Her parents owned a flower shop on Lexington around 70th Street called Plaza Florist. Sometimes I would go with Alexandra when she helped her mother in the shop after school. I remember watching her mother, a petite blonde, at a long table trimming flower stems and creating arrangements. One day when she was working with gladioli, she asked me if I knew the flower's name. I didn't, so she told me they were called "goes-inta" and I realized that she had been doubling up the blossoms, putting one into the other to make each one look bigger.

Once, Alexandra invited me to sleep over at their very modest home on Long Island. Their home life was totally different from what I was used to. When I woke up in the morning, I observed the family's routine and I never forgot it. Alexandra's mother made breakfast for us and then braided Alexandra's beautiful long, black hair. All of us were out of the house before seven o'clock to get into the city for work and school. I loved the routine and rhythm of their home life, but I was especially struck by how they did everything together—working, commuting, eating—it was so different from my own life. My siblings and I were separated from our parents' day-to-day lives. We ate, played, bathed, and slept in the nursery.

A few years ago, I walked up Lexington Avenue to see if Plaza Florist was still there. It was, so I entered and asked for Mr. Plaissay. A man wearing an apron who looked just like Alexandra's father came out from the back. "I'm Mr. Plaissay," he said. Alexandra's brother Constantine—the pesky little boy that Alexandra used to complain about—was now the manager of the family florist.

Another student I remember from class was a Russian girl whose parents were ballet dancers. She sat right in front of me in class, and I remember how she carried herself—like a dancer—but her blouse was never quite as white as other girls', and her nails were bitten down. Ballet was her passion, and the details of her appearance were not important to her, I guess. Or maybe her parents were so busy with their dance careers that keeping her hair brushed neatly and her shirts cleaned and pressed went by the wayside. We never became friends since she would go to ballet lessons directly after school every day.

Vivien and Minkie at Kenilworth Riding Club, Rye, New York, c. 1940s.

CITY LIFE

It was the early 1940s, and New York City was safe enough for a child like me to walk to school, ride the subway, and play in the park alone. On Saturdays I'd get on the subway at 55th Street and join my friends at the Loews movie theater on 72nd Street to watch the newsreels, cartoons, and a double feature—all for a quarter!

Every week I would walk to the Lexington Avenue branch of the New York Public Library. First, I went through every book in the card catalog pertaining to horses. After that, I started on dogs. At that point, the librarian called my mother and advised her to encourage me to expand my subject matter. My mother asked me if I was interested in fairy tales, and when I said no, she dropped the subject.

When I was around eight years old, my mother found me curled up on the sofa in the library reading Richard Wright's *Native Son*. She asked, "Sweetie, what are you reading?" When I told her, she said, "But don't you think that's a little old for you?"

I replied, "Oh, no, Mommy, I'm at the best part. He's cutting her up and putting her in the furnace." She told me later that she always believed, "To the pure, all things are pure."

She let me read as much as I liked, and she didn't mind what I read, because it was obvious that I loved to read. Reading was a way for me to create private space for myself, as I was surrounded by younger siblings and still living in the nursery. I was able to screen out the noises around me and focus completely on the task at hand—something that I can still do to this day.

Growing up in New York City was so exciting. There were so many entertaining things to do. At Christmas we always went to Radio City Music Hall to see the Christmas Spectacular. My grandmother knew the producer, who would take us backstage to see the animals—the camels, llamas, sheep, and, of course, the horses. Another annual family event was Ringling Brothers and Barnum and

Bailey Circus. Daddy would take us, and whatever the vendors were selling, we wanted—the lights on a string, the spun sugar candy, the (live) turtles, and the chameleons. Once, on our way out of the circus, we ran into a friend of Daddy's. We were loaded down with goodies, and I'm sure Daddy looked a little battered and worn. He told his friend, "Thank God it's only once a year."

Daddy always teased me about what he called "Vivien's progression at the circus." At five years old, I would only watch the "roustabouts," who worked the ropes and trapeze lines. The next year, I spent the entire time reading the program. And finally, at seven, I looked up and noticed the horses. The horses, the horses, the horses.

Daddy also took us to the rodeo at Madison Square Garden, where there were tons of horses—the broncs, the roping horses, the outriders. It was thrilling to see how well the cowboys rode. I remember we had front-row seats one year, and I was resting my hand on the wall of the ring. A cowboy who was running away from a loose bull jumped up and landed on my hand. I had never felt that rough denim before. It was strange to me, and I didn't know what to do, so I didn't move. I just waited until he jumped down, probably unaware that he had been sitting on a little hand.

Though I went to the theater to watch cartoons and newsreels with my friends, the first grown-up movie I went to see was *For Whom the Bell Tolls* with Mommy and Abuelita. I suppose they chose this film because the story is set in Spain during the Spanish Revolution. Abuelita barely spoke a word of English, and there were some scenes that went over my head. I recall one scene where Ingrid Bergman is being attacked, and one of the bad guys says, "commence" with her. Though I didn't understand what that word meant in this circumstance, I knew it was not good.

Although my childhood summer days were mostly idyllic, there was a pall cast by the polio scare. While vacationing on an island near Maine with his family, Franklin Delano Roosevelt had gone swimming and sat on some rocks in a wet bathing suit. He later got a fever and a chill. Soon after, FDR contracted this paralyzing disease. This event led many to believe that polio was caused by catching a chill in the summer. At the time, polio was also thought to be contagious (this part, of course, turned out to be true), which added to the general sense of alarm. I remember being changed immediately and dried off after a swim; we were never allowed to sit in a wet bathing suit. One of the friends we played with that summer, Lee DeBaros, contracted polio. His parents took him immediately to the famous Sister Kenny for her treatment, which consisted of wrapping her patients in hot packs and a series of exercises for their affected limbs. She was considered a miracle worker because she saved a lot of children from paralysis.

That same summer, my friend Elizabeth's aunt contracted polio. She was not much older than we were, and she also went to Sister Kenny, but the treatment failed. She never walked again and ultimately died at a young age.

BECOMING A RIDER

As far back as I can remember, when someone said the word "beauty," I would see in my mind's eye a horse galloping across a meadow into the woods. Even before I owned a horse, they epitomized beauty to me. It's a mystery to me how I became "hardwired" to adore horses. My parents liked horses, but they didn't have the same passion for them that I always did.

When I was five, I remember an outing to the Westchester Country Club's polo field (the current site of the driving range), where a horse show was taking place. I was there with my grandparents, father, and aunt. They were all talking, and there I was, literally "cantering" like a horse in a circle around the grown-ups. "Vivien," said my tall and handsome grandfather, looking way down at little me, "would you like to have riding lessons?" I said yes, and that's how I got started riding. From there, riding became a part of daily life.

My first instructor was a German named Konrad Fischer, who ran the Kenilworth Riding Club on Kenilworth Road in Rye. Before coming to America, he had worked at the Spanish Riding School in

Vienna, and he brought several Lipizzans with him. I rode a school horse and never rode the Lipizzans, but I drove them in tandem formation—one behind the other. I took lessons with Mr. Fischer at least three times a week, and his training focused on dressage. He seemed to like me, and always said I had a wonderful seat.

I just loved to be in the stable. When I walked into the aisle, I was in ecstasy. I can still remember the sights, the sounds, and the smells that surrounded me—horses, hay, tack—so very different from the world I came from.

When I arrived for lessons, I would check the list to see which horse I'd be riding that day. I can still remember some of their names: Jackson, Dubonnet, Gold Coin, and Flying Colors. In the old European tradition, we riders did not groom or tack up our

Royal Canadian Mounted Police performing at the National Horse Show at Madison Square Garden, 1975. (Photo by Jill Krementz.)

horses. They were all tacked up, standing in the aisle ready for us to mount, and we got right on.

The grooms at the Kenilworth Riding Club were all European. I remember one in particular, named Paul. Although he would go off on drinking binges, he was also incredibly talented at braiding and would fashion French braids and plumes for the Lipizzans' manes and tails when we had musical rides. It was quite grand.

In a musical ride, horses and riders perform complicated choreographed maneuvers set to music. We would thread the needle, execute small voltes, and eight horses were ridden abreast in a wheel pattern, all at a brisk trot.

I also competed in the horse shows held at the barn. During one class, I was riding Dubonnet when she spooked at the sun flashing off the trophies displayed on the judge's stand. She bucked me off right in front of the judge. My mother recalls that I got up and said, "Well, there goes the blue ribbon." But, supposedly, I got it anyway.

We all wore our britches, boots, and helmets to ride. When I was older and we moved to Rye, I wore my riding clothes to school. Until, that is, the headmaster at Rye Country Day School made me stop. We had a very strict headmaster, Morton Snyder. His office looked out on the yard in front of the school, and one day as I cartwheeled while waiting to be picked up, he came out and said, "Vivien, you're getting too big for your britches. Don't wear your riding clothes to school anymore." That was hard for me because I wanted to be on a horse the first second I got picked up from school.

I had a "boyfriend" in those grade-school years. His name was Johnny. I think we became boyfriend and girlfriend when we were eight. He adored me, but he was quite chubby and not especially smart. He told me, however, that he was rich and said we would get married, buy a ranch, and have horses. So that was it—I was all over this boy!

Johnny came to my eighth birthday party and we had pony rides, of course. We were having a wonderful time, but Johnny got kicked in the stomach. He wasn't hurt, but the pony left a big imprint of a horseshoe on his tummy, which Daddy found quite amusing.

Vivien and Gold Coin at Kenilworth Riding Club, Rye, New York,
c. 1940s.

Johnny didn't like horses after that. He told me that Mr. Fischer
was a Nazi, that he wasn't going to ride at Kenilworth anymore, and
that I shouldn't either. When I told my father what Johnny had said
about Mr. Fischer, Daddy said, "Don't worry about it. Don't be silly."

My father was only intolerant of one thing: hypocrisy. He and
my mother certainly had their opinions about people they knew socially, but they didn't seem to succumb to the pervasive fear of all
things German during and after World War II. However, lots of
people were against anything German in those days.

Horses were such a big part of my life, whether I was at the barn
or not. We had no Breyer horse models or fancy horse toys, but my
friends and I would cut out every photo we found of horses, paste
them onto cardboard, and make our own toys.

My Grandpa Goodman, who recognized my early passion for
horses, would take me with him to the Jamaica Race Course and

we would visit the paddock before every race. I loved seeing the Thoroughbreds up close, and apparently, I had a knack for picking the winners. Grandpa's friends quickly caught on and would ask him, "Who does the kid like in the seventh?" I remember seeing the 1941 Triple Crown winner and Horse of the Year, Whirlaway, there with his legendary beautiful, long tail. He won that day like the champion he was.

When I was about fourteen, I experienced firsthand that amazing feeling of speed when a friend of mine who lived nearby let me ride her horse while she was on vacation. He was a Thoroughbred off the track—Son of Bean was his name. I was welcome to ride him whenever I wanted, so I'd hop on my bike, wearing just shorts and sandals, and ride over to her barn. I'd take Bean over to the Blind Brook polo field where there was a track, and I'd get up on him—no boots, helmet, or britches. I'd just cluck and Bean would gallop away with me suspended on his back and nothing but the wind around us. I adored the feeling of that horse—free, in his element, out of control. I was just a passenger.

Mr. Fischer was a dressage trainer and was against teaching his students to jump. But after begging him to let me jump, he finally relented. On my first attempt, I fell off a horse named Flying Colors. I landed on my head with no helmet on and ended up going to a chiropractor. I was okay at the time, but I believe that fall affected my neck later in life.

Looking back, I can't believe the risks I took, but luckily, I was never seriously hurt. Despite that early tumble, I still love speed. I love going fast and I love to jump. To me, riding without jumping is nothing!

NANNIES: THE GOOD, THE BAD, AND THE UGLY

No autobiography of mine would be complete without some discussion of our nannies. I've described my beloved Tata, who couldn't accompany me from Cuba to the United States. Tata's first successor was . . . a Fräulein. This was before my sister Minkie was born, and German nannies were very much in vogue at the time.

My siblings and I were raised by several nannies during the course of our childhood. In those days, families of means frequently employed nannies to take charge of the day-to-day care of their children. We children lived in "the nursery," which was the nanny's domain, and she was in control of every aspect of our daily lives. The routine of our days was dictated by our nanny, not our parents, from dietary choices to bedtime routines. Although I was five and a half years older than Minkie, I lived in the nursery with her and, later, my brother, Eddie.

Fräulein wanted me to eat. "Eat, mein leetle fish," she'd say to me. The Fräulein diet at dinner was typically string beans, some sort of meat, and pink Junket. I hated Junket. It tasted disgusting and I wouldn't eat it. In fact, I wouldn't eat most of the food served to me. I would stuff it in my cheeks until Daddy told me I looked like a chipmunk. Fräulein's response to this was typically harsh: She would put my uneaten dinner plate in the fridge and I would have it served to me cold and greasy for breakfast, or lunch, or dinner the next night. Of course, I would eat something at some point and the adults thought they had won, but the next day it started all over again.

It was common for Fräulein to administer harsh consequences on a regular basis, but she saved the single worst punishment for when my parents were away on one of their numerous trips to Europe. Mommy and Daddy traveled a lot to France and Italy for the fashion shows, with accompanying dinners and luncheons, often for six weeks at a time. It was during one of those trips, when I was no more than four years old, that I went into the library at home and was looking at some books, and apparently I tore a page out of one of the books. Maybe it was a picture of a horse— I'd like to think so.

Fräulein decided that the appropriate consequence would be to put my hands in the hot oven. I remember her taking me into the kitchen, opening the oven door while the cook was using the stovetop, and putting my hands into the oven until they were burned. Afterward, as she wrapped my hands in gauze, she warned me to tell my parents that I had burned my hands on the radiator and threatened me with a worse punishment if I told them the truth. My parents only found out the truth weeks later when they fired the cook and she said, "Well, being I have to leave, you might as well know what Fräulein did to your daughter."

Fräulein was fired posthaste, with a few words about her behavior. Both cook and nanny went packing. A few weeks later, Grandma Goodman received a visit from Fräulein, who wanted a recommendation. Grandma said, "Get out of here, before I call the police!"

Next came Mam'selle. I suppose my parents felt more comfortable with her as they traveled frequently to France for business. She was mean, though, and frankly, not very clean.

Clockwise, from back left: Andrew, Didi Nethercott, Vivien, Eddie, and Minkie, preparing to board a ship to visit family in Cuba, c. June 1941.

Mam'selle had worked for people who owned a famous racehorse called Bold Venture. I constantly questioned her to tell me more about this horse—that was her saving grace in my eyes. Mam'selle did not last long. Before Minkie was born, Mommy decided to hire a baby nurse instead of keeping the nanny. She chose an English-woman named Didi Nethercott. Didi was the real thing—trained by the book.

Didi was a bit ahead of her time. Starting when Minkie was just a week old, Didi would lay my baby sister across her knees, massaging her whole body with oil. She had Minkie so programmed that after she drank her formula and made that red face that babies do before they poop, Didi would get the potty and put it under the appropriate part of Minkie's anatomy, so she would "learn" to be potty-trained.

Didi was fully committed to our well-being and went to great lengths to fulfill her duties. One night, she was using an eyecup (the predecessor of the eyedropper) in the bathroom and did not turn on the light, not wanting to wake us. In the dark, she reached for the wrong bottle and put boric acid in her eye, almost blinding herself. Mommy was, of course, sympathetic, but said, "Didi, why didn't you look at what you were going to put in your eyes? Why didn't you turn on the light?"

"I didn't want to disturb the children in the nursery," she re-plied. To this day, I check before I put drops in my eyes.

I am glad that I had a bona fide English nanny. Didi told us that some of the nannies she had trained with in England had gone on to work for the British royal family. I learned a lot about discipline, cleanliness, order, and the benefits of fresh air from Didi, God bless her. Her influence was strong—to this day, I still say "bean" and not "bin" for "been"—very British.

Didi stayed with us for about six years, until my brother, Eddie, was a toddler. While we loved Didi, she was essentially a baby nurse—and a very good one. Among my parents' friends, Didi was in high demand, but when my parents told us she was leaving, I was not only sad, I was also furious.

We had a huge walk-in closet in our nursery at 417 Park Avenue, and it was there that I told my younger siblings, "When the new nanny comes, we're not going to do anything she says. We aren't going to like her. We want Didi back." Nobody argued with me, they just looked at me, dumbstruck.

The new nanny's name was Nora Dooley; we called her Lolly. Before she arrived, Mommy told us Lolly's story: She was Irish, and before coming to America, she had worked for a wealthy Spanish family with four sons. When the Spanish Civil War broke out, the boys' parents were afraid that their children would be killed or taken from them. They entrusted Lolly with getting their sons out of the country to safety. During her employment interview, Lolly had shown Mommy a letter from these parents telling the story of how she had saved all four of the boys.

To get them safely out of the country, Lolly had hidden their identities by dressing herself and the boys as peasants and traveling through

Left to right: Minkie, Eddie, Vivien, and Spunky, Central Park, New York, early 1940s.

Spain to France, England, and finally, to Ireland. They traveled by train, by boat, and on foot, under constant threat of discovery. Later, the parents were able to come and be reunited with their children.

So, Lolly had quite an impressive letter of reference. The boys' mother wrote, "To whomever is lucky enough to have Lolly, she saved our children and she's a wonderful person." However, I was still upset about Didi leaving.

My life changed when Lolly arrived. Petite and fun-loving, Lolly was a dream come true. She was like a big sister. She was funny and loved to play with us, including ball and tag. She was very strict, too, but she knew when to be tough and when to ease up a bit. Lolly was a major influence on all of us.

We would go to Central Park with our white gloves and our nice clothes on, and Lolly would bring a washcloth in a little bag. She'd let us play, and before we left the park to go home, she would wipe off our knees and our hands and brush our hair. Thus groomed, we'd go back across to Fifth and home to Park Avenue.

Lolly presided over a happy and well-run nursery. A lovely large, sunny room with several windows overlooking both Park Avenue and 55th Street, it was painted a pale blue with murals on the walls, including one of a scene from *Jack and the Beanstalk*. There was a long table with chairs where we did our schoolwork, played games, and ate our meals, and Minkie and I both had our beds in the nursery—it was that big. Lolly's room and the bathroom were just off the nursery, and Eddie slept in his crib in Lolly's room.

Bathing was part of our daily routine, and Lolly supervised our bath schedules. We bathed one by one, in order of age, so I went first. There was a tin cookie jar in the nursery, and after my bath, I would sneak cookies from the jar and fill up my bathrobe pockets. Chomp, chomp, chomp.

Then our dinner would come, which was always pretty lousy— which is probably why I would fill up on cookies. The cooks never bothered to make our meals appealing, as they were busy making fancy meals for the main table. We were just supposed to eat things that were good for us: cereal in the morning, a sandwich for lunch, and usually string beans and some kind of meat for dinner. I always looked forward to Sunday night dinner, though, because we'd have French toast. That was the best meal we had all week.

We were disciplined the old-fashioned way. When we were naughty, we had to sit facing the corner. These days, the use of "time-out" makes me laugh because the child just sits, watching everything, and is still part of what is going on. But when we sat in the corner, all the wonderful stuff was going on behind us. Everybody was having a good time, talking, laughing, and playing while we sat in the corner looking at the wall. We had to wait until Lolly said, "All right, you can come out of the corner." I don't remember her doing much spanking or slapping—she really didn't need to, because we just adored her.

I consider Lolly central to my early understanding of being a Catholic in my daily life. Although I went to the Dominican Academy and learned about my religion from the nuns, it was Lolly who helped me to put my faith into practice at home. She was very religious and we all went to Mass with her.

I remember I received my First Holy Communion while she was taking care of us. It was a glorious, chilly day in May and I was wearing a beautiful white dress and veil. My parents took me downtown to a fancy restaurant with an outdoor café, I believe near One Fifth Avenue. We sat outside and had breakfast together—Daddy, Mommy, and I. It was very special, but I was freezing!

Over the four years that Lolly was with us, we grew to love her more and more. Mommy always said it was just a matter of time before she would leave us to get married because she was so young and pretty. When she did leave us to wed, we were all so sad, but she married a very good man named Thomas Cunningham, and they lived in Forest Hills. I loved visiting her at her home. I remember the house being quite bare. There weren't many pieces of furniture, and the floors were wood with no carpeting. Though it felt sparse, her home was clean as a whistle.

I remember helping Lolly rinse the empty milk bottles before returning them to the local store. Lolly wore a wedding ring now, and it would clink against the milk bottles as she rinsed them out. I had never really seen anyone washing dishes or rinsing out milk bottles or bringing them back to the store before. Maybe that is why I enjoyed the whole process: the care that was taken to make sure the bottles were clean and placed in the wire carrier and returned properly.

Lolly died of bone cancer at a fairly young age. I was a young mother at the time of her death and I didn't go to her funeral. I kick myself over and over . . . I can't understand why I didn't go, but it had to have been something serious. I think one of my children must have been very sick for me not to attend. Both my sister Minkie and my brother, Eddie, went to the funeral.

Before Lolly died, I remember taking my oldest son, Andrew, to visit her at her home. I had him all dressed up, clean as a whistle, and on his best behavior. It was important to me that Lolly approve of me as a mother.

Lolly had a daughter who eventually became a nun. I kept in contact with her, even though she joined a very strict cloistered order. The nuns couldn't communicate with the outside world more than once a year, and unfortunately, I lost touch with her over time. I also kept in contact with Lolly's husband until his death.

Lolly was our last nanny. When I was twelve, we moved to Washington, D.C., where Daddy, a naval officer, had been stationed at the Bureau of Supplies and Accounts. There, we had maids and other household help, but no nanny. It was a new world.

Lt. Andrew Goodman, U.S. Navy, World War II.

Three

DADDY'S OFF TO WAR

IN 1941, WHEN DADDY WAS THIRTY-FOUR, HE WAS DRAFTED INTO THE navy. He didn't want to go into the army, and thank God, he was rejected as a foot soldier because he had flat feet.

I remember him marching up Park Avenue with the rest of the newly commissioned officers and some noncommissioned officers behind them. We all went to the window as they passed below and Daddy waved to us. Mommy was crying quietly because she said he was "going off to war." She was scared.

Daddy became a Lieutenant Junior Grade (LTJG). His first assignment was a ten-day stint in Hawaii, a cushy way to start war duty. He said Waikiki Beach was not even close to being as beautiful as Cuba's Varadero. He described Waikiki as a narrow strip of beach whose sand was nothing like the talcum powder–soft sand in Cuba. In Varadero the beach stretched way out into the water, so you could walk on and on from the houses into the shallow water and way out into the ocean. Daddy came back from Hawaii with a beautiful tan and everyone teased him about that.

When he got home from Hawaii, he traveled directly to his post in Washington, D.C., at the Bureau of Supplies. Basically, Daddy said that after the government drafted him, they didn't know what to do with him. Because he was in the "rag trade," I guess they figured he could do a good job supplying the uniforms for all branches of the navy— including the WAVES (Women Accepted for Volunteer Emergency Service).

The first summer of the war, we rented rooms at Westchester Country Club. Mommy would take the train down to Washington and spend every weekend with Daddy. While there, she and Daddy looked for a house to rent and decided on schools for us. Their plan was to move the family to Washington so we could all be together.

They found a house in Rock Creek Park, located just outside downtown Washington, a lovely neighborhood where many foreign dignitaries and ambassadors had homes. The furniture was painted black and the walls were painted red. It was totally foreign-looking to us. Mommy and Daddy thought the decor was hideous, but the house was in a nice neighborhood and we would all be together again ("all" meaning the children, the cook, the maids—the works).

The owners said that we all had to be very careful not to touch the precious antiques and artifacts. The immediate result of this warning was that Eddie carved his initials into the top of a black desk in the living room, and Daddy had to pay for the expensive repair.

The house we rented was situated near one of the park entrances, on a quiet, hilly cul-de-sac, where we could play in the street. I remember our driveway was very steep, sloping way down into the garage. Even though it was wartime, we had a car; Daddy had borrowed a big, heavy Packard from our great friends the Kahns, from Baltimore.

Mommy or Daddy would usually drive us to school. When Mommy would drive us, she would wake up, put her mink coat on over her negligee, and say, "Okay, let's go! I'll take you to school." One of Mommy's favorite stories was when the Packard got stuck in the snow on the way back from school. She would laugh as she remembered the scene: There she was, wearing her slippers, negligee, and mink coat in the middle of downtown Washington. Not wanting to get out of the car, she beckoned for help from the driver's seat, and who knows what those passersby thought she had in mind.

I remember our next-door neighbors were Orthodox Jews, who were always kind and friendly. They kept kosher and had separate plates and silverware for meat and milk products. They had two girls about the same age as Minkie and me. One was named Miriamne, a variation of the Old Hebrew *Miriam*. The father wore a yarmulke, and the mother and girls wore long skirts and always had scarves on their heads. Even when we played after school, the girls had their skirts on—they never wore pants like Minkie and me. I was fascinated by their whole way of life.

Once, one of the daughters was somehow locked in the house, and Daddy was the hero. He told her to get bedsheets and tie them together and then come out on the balcony and climb down. He was on the ground to pick up the pieces, but it all came out safely. This adventure made us all closer friends, and they adored our family from then on.

When it came to school for Minkie and me, Mommy chose Holy Cross Academy. The nuns wore black with a royal-blue bib and a stiffly pleated halo-type veil. With their elaborate veils, they all seemed very tall. They each wore a rosary as a belt and it clinked when they moved. They used those "clickers" all the time! Click. You are doing something bad, so watch out! Click. Look at me! I need your attention. Click. Move to the next pew!

I didn't learn anything at Holy Cross, but Sister would read to us, and that I loved. They were all sweet stories about, of course, good people suffering some sort of pain, poverty, etc. That was the best part of school.

Eddie was sent to a small kindergarten, it may have been public, but my parents knew he would be going back to New York after a year or so, so not much fuss was made about which school he would attend in Washington. I, however, was miffed that he was not going to a Catholic school or to CCD class (instruction for children who were not going to Catholic school, which prepared them for the sacraments of Penance, Holy Communion, and Confirmation). So I took it upon myself to give him a good religious education.

One day, Mommy got a notice from Eddie's school saying that he was terrifying the other students in show-and-tell. Their parents were calling up to say the children were having nightmares, wetting their beds, throwing up. When Mommy asked Eddie what he was saying, he said that he was telling them all about hell and what would happen if they were bad.

Mommy got to the bottom of it and asked me to explain what I had been telling Eddie. "Well," I said, "I told him about the pitchforks, the devils, and the burning." I guess I hadn't gotten to the heaven part, which was not as interesting to me. My mother called the school to apologize, and I was told not to tell Eddie scary things like that anymore.

I think my Jewish friends next door got a taste of it too, which did not go over well at all with their parents, who, I learned, didn't believe in heaven or hell.

One day when I was in sixth or seventh grade, Mommy was horrified when she got a letter stating that my eyes had been tested in school and I could not see the blackboard. The letter went on to say that the school would send me to an ophthalmologist if our family could not afford one. Mommy could not believe it—I read like a fiend, and I never squinted or complained. Thinking back on it, I realize children don't know if they are seeing the world as everyone else does. For me, close was clear, and far away was blurry. Children accept things as normal, unless shown otherwise.

Mommy immediately got an appointment with the best ophthalmologist in the Washington area. She was in the room when I was tested. When the doctor told me to look at the board and read the first letter, I couldn't see anything! Mommy almost fainted.

So, at least all was not for naught at Holy Cross. I got glasses and life changed. For the first time, I could see the blackboard, which was a relief, as the classroom was much larger than the ones at my school in New York.

But Mommy was upset because I wore my glasses so much. "Boys don't make passes at girls who wear glasses," she said, something that Dorothy Parker had quipped and Mommy believed it. So it was a constant battle. "Take off your glasses." "You don't need your glasses all the time." Or, "Your eyes will get weak if you wear them all the time."

During those years in Washington, I realized I didn't want to grow up. I didn't want to wear grown-up clothes or shoes or have my hair done like a grown-up or almost-teenage girl. I was having a wonderful time being a little girl, and I think I was scared of growing up. I still played with dolls, and I would beg Mommy to take me to the five-and-ten to buy baby clothes for one of my dolls that was very lifelike, not a Barbie-type at all.

I brought my doll with me when I went to the movies. I remember when we went to see Judy Garland in *Meet Me in St. Louis* and the theater was packed, so I had to sit on the steps of the aisle with my doll. I learned every single word to every single song in that movie. "The Trolley Song" was a favorite.

Life was different for us in Washington. We didn't have a nanny anymore, but Mommy still had wonderful help—a German cook, Louise, who came with us from New York, and two Cuban maids— and we got along just fine. We children were at school most of the day anyway.

One maid was a lovely, young Cuban woman called Blanca. Her skin was quite light and she was really beautiful and tall. An ambassador saw her at one of my parents' cocktail parties and invited her out to dinner. So Mommy said, "We're going to get you all dressed up." She lent Blanca clothes, and she looked stunning. The ambassador came to pick her up in a limo, and we were all excited that Blanca was going on a date.

She was back in about two hours. She said to Mommy, "Oh, this was not nice. This was not a nice man! I had to leave him quickly." In other words, he just wanted to take advantage of her, as they say. Mommy was furious, because she had been led to believe it would be a proper date.

Our time in Washington also generated many wartime memories. I remember pulling down the blackout shades before we turned on the lights in the evening. And we needed coupons for lots of things, which made everything difficult. My mother used to ask all of her friends if they could spare some of their shoe coupons because we kept growing, and we only had a certain number of coupons per child.

During the school year, my contribution to the war effort was knitting scarves because I couldn't do socks. Mommy would knit socks, all in that horrible olive drab color. I remember saving every little piece of tin foil, and we'd make balls of it. And balls of rubber bands too, which were collected to help with the war effort.

Mommy sold war bonds, as a member of the American Women's Voluntary Service or AWVS. She had a uniform, which she had altered to fit at Bergdorf's, and looked gorgeous in it, of course. She and her other glamorous friends would sit in the lobbies of Wall Street office buildings and sell a lot of bonds.

My mother was also trained to drive an ambulance. She had to take a test, which was a blank map of Brooklyn, because if the Germans invaded, the plan was to take down the street signs, so all the ambulance drivers had to know the streets by heart. Mommy said she really wanted to pass the test, so she asked the girl next to her if she could help her pass, and she agreed. I am glad the Germans never invaded for many reasons, but thank God that we never needed Mommy at the wheel of an ambulance where there were no street signs. Everyone gets lost in Brooklyn even *with* street signs.

We also needed coupons for food during the war, which made things complicated. One of my mother's cousins said to her, "Listen, I know a butcher in New York and he can get you some good meat.

He might pinch my bottom, but you'll get meat. So give me your coupons and I'll go get it. You know, he does it under the counter." So Mommy gave her the coupons, and she would get us eggs and beef.

When Mommy wanted to have a party, she would go into the kitchen and say to Louise, our cook, "I'm having some people for dinner on Saturday." Louise, who was German, would say, "High company or low company?" Mommy would answer, "Well, it's the Kaufmans and so-and-so." And Louise would decide whether they were high or low company, and cook accordingly.

Louise was an incredible cook. Mommy would look in the refrigerator and see that Louise had saved tiny bits of food, like two peas and one string bean. And she'd say, "Louise, just throw them out. It's silly to keep all these little pieces and bits and things." Louise answered, "Mrs. Goodman, during the First World War in Berlin, we were eating rats. We were starving." She could not throw food away for the rest of her life.

Once when Mommy wanted to entertain, Louise told Mommy that she was going to cook tongue. So Mommy said, "I'll go to the butcher myself." She went to the butcher and she said, "I'm having some people for dinner on Saturday night and I'm going to be serving tongue. I'm having fourteen people, so I'd like fourteen tongues."

The butcher looked at her and said, "Mrs. Goodman, come with me." He took her into the walk-in freezer to show her all the meat hanging. He pointed to one thing and said, "That's one tongue." It was huge, and Mommy gasped.

Usually, Mommy would call the butcher and say, "Lay-o-nard?" And he'd say, "Yes, Mrs. Goodman?" And she would say, "How do you know it's me?" And he said, "Nobody calls me 'Lay-o-nard.' Only you, Mrs. Goodman. To everybody else I'm Leonard."

Louise missed New York as much as we did. On her days off, she would get all dolled up and put on her stockings (which were hard to get during the war), rolled up just above her knee. She was a pretty rotund lady. She loved to dance and especially loved the polka.

She would go to dance halls, like Roseland, and to one that was all German, where they played only polkas and danced all evening.

Washington was especially a big change for Daddy. He was so bored the whole time he was in the service; he had so little to do on the job. The building where the Bureau of Supplies was located had a beautiful view of the White House. The officers and staff parked in front of the building in a parking lot until word came down in the form of an order from the president, FDR, that the cars spoiled his view from the Oval Office. No one was permitted to park there again.

Ultimately, Daddy got a parking ticket and needed to go to the police station to pay it. He told Mommy he was going to bring along Eddie, then seven, to show him how justice worked and how, if you didn't follow the rules, you were punished and fined. So off he went with little Eddie to the police station to pay his ticket.

As they entered, a burly captain was sitting behind this huge, high desk. Daddy was dressed in uniform and he had Eddie by the hand. He said good morning to the police officer and said he had come to pay his parking fine. He handed the ticket to the officer, who said, "Get out of here, and take your child. You are defending this country. Don't worry about the ticket. Get out, get out!" Daddy dragged Eddie and hurried back out to his car. He later told us, "So much for trying to give Eddie a lesson in jurisprudence."

There was another lesson to be learned about government, and Daddy wanted us to be sure to remember it. One day, the admiral called him and said, "Andy, you must have all sorts of contacts with shirt makers. I want you to see if you can get six hundred dozen white shirts for the officers, quickly, and at a decent price. My secretary will tell you all the details, style, and sizes."

Daddy said, "Aye, aye, sir," and went to work. He made some phone calls to the heads of Arrow, Hathaway, and Van Heusen shirt makers. He completed the task, got the shirts delivered, and called the admiral for an appointment because he had a check from one of the shirt companies for $100,000, or $1.5 million in today's dollars.

He had not spent all the appropriated money. When he handed the admiral the check, the admiral said, "What the hell is this?" Daddy said that he had saved some money, gotten the order done as told, on time and at a lower price than had been budgeted by the government.

The admiral was livid and said, "What the hell am I supposed to do with this? Don't you understand what will happen if the powers that be realize we don't need the money that we ask for every year?" He told Daddy to give him the check and he took it quickly, put a key in the drawer, put the check in it, and locked it. "Now get out of here, Andy."

Lesson: The government will always ask for more. Daddy said, "When you go into the voting booth and there are propositions to spend money, pull down the lever 'no.' The government will get the money anyway, so don't give them any extra to waste." It may sound silly, but to this day I do it. So did Harry, but when I do it, I say to myself, "Daddy, this is for you."

RYE

We lived in Washington for most of the war, going back to Westchester in the summers. We stayed at the Westchester Country Club and had a regular routine there. With the wartime gas rationing, WCC had a horse and buggy to bring people to the beach. I loved riding in the buggy—I was in heaven!

For most of my summers in Rye, from about age eight to fourteen, I was swimming a great deal. We had swimming classes at the WCC, with a wonderful coach. I was really into it and was down at the beach and the pool as much as I could be. I became a pretty good swimmer. I won at twenty-five yards, which was once across the pool, fifty yards, and in every stroke: breast, back, and freestyle.

But the worst part was sitting poolside, freezing, while we waited our turn. I'd have one towel around my shoulders—those towels were skinny and not very absorbent—and we'd just have to sit there and wait, with our feet in the water or on the side.

For the beach, Grandma Goodman gave me a terry-cloth robe, but it didn't look very good on me—it was too big. I just loved to wear that robe, but my grandma and mother would beg me not to wear it. Mommy would say, "Take that off! It looks terrible. And take off your glasses!" She wanted me to be vain, to be *presumida*, and I really wasn't at the time.

As I got older, I competed in long-distance swimming in the Sound. I don't know if it was one mile or five miles, but it was a long, long way. I ended up being the female long-distance champion.

Believe it or not, I would eat a big meal before I swam in a meet. My favorite was a grilled cheese sandwich with bacon. I'd have two of those, and then for dessert I would have strawberry ice cream with Marshmallow Fluff on top. Unbelievable. And then I would swim! I later read that Michael Phelps also ate tremendous amounts of food before a race.

I loved those summers at the beach, and I remained close to the friends I made there, even when we were all married couples. Frannie Santangelo was the male long-distance swimming champion, and we've kidded each other all of our lives that we were co-champions.

Every August, we put on a show at the main clubhouse called The Big Little Show, where we danced and sang musical numbers. We had a wonderful director and we rehearsed down at the beach all summer long—we'd come out from swimming, dry off, put on ballet shoes, and go to rehearsal. The show was held at night on the chipped terrazzo dance floor of the main club. Some of the numbers were with tap shoes, and we loved the sound of the shoes on that surface. We felt so grown-up and professional on the stage and had a lot of fun.

During those summers there was also more time for riding, including long trail rides through the woods instead of at the indoor ring.

It was always a fulfilling time, and I have many joyful memories of my summers, but one year the death of my beloved abuelita changed all that. Abuelita always spent the summers with us in Rye. I remember so well the night it happened. Mommy told me that she and Daddy were going out. Mommy kissed Abuelita good-bye, and Abuelita, who never complimented Mommy much, said to her, "You look like an angel." Later, it seemed to me that Abuelita may have known that she was almost with the angels.

Mommy and Daddy came home to an ambulance and police cars in front of the house. Mommy dashed up the stairs, to find Abuelita in some sort of oxygen tent. Mommy was, of course, upset and crying, and I heard that Abuelita said, "Don't worry, darling. I am happy. I will be with Eugenio again." She knew she would be reunited with the husband she had adored, who had died so young.

This happened right before my tenth birthday. I remember I'd asked for a two-wheel bike, which I later named "Betty," and I pre-tended that the bike was a horse, a chestnut mare. A few days be-fore she died, Abuelita had helped me push my old bike, my tricycle, up a hill. I remember that she was panting from the effort, and I thought that was what had caused her to die. She already had a bad heart, and I thought it was my fault. I cried and cried to my nanny, who I had been left with when everyone went to Cuba to put Abuelita to rest.

There was one summer during the war when I went away to Camp Adeawanda, in Maine, for eight weeks. Because of the wartime gas situation, Mommy and Daddy never came up to see me the whole sum-mer. Eight weeks! What a change from my sheltered life at home.

Like most adults, I have dozens of stories from my camp days. One vivid memory is finding out about the facts of life. Two girls took me under the cabin, which was on stilts, and taught me every-thing. I was about ten. I said, "Impossible. It's impossible. That's dis-gusting. That's horrible. My mommy and daddy wouldn't do that." I didn't believe them.

That was an awful thing to learn from two children, especially since I was far from Mommy to verify it, which of course I did when I got home. Mommy called it "making love" and left it at that.

There were other lessons to be learned at camp. Once we went camping overnight in the woods, and in the morning, we were all sent to pick blueberries, the little tiny ones. I was so hungry, and I was eating more than I was picking and putting into my berry pail. When we returned to camp, we all lined up to give the counselor our berries to add to the pancakes. When she saw how few I had, she asked me what happened. I told her I was hungry and ate most of my berries, and she said, "No pancakes for you!" What a lesson: What you put into the pot, you get out of the pot.

We had pretty basic food at camp. Rabbit for dinner sometimes, and we thought it was chicken. The little camp store typically had almost no candy, but one day, word was out that there was candy at the store, and we were allowed to buy one Milky Way candy bar each with our camp scrip. No Milky Way has ever tasted as good since.

I signed up for hours and hours of riding at camp, out by the bean fields. Speaking of beans, I got an award for being the best bean picker at camp. Daddy used to laugh at this story. We had a Victory Garden at camp, where we raised beans for the troops. Daddy would say, "What? Are they using these kids as slave labor?" We would be piled into a truck and go out to this field, and we'd pick beans for the cause.

Mommy hardly recognized me when I returned from camp that year. I got off the train sunburned and growing out of my clothes. The sleeves of my jacket were halfway up my arms and my skirt was too short. She missed me though, and I never went away to summer camp again, although I did enjoy it.

Other summers, we traveled as a family to visit our friends the Kahns at their camp in the Adirondacks—Camp Midwood, at Lake Placid. It was a family compound, with several cabins and houses for dining and recreation. We could fish, water ski, and swim. I remember wonderful lunches and cookouts with Bill the Woodsman. I can still smell the steak, potatoes, and corn on the cob. Eleanor, the Kahns' daughter, and I would entertain everyone by putting on "shows," like *Oklahoma!* and *Carousel.*

Toward the end of the war, I discovered that Mommy was a closet Democrat. The Goodmans were Republicans, and when I was growing up, there was a great deal of distaste, to say the least, for President Roosevelt.

Anybody with money was against Roosevelt. They said that he was empowering the unions, and the unions were going to ruin everybody's business. There was a great fear of what he was going to do with a powerful central government. My parents and grand-parents feared that Roosevelt would destroy what all these self-made men had built up.

One time, my parents had a large dinner party. I wasn't at the big table but was invited to sit down with the grown-ups. Grandpa and Grandma were there, and they asked me who was the president of the United States, and I said, "President Roosevelt." And they said, "Have you ever known any other president?" And I said, "No." And then Mommy said, "Do you realize that she always has had just one man as president?" And I said, "He's like a king." And that got everyone laughing, and saying, "You see!"

I didn't know where Mommy's heart lay for quite a while, but one day I remember coming home from school and I found her in the den, lying on the sofa, with an ashtray absolutely full of ciga-rettes nearby, and she was crying. I had never seen my mother cry—ever. I said, "Mommy, what's wrong?"

"Roosevelt died!" she replied. I was shocked, because I'd been taught not to admire him or like him.

Then she told me that Roosevelt had started the Good Neigh-bor Policy in Latin America. Because she was living in Cuba then, she was very grateful to him. Suddenly, that part of the world was being recognized and helped with aid and trade. She told me what a wonderful thing it was for Cuba and for South America. She loved Roosevelt very much. But she never mentioned that when anybody else was talking politics.

Vivien (standing, far right) and dormmates on graduation day, Wellesley College, June 1954.

DAY SCHOOL TO DORM

The war ended and we moved back to New York City. Once there, Mommy and Daddy began their annual search to rent a summerhouse in Rye, New York. As usual, they boarded a train at Grand Central and took it to the Rye Station, where they got in Charlie's cab. Charlie knew all the local goings-on, and my parents would ask him about good prospects for a summerhouse. This particular year, Charlie told them they should consider *moving* to Rye because there was a nice house for sale on Hilltop Place, so Mommy and Daddy decided to take a look at it. They purchased the house, and soon after the move, my youngest sister, Pammy, was born, in 1946. The house on Hilltop Place became our family home, and my parents lived there for fifty-two years, until both of them passed away.

The year we moved back to New York, first to Manhattan and then to Rye, was a very difficult time for me academically. When we moved from Washington, it was the middle of the school year, so I went back to Dominican Academy for the last part of the term. I quickly realized that I was behind in math and other subjects. The rest of the class had spent the first part of the term studying the State of New York, which was a major topic for the state Regents Exam and was not a part of the curriculum in D.C. My teachers were shocked that I had lost so much of my education along the banks of the Potomac.

When we moved to Rye, I transferred—for the second time in two years—to Rye Country Day School. RCDS was an academically rigorous environment, and I transferred in at tenth grade, when all the typical high school groups and cliques had formed. I floundered academically. I didn't flunk out that first year, but my grades were mostly Ds and one C. Math was a dilemma, and geometry was like Japanese to me—I didn't understand it at all. In my day, there was no hand-holding, no tutors or academic support, and my classmates were so advanced in everything. It was sink or swim, and at first, I sank.

We had a small class of around thirteen students, which was divided into two groups: the "Rye group" children of the old, moneyed families, and the "train group," who came from lower Westchester towns like Larchmont, New Rochelle, and Mount Vernon. The Rye group families belonged to clubs like Apawamis, Manursing Island, and the American Yacht Club. They were all WASPs, no Jews or other ethnic groups. Yet, the Rye group literally wooed me. I was never sure why. After all, I was the new girl, supposedly half-Jewish. I guess where I lived and my family's wealth trumped everything.

I preferred the train group, as they were smart, interesting, and varied. One member of that group, Greta, lived in Harrison, which is adjacent to but not in the nesting ground of Rye. She was a talented pianist who was smart enough to whip through her homework and still devote hours to piano practice each day. She was a straight-A student and my idol. I used to sit under the grand piano in her house while she practiced and do my homework. Being five years older than my closest sibling, I learned to concentrate easily while bedlam ensued in the nursery. This skill carried into my adult life: I could still read a book while my husband, Harry, watched TV.

My friend Greta's music teacher was a famous harpsichordist in the city, and Greta also took lessons from a very handsome local piano teacher. Greta's father was a wealthy but unattractive man— bald, short, and chunky—and her mother was truly gorgeous. Greta and I always wondered if there was something going on between her mother and the handsome piano teacher. Despite our musings, it was clear that Greta was the center of her parents' lives. Years later, I had a similar role to play, as our Debby rode horses and competed successfully. Like Greta's parents, I was living with talent, nurturing it, sacrificing for it, enjoying it, and being very proud of it.

My other friends were also admirable. Charlotte Beebe and Penny Kimball were close friends who were bright and fun. We used to meet in New Rochelle on Saturdays and either go to Iona or New Rochelle High School for the football games or to the movies. We all had crushes on Robert Mitchum, Van Johnson, and Montgomery Clift. We had lift-top desks at school, and we'd cut photos of stars out of movie magazines and Scotch tape them to the inside of the desk top. When you lifted the desk top, there they were. We loved *Life* and *Look* magazines, and when a new issue arrived in the mail, we'd call each other and go over each page, especially the cover . . . we were always excited to find out who made the cover.

Another good friend of mine was Barbara Briggin, who lived in Larchmont. Unlike Penny and Charlotte, Barbara had a sad life. Her mother had died just before I came to RCDS, and her father was distant and strict. She was the middle child with one older brother and a younger one. Although her family was comfortable enough to employ hired staff, her father insisted that Barbara take on a "parental" role with her younger brother, coordinating doctor and dentist appointments, clothes shopping, and other school-related chores.

Barbara Briggin and Vivien (pregnant with Andrew), Westchester, New York, 1957.

Barbara confided in me that she felt unfairly burdened with this responsibility and would rather "act her age" and spend more time with her friends.

However, I spent a lot of time with Barbara, and on Sundays, when it was Barbara's job to pick up supper, I would accompany her to the deli. We'd pick up bread, meat, and delicious pickles. It was all we could do not to eat a pickle on the way home; the smell was so enticing. Once, we did eat a pickle in the car on the way home, and her dad went ballistic.

I always had the sense that there was a deep, dark secret within Barbara's family, but I was never able to find out what it was. Whenever I mentioned Barbara, Daddy would ask me about their name. "Briggin? That sounds like a changed name," he'd say. He suspected that they were Jewish. Daddy could not abide hypocrisy, and he was particularly upset when he heard about Jewish families changing their names to gain access to private clubs. I also wondered about Barbara's mother. She had died before I knew Barbara, and looking back, I wonder if she didn't suffer, as Barbara did, and perhaps took her own life.

As adults, the boys turned out all right, but Barbara did not. She graduated from Sarah Lawrence College and became a therapist, working with children with special needs. She lived alone in New York City and never married. She attempted suicide, survived, and finally died of natural causes some years ago. When I was asked to speak at her memorial service, I said that when they handed out lives, Barbara got a sad one.

In contrast to Barbara, I was very lucky. Although I struggled with academics in high school, it did not ruin my life. Everything else was just fine. I kept on writing and riding horses, I had friends, and I loved life in Rye even though I knew my parents were upset about my marks. Education was important to them, and they made sure our home life focused on supporting our schoolwork.

For instance, at our dinner table discussions, if anyone stated a fact that Daddy didn't believe or on which we needed more information, he would say, "get *The World Almanac*." It had every fact and figure in it and resolved many disagreements. Later on, when I was dating Harry, he and Daddy would argue over how many troops died in a particular battle or war. The answer was always, "Look it up!" Someone would get the WA out of the library to resolve the dispute. Each year, when the new edition was published, it was an important occasion for our family. We had the book of facts at the ready for the new year.

At school, my marks gradually improved and I began to catch up with my classmates. By senior year, my grades were okay. One of the key factors in my improvement was a wonderful teacher who believed in me, loved my writing, and inspired me. However, in those days you were either "college material" or you weren't, and if you weren't, you were not allowed to take the SATs. I don't know if that decision was based on protecting RCDS's high academic standing, but I was not allowed to take the exam. My choices for college were therefore limited to schools that did not require the SAT, and I ended up choosing

Bradford Junior College, as Daddy felt that Sarah Lawrence, another possibility, was too liberal.

My ultimate goal was to get into Wellesley College, where most of my friends went. Like Wellesley, Bradford was located in Massachusetts, so I would visit my friends often, which kept me motivated in my studies. Bradford was more like a finishing school, and most of the girls seemed more focused on dating than studying. Not me.

For me, Bradford was the means to get to Wellesley, so I studied hard. The teachers adored me because I earned straight As, and they weren't used to that. While the other girls went on dates, I studied hard or worked, either in the library or the snack bar, where I would work the breakfast shift. I made so many English muffins that to this day, I can't eat or look at an English muffin, even when it's on TV.

The headmistress at Bradford had ties to Wellesley and wrote a glowing recommendation, so I transferred for my sophomore year. I was so happy to be there with my friends. I roomed with one of my classmates from RCDS, Penny Kimball, in Shafer Hall on the quad.

Vivien and classmate, Wellesley College Class of 1954's fiftieth reunion, 2004.

My transition was a glorious one. Having achieved my goal, I felt so lucky to be there, and during my three years at Wellesley I milked it dry.

Whatever there was to do, I did it. I hosted the classical music program on the college radio station; I joined Shakespeare House and performed in several productions; my friends and I would take the bus into Boston and attend Broadway previews or rehearsals with Leonard Bernstein and the Boston Philharmonic. Though I tried out for a part in our Junior Show, I didn't get it and was named stage manager instead. I sat in the orchestra pit, and if a performer forgot her lines, I would mouth them to her.

My roommate, Penny, was an absolute genius. She has the kind of mind that can grasp the gist of an entire page in a second. Penny and I have reconnected at our fortieth and fiftieth high school and college reunions, and I continue to admire her spirit of adventure. One night at college, when I was studying in our room, Penny came in, saying, "Vivien, you've got to come to the observatory right now. The sky is so clear." I tried to beg off because I had so much homework, but Penny persuaded me and we headed off into the chilly night. We climbed the observatory stairs to the telescope, where Penny adjusted the lens for me. When I looked into the eyepiece, I couldn't believe what I saw: stars of all different colors bouncing and dancing. Thank God she made me come, I thought, because I never would have gone myself and probably wouldn't again. Moments like that were so special.

Another good friend at Wellesley was Bobby Romano. She was from Yonkers and dated a boy who was attending Harvard Law School. I had never met him, and one night Bobby confided in me that her boyfriend was blind. She was not sure if she loved him out of pity or just love. I told her that it was clear that she loved him, and of course she has pity for him, but to look at what he had done with his life. I knew that he rarely asked her for assistance, but with the help of his classmates he graduated from Harvard Law School. In those days, there were few law textbooks available in braille, so his classmates would take turns reading his law books to him. At my fiftieth college reunion, Harry and I sat with Bobby and her now husband. They haven't changed a bit—both wonderful, caring people. He has a successful law practice and she teaches English as a second language to newly arrived immigrants.

I majored in English and also studied Spanish literature and political science. I remember telling my mother I didn't like "poli sci," and she said, "Oh, honey, you have to be nice to everyone because you never know, sweetie. Be friendly and pleasant."

"Mommy," I said, "it's a course, not a person!"

My mother was so gracious to my college friends and also to Minkie's and Eddie's. Later in life, I would meet classmates who reminded me of how kind my mother had been, inviting them to our home for the holidays if they couldn't go home, or for summer weekends.

Mommy and Daddy were darlings. They came up to visit me often and brought me goodies from home. We'd go into Boston and stay at the Ritz-Carlton. On one such weekend, we saw the pianist Vladimir Horowitz and his wife in the hotel dining room. He was performing with the Boston Philharmonic and was dressed in a white tie and tails. I remember his very long fingers and still feel what a thrill it was to be so close to such a genius.

Other family members visited me too. My uncle Jorge, who had graduated from Harvard and the Sorbonne, came to visit one weekend. He was so proud that I was attending Wellesley. It might have been on that visit that he said to me, "Vivi, you have to get your mother to read more."

"But she does, Tio Jorge."

"I know, but it's not the right kind of reading."

"I don't think you have a shot," I told him.

Jorge wanted Mommy to read for edification instead of recreation, but Mommy always read romantic novels and light fare. Though not an intellectual like Jorge, she was wise. She understood the value of a good education, and she made sure that we children understood it too. My siblings all graduated from top schools: Minkie from Smith College, Eddie from Yale, and Pammy from University of Wisconsin–Madison.

The year after I graduated from Wellesley, I spent five months in Cuba visiting my uncle Jorge and my aunt Margot. I loved my time there and so enjoyed being in such an intellectually stimulating environment. Jorge was a professor of philosophy at the University of Havana, and every day after lunch his students would visit him in his study. I saw firsthand how much they respected and admired him. A highly respected author, essayist, and statesman, he also hosted a very popular weekly television show, Cuba's version of *Meet the Press*.

Mommy would call often, asking when I was coming home, but I wanted to stay as long as I could. Being with my uncle was like a postgraduate education for me, and I wanted to prolong my intellectual growth as long as possible. Jorge was an "absentminded professor," to be sure, and my aunt Margot kept his life organized. They were not wealthy, but both seemed content to weather life's economic ups and downs. I felt surrounded by love and, in particular, felt such affection from my uncle. Knowing now what a pivotal role Jorge played in my life from the beginning, I wonder if he felt he was a father figure to me. He was genuinely interested in my intellectual life and treated me not only as a beloved niece, but also as an intellectual *compadre*.

During my college days I dated students from Harvard Law and Medical Schools. I didn't date undergraduates, and I found Business School boys boring and narrowly money-minded. When I dated law students, I'd accompany them to their classes, and I attended some very interesting lectures. Although I was invited on weekend dates to Dartmouth, my friends advised against it. "Don't go. They're wild men up there in the woods because there are no girls there. Forget it!"

But I was always more of a student than a social butterfly. If I had to choose a favorite class, it was undoubtedly my Shakespeare class. The professor made the plays and sonnets come alive in so many ways. She was a very interesting person herself, so when Mommy and Daddy came to visit, I would bring them to one of her classes. They loved it too.

In those days, there weren't many Catholics at Wellesley. I knew of only one other Catholic girl with whom I shared classes, Lois Cochran. There were two professors in particular who challenged me to articulate my beliefs as a Catholic. The first taught a class on the eighteenth-century English novel. I had written a paper on *Moll Flanders*, by Daniel Defoe, in which I asserted that all humans are born "good." After receiving a C- on the paper, my professor and I met to discuss my mark. "You're a Catholic, aren't you?" she said. She challenged my assertion that all are born good and asked if I believed in baptism as the means to wash away original sin. I was taken aback and agreed to edit my paper, though she never changed my mark.

At Wellesley, every student had to a pass a Bible study class, and most of us took the class during sophomore year. Mr. Buck, a young Protestant minister, taught my section. One day he called on me and said, "Miss Goodman, you're a Catholic, aren't you?" When I answered yes, he asked me to name the different types of angels. "Cherubim and seraphim," I answered. He took me to task, saying that these were only two of the nine types of angels, and that I had better find out about the other seven. I took this as a challenge, and endeavored to become more knowledgeable about Catholicism, which, in turn, strengthened my faith. Every time I was presented with a question about Catholicism that I couldn't answer, I would consult *The Catholic Encyclopedia*, a huge tome kept on a stand in the library.

I stopped taking my religion for granted. I never felt the need to stand on a mountaintop and screech about it, but I realized that I had to be able to defend my beliefs, in ways both big and small. For instance, when classmates would ask why I didn't eat meat on Friday, I realized that not everyone understood this practice. Though considered a small sacrifice, I explained that since Christ died on a Friday, we didn't eat meat on that day out of respect and remembrance. It was a small sacrifice for us. After all, he gave his life for us.

I loved my college years and I am very proud to have graduated from Wellesley, because I worked so hard to get there. It was always very important to me to make my parents proud and to measure up to my siblings, who are each brilliant in their own way. They are incredibly well-read, well-spoken, successful in their selected professions, and active philanthropists. I didn't want to be the adoptee that turned out to be "the dumb one."

Vivien and Harry at Houghton Memorial Chapel at the Wellesley College Class of 1954's fiftieth reunion, 2004.

On graduation day in 1954, I was awash in tears. I knew that this precious time and place in my life was coming to an end. While I didn't know exactly what I was moving on to, I did know that I would never again have the luxury of being in this "ivory tower," with the time to pursue my studies. I knew from then on it was the real world, whatever it was going to bring.

In 2003, the movie *Mona Lisa Smile* came out and it was all about Wellesley and the class of 1954. I thought it was incredibly accurate, although some aspects were overdone. In the movie, there is a scene showing a class on how to set a table, when to wear white gloves, and the like. I never heard of such a course and neither had any of my classmates.

But the movie did portray many things about Wellesley correctly. For instance, we did have curfews. On weeknights we had to sign in to the dorm by 10:00 p.m., and on weekends we needed to sign in by midnight. Also, students in a dorm could invite a professor over for dinner. After dinner, the professor, usually a young, handsome man, would sit with us in the living room and answer our questions. If the professor was particularly gorgeous, the room would be packed.

Seeing the movie reminded me of the traditions and routines that made up my daily life on campus. Students were expected to contribute to our community. My dorm, Shafer, like all the dorms, had a schedule of chores that students were expected to sign up for each month. I remember waiting tables in the dining room and being "on bells." The student on bells announced the arrival of guests to the resident students in the rooms above. For example, she'd call up to the floor and say, "Goodman, you've got a caller." One evening I had a blind date, and I asked the girl on bells to give me a hint about my date's height—because I was fairly tall, I wanted to know what size heels to wear. When she called up to the floor, she said, "Goodman, your caller is here. Get on your knees."

Mona Lisa Smile was playing in movie theaters when the class of 1954 had its fiftieth reunion. During Wellesley reunions, each returning class parades wearing their beanies, which in our case were purple, led by the class officers holding their class banner. To match the beanies, I had donated light purple Bergdorf Goodman scarves for everyone to wear. But the highlight of our fiftieth reunion parade was clearly the Mona Lisa paddle masks that a friend of mine provided for everyone. We waited until we were at the base of the chapel steps to put the masks in front of our faces and then processed into the chapel—the crowd loved it.

WORK AND TRAVEL

Most of the class of 1954 graduated and then got married or did some sort of work while waiting to get married. The logo on the school shield says *Non Ministrari, sed Ministrare* ("Not to be ministered unto but to minister"), and we used to joke, "Not to be ministers but to be ministers' wives." There wasn't a push for graduate school, and very few graduates went on to a full-time career. Most of my classmates either did volunteer work or went to secretarial school—I did both. I went to secretarial school and also volunteered at an orphanage, the Cardinal McCloskey School and Home, in White Plains, New York. I didn't last long there because I couldn't take it—it was too sad.

The children would be told that a parent or relative was coming to take them out for the day, and we'd get them all dressed up and they'd sit on a bench in the front hall waiting all day for someone to come. When no one came, one of the volunteers would just scoop them all up and take them for ice cream. It was horrible to watch. Many of the children would tell me they weren't orphans, assuring me they had a mommy or daddy who was coming to take them home. It would kill me to hear them call out for their mommies.

Although it was a sad place, there was a wonderful nun there. When she entered a room, all the young children would run to her and hug her. She would kneel on the floor, and the children would cling to her habit. I remember that she would look at me kindly and

Left to right: Vivien, Nena, Eddy, Andy, Minkie, and Belle.
Off to Europe, aboard the USS *Independence*, summer of
1954.

say, "I have the most important job in this orphanage. I have to
teach these children how to be in an institution—most of them, for
the rest of their lives."

I attended secretarial school and learned to type quickly, but
not quickly enough for *The New York Times*. I had asked Daddy to
get me an interview there and he called one of the top editors. Sec-
retaries at *The Times* were required to type sixty words a minute,
and I wasn't quite that fast. Also, my interview did not go very well.
The editor asked me about my education and experience, and I told
him that I had graduated from Wellesley as an English major. He
looked at me over his glasses and asked, "Do you know how many

English majors want to work at *The New York Times?*" He asked if I had other experience, and I said that I'd done volunteer work and traveled. He replied, "Thank you very much, Miss Goodman, but you must realize that you have to put something into the pot to get something out of the pot." (Which I had, once before, learned at camp.) That was the end of the interview and any thoughts of a journalism career.

I took a couple of memorable trips to Europe as a young woman. I first traveled to Europe with a tour group just before entering college in the summer of 1950. It was shortly after the Second World War, and Europeans were still dealing with shortages and rationing. When I checked in to my hotel in London, I received ration coupons to use during my stay. While I was there I planned to visit Pam, my high school pen pal, who lived on the coast.

On the train from Victoria Station, I ordered oatmeal and asked for sugar. Even though I had coupons for it, the waiter told me there was no sugar to be had. I hadn't realized sweets were so rare, and I figured it would be a wonderful surprise if I arrived with chocolate. In addition, before I had left New York, I asked Pam what I could bring as a present, and she asked for much-needed soap for the family and stockings for her mother. When I arrived in her town, I found a candy shop, put all of my ration coupons on the counter, and asked for all the chocolate they could provide. The store clerk looked at me and said, "But Miss, if I do that, there will be no chocolate for the whole town." This was a shock. The war had ended four years ago, and during that time the United States had returned to business as usual—shortages and rationing were a thing of the past. So I took back most of the coupons and settled for a smaller gift of chocolate for my pen pal. I remember starving for sugar the whole time I was in England.

I also traveled to Italy on that trip and remember going into a store to get some hairpins. I didn't know much Italian, but I pointed to the card of hairpins underneath the counter. The clerk took out the card and handed me one hairpin. I was so embarrassed, because I wanted the whole card. Again, I realized how limited supplies were, even for everyday items that I took for granted.

Later in the trip, we were crossing a border close to Eastern Europe. Armed border guards entered the train cars and asked for everyone's passports. When they checked the passport of one of the girls in our group, they made her get off the train and wait while the train pulled away. It was very scary because we couldn't do anything for her. We felt powerless to help because the guards had guns, which were big and frightening.

Our tour guide explained later that the guards had a travelers' list, and if the passenger list or passport names didn't exactly match their list, they could detain someone until they figured it out. It was pretty scary to realize how people could have their freedom taken away so quickly and easily.

About four years later, just after I graduated from Wellesley, our family took a wonderful trip to Europe. My brother, Eddie, was twelve, Minkie was eighteen, and I was twenty-two. I pored over guidebooks at the time and read up on every place we visited. I also wrote about our experiences in my travel journal. When we'd arrive in a town, I'd start the "lecture." When we went to Arles, France, where Van Gogh painted, I'd exhort everyone to notice the brilliant sun, sky, and landscape. I was truly inspired, but at that point in their lives Minkie and Eddie weren't. This did not discourage me, however, because I didn't want my siblings to miss out on anything.

We also traveled to Spain, where we dined at traditional inns called *paradores*. At many of these inns, the bathroom was a hole in the ground, so Mommy wouldn't let us drink the tap water. It was summer, so it was quite hot, and of course there was no bottled water then, so at lunch Mommy would let us drink from the big pitcher of sangria on the table.

She never understood why Eddie, Minkie, and I would all fall asleep in the car after lunch.

My Grandmother Goodman traveled with us on that trip. She

was known for her terrible temper, which we experienced firsthand one evening at dinner. We were at a fancy restaurant and Eddie did not want to finish his meal. Minkie and I decided to cover for him, splitting his meal between our plates and finishing it so he wouldn't get in trouble with Grandma. She noticed what we were doing and had a screaming fit in the middle of the restaurant.

She yelled at us, "You girls, you're not getting my ring! Eddie's going to get it." We didn't know what she meant at the time, but as it turned out, the ring in question was a big, beautiful diamond ring. She kept her word, giving it to Eddie, who gave it to his wife, Lorna. So much for Minkie and me trying to save his ass.

Truth be told, I am an eternal student. I love to learn, and between my college days, travels, and jobs before marriage, my world enlarged—yet at the core were always my family and horses.

Consuelo Mañach,
Vivien's abuelita, at
around age twenty,
the future matriarch,
Madrid, Spain.

Nena and her
mother, Consuelo,
Madrid, Spain,
c. 1911 or 1912.

Left to right: Jorge, Eugenio, Consuelo (Abuelita), and Manuel Mañach, Madrid, Spain, c. late 1890s or early 1900s.

Nena's father, Eugenio Mañach, Madrid, Spain, September 22, 1911. *"To my little daughter: Be good, hard-working, and humble and you will always have the love of your father. –Eugenio"*

Rafaele "Lello" Matacena and his mother (Vivien's grandmother), Filomena Matacena, in Venice, Italy, 1929.

Lello and Filomena at Teatro San Carlo, Naples, 1959.

Lello Matacena, around three years old, in
Naples, Italy.

Vivien Matacena in Havana, Cuba, c. 1934.

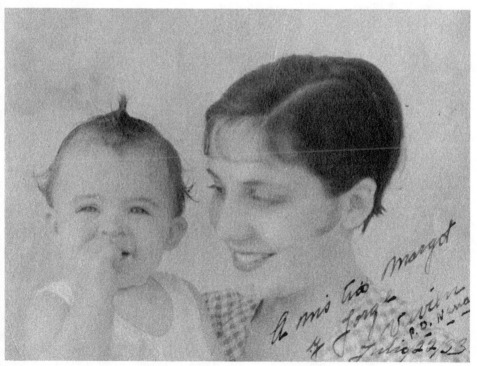

Vivien and Nena, Havana, Cuba. Photo inscription to Vivien's godparents: *"To my Tios Margot
and Jorge, Vivien via Nena, July 22, '33."*

Lello's cousin Raffaellino, Nena, and Orestes Ferrara (Cuban ambassador to the U.S., and uncle to Lello and Raffaellino), c. late 1920s or early 1930s.

Nena Mañach (far right) with friends, including Silvia Rosen (far left), at Varadero Tennis Club, Varadero, Cuba, c. 1920s.

Nena Mañach Goodman posing in front of a store with a familiar name (*mañach* in old Spanish means "blacksmith").

Apartment building in Cambridge, Massachusetts, where Nena and her family lived while brother Jorge attended Harvard, c. 1914–1921. (Photo by Vivien Hanson.)

RIGHT, TOP AND BOTTOM: Nena, Andy, and Vivien in studio portraits taken for Andy and Nena's engagement announcement, New York City, 1935.

Mrs. Manach Betrothed to A. Goodman

Senora Consuelo Manach, of Havana, announced the engagement of her daughter, Mrs. Nena Manach, to Andrew Goodman, son of Mr. and Mrs. Edwin Goodman, and the brother of Miss Ann Goodman, of 2 W. 58th st.

Mrs. Manach was born in Spain and is a cousin of Countess Covadonga, who recently married the eldest son of former King Alfonso of Spain and former heir apparent to the Spanish throne.

The count and countess are now visiting in New York.

Mr. George Manach, brother of Mrs. Manach, and his wife are also sojourning in New York, where he is a visiting lecturer at Columbia University in the Spanish and Pan American departments. Two other brothers, Manuel and Eugene Manach, live in Havana.

Mrs. Manach attended the Sacred Heart Convent in Boston and the Sacred Heart Convent in Havana.

Mr. Goodman attended the Horace Mann School in New York, the Hackley School at Tarrytown and the University of Michigan. He was apprenticed for a year to Patou in Paris and since has taken an active part in the mnagement of Bergdorf Goodmn, and is now vi e-president.

Mr. and Mrs. Edwin Goodman and Miss Ann Goodman will fly to Havana to attend the wedding which will take place soon. The couple will make their residence in Nw York.

ABOVE: Engagement announcement for Nena and Andrew in *The New York Times*.

Home movie stills of Nena and Andy's wedding, outside Havana, Cuba, September 29, 1935. They were married at the home of family friends, the Kaffenburgs.

Vivien and Minkie
in Central Park,
New York City,
1937.

Vivien in
Rye,
New York,
1936.

RIGHT and BELOW:
Andy and Vivien at
the Westchester
Country Club
beach club,
summer 1936.

Vivien, always a lover of dressing up, in her Tyrolese outfit, Westchester, New York, 1936.

Vivien at the Westchester Country Club beach club, summer 1936.

Eddie, Minkie, and Vivien, New York City, 1940.

Eddie, Minkie, and Vivien in Central Park, New York City, winter 1942.

Minkie and Vivien at Cienfuegos Yacht Club, Cuba, 1940.

Vivien on Gold Coin at Kenilworth Riding Club, Rye, New York, c. 1947.

Vivien dressed for
the Little Big Show
at Westchester
Country Club, Rye,
New York, 1944.

Dormitory portrait outside Shafer Hall, Wellesley College, fall 1953. Vivien is in the second row from the top, sixth from left.

Wellesley College Class of 1954's ten-year reunion, June 1964.

Vivien and Harry at their wedding reception, Westchester Country Club, Rye, New York, January 12, 1957.

COURTSHIP AND MARRIAGE

IN MARCH 1954, DURING MY SENIOR YEAR AT WELLESLEY, A BOY I didn't know called me up and asked me out on a blind date. I said no because I didn't go on blind dates anymore; I was a senior and I'd had some awful blind dates by then.

Then he told me he had gotten my name from Paul Pileckas. Paul was a young man I had met a few years earlier as a teen at the Popponesset Inn on Cape Cod, where my family and I had spent part of the summer. When I was a sophomore at Wellesley and Paul was at Colgate University, we dated and were pinned for a time—being "pinned" meant you were seriously dating but not quite engaged.

Knowing that Paul wouldn't give my name to some jerk, I agreed to go out on a double date with him. He said he'd find a guy if I could find a girl. I yelled down the hall to my friend Lois. "Do you want to go on a double date just for a drink tonight?" She didn't want to go, but I talked her into it.

Looking back, it's a miracle that date ever happened. I was performing in a Shakespeare play that night and wasn't available until

10:00 p.m. Due to curfew, we would have to be back to the dorm by midnight. Our dates were naval officers who were driving up from Newport, Rhode Island, where they were stationed. It seemed like a pretty big schlep for a drink and a two-hour date.

When they arrived to pick me up from the theater, Lois was already in the car. Harry was driving, and his friend—my date—was drop-dead gorgeous. He was six-foot-three and blond with a great physique, and for the life of me I can't remember his name. Harry called him "Bolivar."

We went out for a beer, and frankly, the tavern we went to was a dump. We got a booth and the four of us chatted. The minute I met Harry, I was instantly smitten. Harry was tall and trim, with auburn hair and hazel eyes, but it was his humor and quiet charm that fascinated me. When he looked at me across the table, I melted—it was kismet.

I certainly didn't make the same impression on him that night. He told me later that I looked so ugly the first time he saw me—I had all that stage makeup on. He said my face looked green, and as I had been playing the Duke of Norfolk, my hair was gray.

Shakespeare House at Wellesley College, 1954.

Ensign Henry "Harry" Malloy, U.S. Navy, at home in Larchmont, New York, c. 1953.

No matter what Harry thought of me at first, I thought he was charming, funny, and cute. I thought he was perfect! He was Irish Catholic, had graduated from Villanova University in 1953, and grew up in Larchmont. When I met him, he was serving as an officer on a destroyer. He would go out on tours for five months at a time, usually in the North Atlantic in winter.

The four of us started double-dating regularly, going to nicer places where we could eat dinner and dance. After a few dates, Harry was shipped off, but I kept going out with Bolivar to find out more about Harry—where he was, what he was doing.

Around Mother's Day, I asked Bolivar what he had gotten for his mother. When he said he hadn't gotten her anything, I insisted that we stop so he could send his mother a box of Fanny Farmer candies. When he got back in the car, he said, "You know, when we get married you have to change your religion." I realized at that moment that I had to stop going out with Bolivar. He was talking about getting married and I had no interest in him at all. The only reason I was dating him was to get news of Harry. After I stopped seeing him, I had no way of finding out about Harry.

A year went by and I was still smitten. I would talk about Harry with anybody who would listen. I had never dated him, but I was crazy about him just the same. I can't explain it, but I just knew in my heart that he was the one. Over the summer, while swimming at the beach club, I saw Ann Harmon, who was really gorgeous and had been named Miss Westchester. More importantly, Harry had mentioned knowing her. Finally, someone who might be able to fill me in on Harry's whereabouts! I remember swimming up to her by the side of the pool and mentioning that I had met Harry. She told me that he was in the North Atlantic and he'd be gone for weeks.

After ending his tour and coming home to Larchmont, Harry called Ann for a date. Luckily for me, she said she wasn't feeling well (although she admitted to me years later that she wasn't sick but was dating someone else). Ann suggested that he call me because she remembered meeting me at the pool.

Harry called me twice and got a busy signal both times. He said to his mother, "The heck with it. I'm just going to go out and have a drink with Peter." Peter Ernst was Harry's friend from Larchmont, who was home on leave from duty on the *Wasp*, an aircraft carrier.

His mother, Ellen, said, "Third time's a charm. Why don't you try once more?" He finally got through, and I always say, "Thank you and God bless you, Ellen."

I couldn't believe it—Harry was finally calling me. Even though I had been carrying a torch for him for more than a year, when he asked me to go out for a drink, I played hard to get, telling him I had some things to do, which was not so. I made him talk me into it, and finally we agreed that he would pick me up at eight. I calmly hung up the phone, then ran screaming down the hall. "Minkie, he called!"

Minkie and I spent the whole afternoon going through at least seven choices of outfits, searching through her closet, my closet, and Mommy's closet. In the end, I chose a very simple dress. That evening, I told Daddy that a boy was picking me up at eight, so after dinner we all went into the library to wait for Harry.

We grew up in a large house staffed with maids and a cook, so when Harry arrived that evening, he was greeted by our maid, who showed him into the library. Coming through the door and seeing all of us sitting there, he later told me, was quite intimidating. But what he didn't realize then was that we gathered in the library every night after dinner.

Harry looked fantastic. He was dressed in his naval uniform, which didn't hurt. We met a few of his navy friends for drinks, and I realized quickly that I couldn't follow the conversation because they were all using navy lingo. I pretended to understand, smiling like a dummy. Because I didn't drink, I didn't know what to order, so Harry offered me a taste of scotch, but I didn't like it. He suggested a grasshopper, so that's what I had.

At the end of the evening, he invited me to go sailing with him the following morning. He asked me if I'd like to join him; his brother, Jack; and his friend Pete, who were going to race their sailboat from Larchmont to Manhasset. I said yes, but I didn't know what I was getting into.

Early the next morning, Harry picked me up for the race. With Minkie's help, I had chosen a really sharp outfit—beige top and pants and nice shoes. Perhaps a little overdressed for a boat race, but what did I know?

The boat was actually a racing machine, as Harry later described it. With just a tiny indentation in the middle, it had no galley or toilet, and you sat on the deck the whole time. I had never been on a racing boat before, so I didn't know anything. For eight hours, I just tried to stay out of the way, and all they had on the stupid boat was beer.

When we came ashore, I had to go to the bathroom so badly I thought I was going to explode. As he helped me out of the boat, he had to grab my leg, and I remember him saying, "Boy, you need a shave." He claimed he never said that . . . but he did. Even though he embarrassed me with that remark, I dismissed it because I was in love.

Harry and I started going out regularly, and one night some weeks later at dinner, Daddy said, "Well, you've been going out with this young man for six weeks. Are his intentions serious?" I told him I didn't know but said that his parents liked me. "Of course they like you, you're local. You'll keep him around." Daddy was nothing if not realistic.

Later that evening when Harry picked me up, I was a little worried. Daddy's words rung in my ears and Harry hadn't given any inkling of how he felt about me. It was pouring rain that night and we were sitting at a red light, windshield wipers slapping back and forth. It was like a scene from a movie.

Harry said, "You're awfully quiet tonight. What's wrong?" I figured, this is it. It's either going to happen or it isn't, so I might as well find out. I told him what Daddy had asked at dinner.

Harry stared straight ahead, not looking at me, and he didn't say anything for the longest time. I thought, *Well, this is it. I asked for it and I'm going to get it.* The light turned green and he finally responded, "Well, I *like* you." That was enough for me.

It seemed fitting, then, that we went for a drink at The Barge, which was literally a barge tied up to a pier in Port Chester. It was nothing fancy then, though apparently it has come up in the world since my day. We had a quiet beer with friends and then headed home.

We continued to go out over the next few months, and in time we became serious. Harry told me he wanted to speak to my father, so one Saturday morning that summer Harry came over. I went upstairs to tell Daddy that Harry was downstairs and wanted to speak to him. "Okay," he said, "send him up." Daddy was in his dressing room and Eddie was running around upstairs, so Daddy told him to get lost.

Mommy and Daddy both adored Harry, so when Daddy and Harry came downstairs that day, it was a fait accompli. Soon after, we were officially engaged. It's funny, but I remember the moment when Harry asked Daddy for my hand more clearly than the moment he proposed to me.

Once we were engaged, we all sat down in the library and Daddy took out the tiny engagement calendar that he always carried with him and said, "Okay, it's July. I think six months is enough time to be engaged and plan the wedding. So, let's see, that brings us to the holidays. Well, we don't want to do it over the holidays. How about January 12? Nothing is happening in January." And with that, the wedding planning began, and it was so much fun.

Harry's father, also named Harry, knew someone in the diamond district, so they went together into New York City to buy my ring. When Harry gave me my engagement ring, he said, "I could have gotten a bigger one, but it had a flaw, and I didn't want to give you something with a flaw."

THE WEDDING

The morning of our wedding dawned sunny and cold. As I got ready in my room, I recall Daddy knocking on the door. I was still in my slip, not yet dressed, when he came in to tell me that there was a "slight problem." Tony Fellan, the florist, had forgotten one of the bridesmaid bouquets, so he was headed back into the city to get it. "Okay, Daddy." I remember feeling that nothing could possibly rain on this parade, and I was in a bubble of happiness. We were married at the Church of the Resurrection in Rye, New York, and though it was cold, the sun was out and there was a beautiful layer of snow on the ground.

My dress was perfect. It was double-faced satin with an empire waist and was made to order at Bergdorf's, of course. Over it, I wore a stunning antique lace jacket. My bridesmaids wore off-white dresses with apricot velvet trim. By chance, the day we were married fell on a feast day that called for apricot-colored vestments that matched our wedding colors exactly. There were not one but three priests, several altar boys, plus eight bridesmaids and eight ushers in our wedding party. As a friend of mine remarked to me later, "Boy, you were *really* married."

We got to the church on time with all of our bouquets intact. I remember standing with Daddy, ready to process down the aisle, when he looked down at the last moment and noticed that the hem of my dress was turned up a little bit. Though I had a dresser behind me, Daddy, dressed formally in his morning coat, quickly bent down and fixed the hem himself. Our wedding photographer captured that moment, which has always been precious to me because it says so much about Daddy. From the time I was young, Daddy would invite me to go down on the floors of the store with him, and I would tag along behind him as he quickly walked through the stockrooms and onto the selling floors. Though he could have easily told someone else to do it, when he saw even the smallest detail out of place, he would see to it himself. He knew the inventory by heart and would point out any mismarked dresses while walking quickly through the stockrooms. Like him, I am quite detail-oriented, and I feel that I learned so much about how to do things correctly from him.

As you can imagine, with Mommy and Daddy's impeccable taste, the wedding was beautiful. My most vivid memory of that day is the feeling of joy—of a dream coming true.

After the wedding, I found out about some of the twists and turns that had occurred during our celebration. We held the reception for 250 guests at Westchester Country Club, and while we were standing in the receiving line, Harry asked a friend to get him an hors d'oeuvre. This so-called friend decided to play a prank on Harry, putting some kind of prescription sedative in his snack. One alarming side effect was to turn urine a terrible red color. Poor Harry—what a trick to play on his wedding day. He suffered through the wedding reception scared to death that he was becoming seriously ill. Harry's brother, Jack, was our best man, and though I smiled and nodded during his toast, his frequent mentions of the word "prosperity" went right over my head.

We headed into the city for our wedding night. Harry's boss had offered his apartment at Hampshire House on Central Park South. Harry and I had been to a party at Hampshire House, where the host's apartment had a beautiful view of Central Park, so I was thrilled to be spending such a special night there. However, the apartment we stayed in was no bridal suite, just a room with a window facing a brick wall. No matter, the next day we flew to Nassau in the Bahamas.

Again, a surprise—Nassau in January is really cold, and I had only packed tropical clothes for the honeymoon. I was freezing the whole time. It was too cold even to lie on the beach.

Our hotel room came with a continental breakfast. I love breakfast and am always very hungry in the morning, so each day I would ask Harry if I could order sausages, bacon, and eggs. After a run on room service, Harry ended up running out of money and had to call his dad to wire more. When his dad asked him why, Harry admitted that I had run up a large room-service tab.

Up until that time, I rarely thought about the cost of things because my parents paid for everything. In those days, the shops in Rye all had charge accounts, so I never carried cash.

Harry's parents, Harry and Ellen, were loving and devoted parents to their two sons, Harry and Jack. They were kind and welcoming to me from the very beginning. When we were first married, I hardly ever cooked a meal because we were either invited to the Malloys or the Goodmans for dinner.

Harry's father was a hardworking lawyer whose main client was Hughes Printing, a large printing company in Stroudsburg, Pennsylvania. He was short and chubby, with a wonderful sense of humor and a big, big heart. His family had come from Armagh, in Northern Ireland, and immigrated to America during the years of the Great Famine. They were Catholic, which was rare in Northern Ireland.

When Harry and I were newlyweds, Dad Malloy showed me the Malloy family Bible. He said, "Look, I put your real name down—Vivien Matacena. I don't want to put you down as Vivien Goodman, since you have no Jewish blood in you. Remember what happened during World War II. If somebody had just a little bit of Jewish blood, just one-thirteenth, they were sent to the concentration camps and the gas chambers."

I know he wanted me to understand why he made this choice, and though I know he did it to protect me, I don't think I ever told my father about it. I did not want to hurt his feelings, and I wanted to protect the Malloys from being thought of as prejudiced.

Harry's mother, Ellen, was tall and slim, the physical opposite of her husband. Her family, the Nevilles, came from Limerick, Ireland, and settled in Brooklyn, where Ellen grew up. The Nevilles were perhaps a little finer and a bit wealthier than the Malloys. Ellen's brothers became firemen and policemen. One brother became a senior detective in New York City. Whenever Harry had a question about safety or security, he'd call his uncle Jack.

THE YOUNG MARRIEDS

By the time we were married, Harry was out of the navy. He had been offered his own ship, but chose to pursue civilian life. He got his first job working for the *New York Journal-American* newspaper in the advertising department. A friend of his from Villanova, Gene Rosenquist, also got a job there, and the two of them would travel throughout the five boroughs to delis, bodegas, and newsstands to display point-of-sale material for their products. They would take the subway throughout the city from one business to the next until they figured out how to get the job done by phone. He and Gene would make the calls, then take off and play golf. They got away with it for a while, but it didn't last long.

Harry's next job was with Ted Bates Advertising. One day, his boss, Ted Bates, saw Harry sitting at his desk around 5:00 p.m. and asked why he was still there. According to Ted, if you'd finished your work, it was time to go home to your family.

For us, that first home was a little garden apartment in Larchmont. This was before the construction of Route 95, and our home was situated right by what is now the tollbooth on the border of Larchmont and New Rochelle. I always said we lived in Larchmont because it was a little classier than New Rochelle. We also wanted to be near Harry's parents, as Ellen was quite ill at that point. Sadly, she died very young.

Mommy helped me decorate the apartment, and it was adorable. She had so much fun helping me furnish it, and of course, she bought everything. She had such wonderful taste, and I still have most of those pieces to this day.

Gene Rosenquist at Hilltop Place, Rye, New York, c. 1957.

We had cream-colored carpet and asked everybody to leave their shoes in the hall before they came into the apartment. Mommy commented that our neighbors would think a Muslim family had moved in.

We moved from our one-bedroom apartment in Larchmont to a house in Rye when I was pregnant with Debby. A nice real estate agent my parents knew told us about Indian Village. Our house on Mohawk Steet was charming, convenient, and near Mommy and Daddy on Hilltop Place. It was a lovely neighborhood with small houses, yards, and quiet streets. Many young families lived there, and we quickly became friends with everyone on the street.

The children played on the street with their tricycles and balls, dolls, and roller skates with no fear of cars tearing along. It was perfect. . . . Until one day when our neighbor's son threw a rock over the fence and hit Andrew on the forehead. He needed stitches, and my life changed. I realized that life for my children was fraught with unseen danger, scrapes, stitches, bee stings . . . there was no safe haven. I was on the alert, more and more.

With Mommy living nearby, I had built-in babysitters for quick trips to the market or various appointments with one or the other of the children. Mommy had the staff and loved seeing her grand-children so often. It was bliss for me as a young mother. When she came to visit, it was always around bath time, when I was pooped, and a helping hand was so welcome. Early dinner and bed and a story with "Dita," as the children called her, ended the day very often.

I was a very busy young wife and mother. We had five children in eight years, so I spent most of the time giving birth and being pregnant. I think the longest break I had was between my fourth child, Mark, born in September 1962, and my fifth and youngest child, Vivi, who was born in July 1965.

We quickly outgrew our small house on Mohawk Street—it and I were bursting at the seams. I was pregnant again and started house hunting. One night at dinner, Harry asked me if I had seen anything I liked that day. I said I had seen a house in nearby Purchase and loved it.

We went to see the house together and Harry loved it too. There she stood in all her glory—past glory really, as the house had not been taken care of very much in recent years—at the end of a circular driveway with gravel, just as Harry ordered. Constructed around 1910 by the builder of the *Lusitania*, the house was built like a ship. It had steel girders, a thick stone foundation, and plaster walls so dense you could not hang a picture with a nail. You needed a drill and a molly bolt—and a handyman, really.

The house had twenty-eight rooms, seven fireplaces, seven bathrooms, and seven maid's rooms. It was huge, and the world thought it was a white elephant, but we bought it. We did not have the money to do anything more than paint, install cheap storm windows, and cover the exposed radiators. It had no barn, but I bought a prefab tractor shed and put the tractor outside and a pony in it. I was going to call the house Lilac Way or Pheasant Run, but my sister Minkie said that the lilacs might die and the pheasants might disappear and suggested an architectural name for the house. We stood in front of the

Five Chimneys, Purchase, New York, spring 1963.

house and looked up and saw the five chimneys. So we looked at each other and said, "That's the name of the house: Five Chimneys." That was the beginning of an era of fun, adventure, great parties, weddings, dinners, and a glorious place to bring up five children.

When I was expecting our first child, Daddy had offered Harry a job at Bergdorf's in the fur department. He ended up working at Bergdorf's for almost ten years. Even years later, former colleagues remembered Harry with affection. He organized an annual Communion breakfast, bringing in leading speakers like the president of Fordham, to address Bergdorf's employees.

Harry came home with wonderful stories about the clientele. His favorite was one about Elizabeth Taylor. At the time, Elizabeth Taylor was living in California and married to Mike Todd. She was in New York en route to Russia, where she would be shooting her next film. She stored her furs at Bergdorf's and came in to pick out some fur coats to bring with her.

When she arrived, Harry showed her into a huge dressing room that was covered in wall-to-wall mirrors. The room had special lighting to show the furs to their best advantage. Harry and the fitter brought all of her furs out, and after trying on the first one, she complained that it was a bit tight. Even though Harry and the fitter were right there, she took off the coat *and* her blouse and was completely topless. Then she just turned and said casually, "Why don't I try on the other one?" Harry loved telling this story to all of his pals.

A few years later, I was in the store at Christmastime with Andy and Debby, and the salesperson told me that Elizabeth Taylor was in Daddy's office. I went up with the children, thrilled to meet her because I loved her in *National Velvet*. Andy and Debby, who were ten and twelve at the time, were beautifully dressed and excited to meet a movie star. Liz was wearing a huge diamond ring that Mike Todd had given her, and my Debby asked, "Is that *real*?" Liz laughed and assured Debby that it was, indeed, a real diamond.

On November 9, 1965, Harry was at Bergdorf's when the Great Northeastern Blackout hit. He spent the night guiding customers and staff down darkened stairs, bringing them to the Paris Theater next door. He couldn't get home, and there I was with five children and three dogs at our house in Westchester, with only candlelight.

After I thought I had the kitchen spotlessly clean, I tucked all the children in bed and went to bed myself. The next morning, I got up and there were crumbs all over the place. I realized that modern fluorescent lighting had made our lives miserable. By candlelight, you couldn't see all the crumbs, and the silver didn't always have to be polished.

After working in the fur department, Harry joined customer relations at Bergdorf's for a time, but eventually left the business to try something new. He started working in commercial insurance and worked in that field for the rest of his professional life. Harry did well enough, but his job was never his passion.

I'll never forget him coming upstairs one evening at bedtime—I was almost asleep—and he said, "Honey, I just want you to know something: I'll never be a millionaire. I've seen those guys, and they never see their families or their children. You and the children are much more important to me." He was a fantastic father and a wonderful husband. And still is, as I am still in love with him and feel him close.

When the boys were little, there was no football league in our area, so Harry and some friends organized the Purchase Panthers. He coordinated the uniforms and equipment, organized practice and game schedules, recruited players (and their families) for the team, and coached.

During one game, our son Andy was playing quarterback for the Panthers, when he was tackled really hard and a foul was called. Andy came off the field with the wind knocked out of him. As Andy began to recover, he wanted to go back in the game, but Harry kept him benched. The more Andy sat, the more he steamed, but Harry kept him out of the game until Andy was completely fired up. Then, and only then, did he let him back in the game, and Andy got some payback on the player who had put a dirty hit on him.

At a game up in Stamford, Connecticut, the Panthers played against a much bigger, tougher team. When the other team emerged from their bus, the Panthers panicked. But Harry told them not to worry, giving them a strategy—not to win, but to avoid getting hurt. He told them when someone is coming to tackle you, just fall down. Even though they were beaten badly by the team, the kids had fun and no one got hurt. Harry loved being a coach. He loved the kids, and they all loved him.

Life at Five Chimneys with the children, horses, and dogs was an adventure in itself. Living in a large, old home inevitably led to emergency repairs. Harry was adept at fixing things, and he had a very organized workshop in our basement. He kept it shipshape and got upset when people moved his tools. "Daddy fix-y, Daddy fix-y" was a refrain when a toy was broken, and Harry could fix just about anything.

FAMILY LIFE

I AM AND ALWAYS HAVE BEEN A VERY ORGANIZED PERSON. I'M SURE that came from my traditional nursery upbringing, where things were very organized. But I never hired nannies because I wanted to raise my children in my own way. I always had household help for cleaning, laundry, and cooking simple meals, but it was a far cry from my own upbringing in the nursery.

There was discipline in big and little things: Everyone used the back stairs because the front stairs were just for company; no one was allowed to put their hands on the walls; furniture was lifted, not dragged across the floor; when walking in the (back) door, everyone washed their hands and took off their dirty boots in the mudroom. All of this made life—and housekeeping—a bit easier in a twenty-eight room house with five children.

In my house, there was order: three meals a day and two snacks. The children were always hungry when they sat down to eat. If they didn't eat their meal, they didn't get a snack. When I see my grandchildren come in and out of the kitchen, getting snacks during the day, I wonder how they're going to eat the main meal that their mother has cooked for them. How could they possibly, if they're always snacking?

In my home, every shelf has to be lined before I put anything on it. Every bottle and can has to be set, one behind the other, like soldiers in a line, so I know how many I have left. I used to have a menu taped inside the kitchen cabinet door so the children knew the menu each week. They all ate well, but they didn't like vegetables that much. Our pediatrician at the time suggested giving them Campbell's vegetable soup because he said it provided every vegetable that they needed.

When I packed their school lunches, the food was always healthy. Andrew would open the refrigerator and complain, "Can't we ever have real food? Do we have to have all this healthy food all the time?"

This was the 1970s, and health food and exercise were not as popular then as they are now. The word *fit* was not in the popular lexicon. I was one of the few people I knew who ran every day and was committed to good nutrition for myself and my family. They ate what I ate: healthy, balanced meals, lots of fruits and vegetables, and grains. It was just a matter of course for me.

During the summers when the children were very little, we would take them to the Westchester Country Club beach club to swim. Daddy and Mommy had bought a little cabana there, so we could spend the whole morning at the beach. But Andrew and Debby both got ear infections from swimming in the pool there. My parents had recently built a pool at their home on Hilltop Place, and our pediatrician advised me to have the children swim in their private pool instead, so that's where we went.

Every summer, Mommy would hire a pool boy. He would come early in the morning, vacuum the pool, put out the cushions, and once Minkie and I arrived with our children, he would play pool games and watch over the kids so we could do errands. The cousins would play pool games all day, so summers were a lot of fun. In the later years, when Mommy would be walking through Rye, former pool boys would stop to say hello. Many of them went on to great futures, owning businesses or practicing law.

When they were young, our children made a lot of their own fun. I'll never forget coming home one day and seeing my children with their eight Malloy cousins—Jack and Cathy's children—in what we called the pine tree field. There they all were, children and ponies alike, adorned with garlands of flowers. When I asked what was happening, I was informed matter-of-factly that they were celebrating a wedding—my nephew Chris was to be married to our pony, Special Edition. Special's mane and tail were braided with flowers and Chris wore a floral wreath on his head for the occasion. I'll never forget that sight, the joyful yet solemn wedding procession through the field carried out with great aplomb.

The children were in bed by eight o'clock, at the latest, when they were little. Though I didn't hire nannies, I established consistent structure for our children, something I experienced in my childhood in the nursery. I think having a consistent bedtime for them was essential, especially given all their work and play outdoors. I would read stories to them until they could read themselves.

When I was a child, our nannies' practice of recording the details of our daily health and habits in notebooks made a lasting impression on me. Once I became a mother, I was careful to record the details of our children's health. To this day, I have a bookshelf of notebooks kept for each child, where I wrote everything down: records of shots, illnesses, allergies, even little drawings of their teeth showing which date each tooth was lost. Our children, some of whom are now parents themselves, ask how I did it. I tell them it was just how I wanted to be a parent—so I just did it.

Motherhood came naturally to me. From childhood, I loved "mothering" my dolls and my stuffed animals—all dogs. Once I had children of my own, I loved being a mother to them. When it comes to raising children, my motto is "Keep things simple. Do everything with kindness and always listen to your children." I was horrified when a friend of mine confided to me that she couldn't wait until the children were grown up. "I hate the babies and I hate the toddlers," she said. I thought that was the most horrible thing a mother could say.

Harry and I raised the children with loving care, but also discipline—definitely discipline. I was extremely strict, and Harry was too, and he always backed me up. If Harry saw one of them doing something wrong, he'd deliver a swift smack on the behind and send the offender up to his or her room. I never had to worry about the children getting mixed messages—we were a united front.

I promised myself I would never say, "Wait till your father gets home," because I said that once and it didn't turn out well. We had given the children little ducklings for Easter, and they wanted to show them off to the boy who lived next door—let's call him Danny. I had forbidden my children to play with Danny because he pushed them around and bullied them. Without my knowing, Andrew, Debby, and Kenneth put the ducklings in their little red wagon and pulled it down the driveway to the neighbor's house.

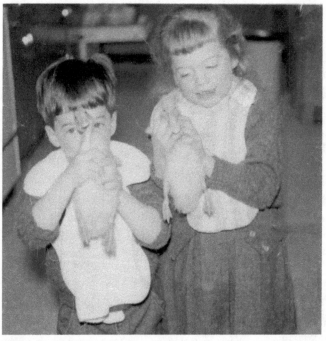

Kenneth and Debby with their ducklings, Purchase, 1965.

When Danny saw the ducklings, he asked Andrew if they could fly. Andrew said he didn't know, so Danny promptly picked up a duckling and threw it into the air. The poor thing dive-bombed down and was dead on impact.

The children were shocked and crying. Not knowing what to do, they picked up the dead duckling and put it in the wagon. This sent the other ducklings into a panic, and they were quacking nervously all the way home.

When the children got home and told me what happened, I was livid. They had disobeyed me by taking the ducklings to the neighbor, and now one of the ducklings was dead. They knew they had done something pretty awful, and I told them—just that one time—"Wait till your father gets home."

Hours later, when Harry got home, I said, "Tell Daddy what happened!" Harry was furious.

He spanked Andrew and sent him upstairs. Debby was crying, thinking she was next in line. But when Harry called her, instead of a spanking, he asked her to tell him what had happened and they had a long talk about it, but no spanking. After that experience, I decided from then on, I wouldn't give him bad news the moment he walked in the door. Rather, I'd wait until he had time to settle in and relax before discussing anything serious.

Along with the children, we always had at least two dogs—corgis, shepherds, Newfoundlands. I adore German shepherds, and we've had five over the years. Once in a while, a stray dog or cat would come into our lives and we'd keep it.

As my children grew, so did Edition Farm. By the time they were old enough to have household chores, they had barn chores. The children would come home from school, get a snack, and go right down to the barn to tack up and ride or help clean. After they'd finished at the barn, they'd come up to the house, have dinner, do their homework, and if there was any time after that, watch television. Andrew once said that none of his friends wanted to come over because I'd put them to work in the barn.

All of my children were offered riding lessons. Andrew and Kenneth preferred golf, which they played with Harry. Mark, Debby, and Vivi all had a feel for riding, so they pursued riding lessons, pony club, hunter paces, and eventually competed in horse shows nationally. One year all three of them competed at the National Horse Show in Madison Square Garden.

I love everything the horse world taught my children. It was a wholesome, wonderful, outdoor life—such a healthy life. Caring for the horses taught my children responsibility and empathy. When you've just finished playing tennis and you're hot and tired, you put the tennis racquet away and take a shower. When you've just finished riding and you're hot and tired, so is the horse. The horse has to be cooled off and made comfortable, he needs to be watered, given clean hay, and brought into a clean stall. Only then do you take your shower. Putting someone or something before your own needs is essential, and sometimes it's tough.

Our commitment to the horses was intensive, and with that plus school, my children were always busy. Harry and I valued hard work and commitment, and their experience living with horses provided our children with a strong work ethic.

I coordinated every detail of Edition Farm's daily operations, and at horse shows I drove the trailer and groomed, which was great. I bought our first two-horse trailer from some people who were moving to England. I repainted it green and white—Edition Farm colors—and drove it from horse shows to hunt clubs to gymkhanas. Six years later, I sold it for the same amount I paid for it.

I had to make two trips to the horse shows because we had several horses, children, and lots of equipment. I would get up really early, hitch up the trailer, and drive two ponies to the show grounds. I'd unload and deliver the ponies, leave one child at the show to stay with them, then make another trip home to pick up the remaining horses and children. Usually, this commute happened at 5:30 or 6:00 in the morning, because trailers were not allowed on parkways. After the show, I'd repeat the same routine.

One time we went to a horse show in New Jersey, and I had to leave early to go to a party. Harry was very adamant that our social life not be affected by the horse show schedules; no matter what happened, I had to be spruced up, looking nice and ready for the party, usually on a Saturday night. On this day, there was no way I was going to be able to get back from New Jersey over the George Washington Bridge with the trailer in time.

So my friend and trainer Judy Richter told me to just leave the trailer in the field with the ponies in it—with hay and water for the night. She gave me her car and drove the children home later in her van. So there I was, in Judy's little Volkswagen with a stick shift, which I didn't know how to drive. I crossed the G. W. Bridge at about four miles an hour in the right lane, praying it wouldn't stall.

I made it home just in time to get to the party, and the next morning, I got up at God knows what time to get to the ponies. I

Andrew and Debby ready for Father Hamish to perform Debby's First Holy Communion, Purchase, New York, December 11, 1966.

drove the Volkswagen back to New Jersey, and to my great relief, the ponies were fine. They even showed that day. But that was the one and only time I did something so crazy. There are so many things that could have gone wrong. What if one of them got colic or tried to lie down?

Shortly after this, Judy hinted to Harry that selling the trailer and buying a horse van would be a great idea. A van could accommodate everybody and everything in one trip. So for my birthday, Harry presented me with a beautiful horse van, painted Edition Farm green and emblazoned with our "EF" logo on the door. It was

Another Pony Club member with Mark Malloy, Jimmy Kingery, and Vivi Malloy at Pony Club Rally, summer 1975. (Photo by Jill Krementz.)

big enough for three to four small horses, the children, and all the equipment. Mommy's eyes popped when I brought it to Hilltop Place and drove around her beautiful circular driveway. "Look what I got for my birthday! Don't you wish I had taken up ballet?" I remember her standing there in her beautiful "at home" outfit, and I can't imagine what she must have thought.

I also had a beautiful antique wicker governess cart, and I taught our pony, Special Edition, to "drive," or pull, the cart. I wanted to show it off, so I drove the children to my parents' home on Hilltop Place, about two miles away, crossing over what would become Route 287, the Cross-Westchester Expressway. There we were, clip-clopping along in this tiny little wicker cart. What a sight. Thankfully, we made it to Hilltop in one piece, but I look back on that adventure now and think, *How could I possibly have done that?* I wasn't an idiot, I was just confident.

Jack, Harry's brother, and his wife, Cathy, lived nearby. It was wonderful for our children to have their cousins so close. Though we thought our family was large, Jack and Cathy outdid us by having nine children. Harry used to joke that it was all his fault. Like Harry, Jack was a naval officer and had to be gone for months at a time. Because Jack was married and, at the time, had two children, Harry spoke with Jack's commanding officer to ask for a better assignment closer to home. Harry's request was granted, and Jack had more time at home . . . and more children. Every time he came home on leave Cathy got pregnant.

Pop Malloy once said that after a while, when Cathy announced she was pregnant, everybody would cry, so she decided not to tell the family until she was showing.

Jack and Cathy had a daughter, Justine, named for Cathy's dad, Justin Moran. They asked Harry and me to be her godparents. I'll never forget that call, because Cathy said she couldn't wait for me to see the baby, that she was so beautiful. A few days before the baptism, Cathy called me to tell me that Justine had a bit of a cold and they were postponing the ceremony.

They woke up one morning a few days later and noticed that the baby had slept through the 2:00 a.m. feeding. Jack found her in the cradle by the bed, and she was blue. He immediately started CPR and they called the ambulance, but little Justine had already died. The cause was crib death (SIDS). We were all in the midst of raising our wonderful, healthy children, and the death of a child was incomprehensible. Harry and I were so proud to have been asked to be the godparents, a role we take very seriously, and it was heartbreaking for us all.

Unfortunately, years later Cathy and Jack suffered another sad loss. Their son Chris, the same one who "married" Special Edition, was home for the holidays from college. He and some of his brothers had been at a party late one night, and he got up early the next morning to return his girlfriend's car. Tragically, he fell asleep at the wheel, the car flipped over, and he was killed.

Harry called me while I was in Florida at a horse show with Debby. I went to find her and saw her giggling and happy with friends. I hated to have to tell her, but I pulled her aside and gave her the sad news about Chris. She collapsed right in front of me.

Despite these horrible losses, Jack and Cathy remain a wonderful, devoted couple. They say that having a good sense of humor gets us through the darkest times, and I think the Malloys have always used their great sense of humor and wit to weather difficulties in life.

EDUCATION

When it came time for the children to start school, I knew I wanted their education to have a spiritual component, but the parochial schools were not of the same academic caliber as the private schools in our area. I read an article about Whitby School, a Montessori school in Greenwich, Connecticut, and was very intrigued by their approach and philosophy. I knew the importance of learning through my own senses. One of my professors at Wellesley had spoken

Vivi ready for her first day of school, Purchase, New York, 1968.

memorably about trusting one's own senses, and that idea stuck with me. The Montessori approach aligned so clearly with mine: the idea that the purpose of education is not to put in, but rather to draw out the innate abilities of children. The value placed on learning through the senses resonated deeply with me.

I mentioned the article to Harry but knew it would be a tremendous sacrifice for us financially, not to mention that it was pretty far outside the mainstream in those days. But one day, Harry came home from work and asked if I'd like Andrew to go to Whitby. I was overjoyed. As it happened, he had met two of Whitby's founding members and invited them to our home to discuss the school.

So Andrew and, ultimately, all of the children attended Whitby. It was a wonderful school and I became very involved as a parent and head of the Parent Association. At home, we tried to replicate the school environment. We bought child-sized chairs, tables, and bookshelves so the children could work comfortably and independently.

The Montessori method is based on respect for the child, and honoring the child's voice. The expectation of mutual respect between adults and children made our children comfortable sharing ideas and conversing with adults. I think this is why they have always been at ease in the adult world from the time they were little.

The toughest challenge our children faced was leaving Whitby. Though we felt that the Montessori approach was wonderful when the children were younger, Harry and I were concerned that, as they got older, the children were not adequately prepared for high school and college. Whitby didn't assign homework or have traditional testing. My alma mater, Rye Country Day School, was an academically demanding, high-pressure environment. Though it was a big change from Whitby, Harry and I felt that it was time, and we transferred all our children. As a condition of acceptance, all the children had to attend summer school prior to entering RCDS in the fall. It was a big transition from Montessori, and it took them awhile to adjust.

Even though they didn't go to Catholic schools, we made sure our children got religious education. Taking a page from the Montessori method, I arranged for a priest from Manhattanville College, Father Hamish, to come to our home to teach the children in a way that I knew would be meaningful to them. They talked about religion and he would tell stories, rather than the traditional catechism I was taught. Later on, in preparation for Confirmation, each of them went through CCD after school. Harry and I also made sure we attended Sunday Mass. Sometimes the children went to church in riding clothes, sometimes in ski clothes. Although we might come late or Harry might leave early, we got there.

TRAVEL

When Minkie, Eddie, and I were all young marrieds, Mommy and Daddy had invited us to Jamaica for a week, where they were vacationing at Round Hill Hotel. We had a wonderful time sailing, water-skiing, snorkeling, and playing tennis and golf. We never

The *Nepenthe*, 1972.

stopped—to the amusement of the older guests. But Mommy and Daddy didn't like Jamaica much and were soon on the lookout for another place to vacation in winter.

In 1972, Mommy and Daddy chartered a small yacht, the *Nepenthe*, to sail the Caribbean. Mommy wanted to find a place to vacation in the winter, since traveling to Cuba from the U.S. was no longer allowed, due to poor relations between the two countries. Because we couldn't all fit on the *Nepenthe* at the same time, each family rotated in, joining my parents as they made their way through the islands. Minkie and her family sailed to the Grenadines and Dominica, and we visited Antigua, Saint Martin, and St. Barts. But it wasn't until Mommy and Daddy went to Barbados that they said, "This is the place."

Barbados became our favorite place in the Caribbean—other than Cuba. Mommy and Daddy would spend two months there every winter, and like the *Nepenthe* trip, they would invite each of our families down for a week.

Our travel was frequently tied to our interests. Harry and I went to Scotland ourselves, and to Germany, Spain, and Italy at various times. Those are the three places where we have roots, plus Debby was living in Germany. Harry and I also had wonderful trips with friends to Ireland and England.

Harry was an excellent golfer, and he played all over the country, as well as in Cuba, Bermuda, Ireland, and Scotland. Whenever we visited Cuba, Harry was invited to play on the beautiful golf course at the Xanadu mansion in Varadero, where Irénée du Pont had gathered the flora and fauna native to the island. It was truly a gift to the Cuban people and was beautifully preserved. It was on one of these occasions that the Iguana Incident happened.

Harry was golfing with the Mendozas and Fanjuls, and after hitting their fairway shots they approached the green. Harry looked at his ball and was pleased with his position, right in the middle of the green facing the hole. He looked around to ascertain his lie and saw, on either side of the green, some rock outcroppings—coral, of course—and on each one was a large iguana. Harry remarked that he had never seen such huge ones and later told me they looked like medium-sized dinosaurs. His golf buddies assured him that they just sit and sun themselves all day and never move. Harry approached his ball and set up for his putt. Suddenly, one iguana tore across the green literally between his legs, while the other iguana jumped down onto it. There ensued a turf war on the golf course with Harry aghast at the blood, hissing, violent bites, and . . . enough said. You had to be there.

And then whatever had started the battle was resolved, and each went back to his own rock. The guys, all Cuban, said, "Harry, that has never happened. We never saw that before." It was prehistoric, like *Jurassic Park* before that movie ever came out. Harry's game was a little shaky after that, as you can imagine.

By the early 1970s, the family was divided between the golfers and the riders, but one sport the Malloys all had in common was skiing. In the early sixties, Harry had gotten interested in skiing. He and I took lessons, and he taught Andy and Debby to ski. Skiing ultimately became a major sport for the entire family, with all five

Left to right: Debby, Vivi, Mark, Kenneth, and Andrew in
costumes from Dita and Popi's European travels, spring 1967.

children progressing from ski school to the Stratton Mountain
School for racing. Harry and I drove up to Vermont every weekend—
four hours each way—splitting five children and the dogs between
the two cars.

Our ski trips are among my fondest family memories. In the
early days, Harry and I endured lots of ski weekends in less-than-
wonderful accommodations. The two of us rented houses with other
couples or stayed in awful motels where we had to climb over beds
to get to the bathroom down the hall. We suffered with mouse
droppings in the closets and bad food.

One time, when we were at Bromley, in Vermont, it was pouring
rain. Harry had read in *Ski Magazine* about this new mountain,
Stratton, so we decided to drive over there and take a look. The first
thing we saw was a building in the Tyrolean style—what a find.
Having skied in Austria and Switzerland, we felt it was a little bit of
the Alps in Vermont. Harry and I had lunch there and decided to
ski Stratton the next day. There were only three trails and one lift at
that time, but we loved it. We found out that a fellow Whitby parent, Tom Cholnoky, was building condos there. The ones he had

Harry with (left to right) Debby, Andy, Mark, and Kenneth in front of the base lodge at Stratton Mountain, Vermont, February 1967.

built on the mountain all sold, so we purchased a condominium under construction on Birch Hill Road.

We bought 1 Moose Maple on Birch Hill Road in 1969. The condos were attached, so I wanted the one on the end with the view of the mountain and one additional window. It was more expensive, and Harry almost didn't go for it. It has three bedrooms, two bathrooms, and cost $22,500. Looking back, it's unbelievable that we paid so little for something that gave us so much. It is a treasure trove of memories, of nights together by the fireplace, of Olympic skiers as guests, of waxing and sharpening the skis in the rec room, with our dogs—usually a Newfoundland and a corgi or two— romping around us. We used to have parties at the condo and call them "stress tests" to see how many people we could cram inside. We had wonderful times. Considering all the fun we've had over the years, it was one of the best investments we ever made.

Once we had the condo, we drove up to Stratton every weekend with all the children and three dogs. All of the families on the mountain had different drills to get their children up to Vermont for the weekend. Some dressed the children in their pajamas, picked up their husbands from the train station (with a martini or two to go for him and dinner in the trunk for arrival), and off they'd go.

Some families, like ours—with lots of children or different schedules—drove two cars up north each weekend. In our family, my car was the less preferred conveyance. I played classical music and quizzed them about school. The children preferred Daddy's car since he let them play their music and stopped at Lou's Gulf Station on Route 30 to buy some of the best fudge on the planet.

Once we arrived, we were all together and it was wonderful. The condo was cozy and easy to set up. We'd turn on a couple of breakers to get the light and heat started, and that was it. I would cook a glorious dinner, and everyone would be too full of fudge to eat it.

We usually wouldn't ski as a group, as we were at different levels. The older children were on the ski team, doing drills on the most difficult slopes. The little ones were in Cub School. After lunch, we'd pick up the little ones (usually only Vivi, who was screaming to join us). But, to be honest, Harry and I were happy when they were in Cub School, so that he and I could continue on the more challenging slopes. We'd pause to watch our older children barreling down between the gates in a ski team practice.

Sometimes I worked as gatekeeper for the ski races, with Harry starting the skiers at the top of the course. Being out in the snow wearing ski boots was torture. Standing still for hours in plastic boots left me with permanently sensitive feet. Nowadays, if the temperature drops below forty degrees, my feet, hands, and one ear get terribly cold.

Sundays were the peewee races, and our condo is still full of the children's race awards. Harry and I would sit in the base lodge and try to pick out which little ski hat was a Malloy racing down the Suntanner, the main slope ending in front of the base lodge. The children would ask if we saw them, and whether or not we did, we would always say, "Yes! What was your time?"

Number 1 Moose Maple on Birch Hill Road is still going strong. Our children and grandchildren still ski at Stratton and love it as much as we do. There was magic about those ski weekends.

Harry and I also took trips with friends to go skiing. We skied in Canada, Switzerland, Austria, and France. In Europe, Zermatt, Switzerland, was always my favorite place to ski. I loved the elegant morning coats on the bellmen at the Grand Hotel and the Oriental rugs in the lobby—very plush, although I hated to walk in my ski boots on those Orientals. We were stepping around in our banana-yellow ski boots, the dernier cri in America but very impractical for walking, which most people did in Europe in the ski towns. We could hardly move, unless we were on our skis and had slippery snow to propel us. Walking was torture.

One afternoon after a long day of skiing, we decided to hail a sleigh to take us back to the hotel. We placed our skis in the flat part of the sleigh behind our seats and asked the driver to take us to the Grand Hotel. All was well until we started to pick up speed . . . lots of it.

I realized immediately that the horse was a runaway, and told Harry so. Our skis were bouncing all over and were about to fall out as we careened around corners on narrow streets. It was not funny, so Harry asked the driver to slow down. The driver, an American, had just started that day and told us he didn't know how to say *whoa* in German. In the meantime, the horse took over and was obviously headed back to her stable. Finally, he managed to slow down enough for us to leap off and grab our skis; I don't know if we even paid the driver. It was a harrowing adventure, certainly. Since then, I have heard of so many cart accidents. It is definitely not safer to ride than to drive—at least in Zermatt.

During that same trip, after skiing in Val-d'Isère, France, Harry and I were headed to Lyon in our rented Citroën, when we stumbled upon a wonderful restaurant and had one of the most memorable meals we've ever enjoyed. I had been suffering an episode of vertigo as a result of skiing down the flat, foggy, treeless slopes of Val-d'Isère, and it was getting toward dinnertime. We drove into a small village, looking for a place to eat.

We turned into a cul-de-sac, narrowly missing driving into a charming garden, and we saw a sign for a restaurant. It was covered in vines, barely visible from the outside, but we decided to try it, thinking: *We're in France, how bad can any restaurant be?*

So in we went, and the restaurant was absolutely charming. In a room lit by candlelight and chandeliers, we were served an outstanding meal by a gracious maître d' and *serveurs*. How we continued driving to Lyon after dinner can only be attributed to our youth, fitness, and nonchalance. Our hotel room in Lyon was just as spectacular as our dinner. The room was round, with French doors looking out onto the most beautiful square.

Our friend Herb Frankel was also in Lyon on business. He and Harry had made reservations before we left the States at the restaurant of Paul Bocuse, one of the originators of nouvelle cuisine. Harry, as Daddy used to say, was a frustrated travel agent because he loved making travel arrangements. Everywhere we went, it seemed like Harry knew someone—a maître d' or an innkeeper—and he would make a point of getting to know people. That personal touch made our trips such a pleasure. It might be a ski lesson with the local ski pro or staying at a lovely inn and feeling like a guest of the owner because Harry had already gotten to know him. On this trip, it was a pilgrimage to have lunch at the birthplace of nouvelle cuisine, L'Auberge du Pont de Collonges.

The three of us drove out into the country the following day, passing beautiful farms and vineyards with cows and chickens all around. When we arrived, we parked and walked through the garden into the restaurant. It was not grand, but very rustic and charming. Always Miss Inquisitive, I glanced into the kitchen and saw young men in long white aprons polishing copper. Pans of all shapes and for all purposes hung from brass hooks above the counters. There were pastry boards, chopping boards, and dough tables, all marble of course.

We were seated by Madame Bocuse. Once we had ordered, the sommelier arrived to take our wine order—for each course. Harry and Herb ordered wild boar, which was wheeled in, snout, horns, and all. Undoubtedly, the best part of the meal was dessert. I ordered mousse and Harry and Herb ordered ice cream. Each of our desserts was rolled out on a cart, presented in crystal bowls chilling on beds of ice.

After that unparalleled meal, Paul Bocuse came to our table. The tall, burly gentleman looked very chic in his classic chef's attire. He was the hero of nouvelle and my hero too. No heavy cream sauces, no more food cooked to death.

Before leaving, Madame Bocuse showed me through the kitchen from top to bottom. The young staff in their long white aprons were still scrubbing, polishing, and chopping—for the evening meal, no doubt. We realized that we were the only table seated for lunch that day and were told kindly that they had opened the restaurant especially for us, since we had made our reservations all the way from the United States. God bless Harry and all his friends and restaurant connections—amazing!

Years later, Debby was riding and competing around the world, and Harry and I visited places we never would have gone, like Tahiti, New Zealand, and Australia. We also returned to Nassau, where we had spent our honeymoon, for our fortieth anniversary. We wanted to see "where it all began," so we gave the address of the hotel to our cab driver, who drove us to a parking lot. We got out, looking for the lovely club where we'd stayed, and were promptly informed that it had been torn down: They literally paved paradise and put up a parking lot, as Joni Mitchell once sang.

Harry and I were married fifty-two years, and every moment was precious. He was the sweetest guy in the world. He loved me. He told me every day how beautiful I looked. I am so lucky.

Seven

GIRLS AND BOYS

ANDREW

When I got back from our honeymoon I didn't feel well and thought I had the flu, so I went to see Dr. Bullwinkle, our family doctor. After the examination he asked me to get dressed and come into his office. "I guess I have the flu," I said.

"No, what you have has something to do with being married. You're pregnant." It was such a lovely way to say it. Thank you, Dr. Bullwinkle—a honeymoon baby!

Toward the end of my first pregnancy, we were at the Malloys for dinner, and Mom Malloy had made a pork roast. It was called fresh ham in those days and it was absolutely delicious—one of her specialties. I think she had made it especially for me, because it was a favorite of mine, and I delved into it with great gusto.

As we were finishing dinner, I started to feel funny. I never get indigestion, so I thought maybe I had eaten too fast. Harry was immediately nervous. "Call the doctor!" he said.

Andrew, Debby, Kenneth, Mark, and Vivi ready for Easter
Sunday Mass, on the front porch of Five Chimneys, Purchase,
New York, April 1967.

I wasn't so sure and didn't want to call the doctor if it was a false
alarm. But Harry insisted, so I called the doctor and he said, "You
are too pregnant for this to be indigestion. Go to the hospital."

I insisted that we pick up my suitcase before going to the hospital, so we tore back to the apartment with Harry driving like an
idiot. I had never seen him that nervous. But I had spent so much
time packing that suitcase with all the little things for the baby's
homecoming, and I couldn't leave it behind.

After all that, it was an uneventful birth; everything was easy. I
don't remember much, but when I got to the hospital I was examined, and the nurse said, "not right away." Awhile later I had a big
contraction and the nurse called the doctor, who said, "right away,"
and I had the baby.

Our eldest son, Andrew Thomas Malloy, was born on October
30, 1957, and named for both of his grandfathers. He weighed six
pounds, fourteen ounces, and was absolutely gorgeous. To us, he
was perfect. Mommy, who was in the waiting room with Harry, was

one of the first to see Andrew. She pointed out that he had a beautifully shaped head and ears, which was terribly important for a boy who has short hair and cannot camouflage these features.

Andrew was a dream child; all he did was smile, sleep, smile, eat, and sleep. He was just a piece of cake. My mother arranged for me to have help during the first week at home with the baby—a very large, grandmotherly woman who did so much to make me comfortable in those early days. She was wonderful. The day she left, I remember watching her sitting in our little kitchen putting on her boots and being terrified of being left alone with the baby.

Before she left she said, "Now, Mrs. Malloy, I've left you a nice cooked chicken so you'll have that for a few nights, and some soup. And you should continue to drink plenty of milk, because you're nursing." Then she left, and Andrew started to cry.

That evening, as Harry and I sat down to the roast chicken dinner, Andrew started crying again. It wasn't time for his breastfeeding, so we decided to make him a bottle. We were new parents and doing everything by the book, so as Andrew screamed in the other room, Harry and I were in the kitchen, nervously making sure the temperature and the timing of the drops were just right. Nobody picked up the baby to soothe him—we knew nothing. Eventually, Andrew was picked up and fed and, true to form, went right back to sleep.

In 1957, there were no classes about baby and child care or internet resources. My mother wasn't much help in this area because she always had nannies, and neither Harry nor I had experience with babies. We were flying blind, with Andrew as our test flight.

After Andrew was born, I still picked Harry up at Larchmont Station every night, leaving Andrew in his crib because he was such an angel. One day my kind neighbor realized that I was doing this and said to me, "Vivien, you can't leave the baby alone." I had no experience and no idea of the risks. So when she said, "What if there's a fire? What if he chokes?" I was horrified—it had never occurred to me. "Just leave the door open when you have to run out and I'll watch him."

"What are we doing on Saturday night?" was a common refrain of Harry's as the weekend approached. Any one of our young married friends was always having a party that night. I would take Andrew with us and put him to sleep on the bed with everyone's coats. When my mother-in-law found out that we were taking Andrew to the parties, she was up in arms. "Don't you ever do that again! Do you know all the germs that you're exposing that child to, putting him on all those strangers' coats? You bring him right here to me and I will watch him for you." From then on, Mom and Pop Malloy sometimes watched Andrew on Saturday night.

Andrew was speaking way before he started to walk. His first word was *Dada*, and *Mommy* came way later. I think he was eighteen months old before he walked, and if I had been reading about developmental milestones, I would have been more concerned. I was unaware and took for granted that Andrew was doing fine. As it turns out, he was, but now I realize that most babies start walking around a year old. I read somewhere that crawling is linked to brain development related to reading, so I think Andrew was preparing to read.

I remembered how, when Eddie was born, our nanny Didi would always stress the benefits of fresh air. So if it wasn't raining, I would bundle Andrew up, no matter the temperature, put him in his pram, and push that pram all over Larchmont. I never saw one other mother doing that.

When Andrew was about four years old, we decided it was time to try to get him into Whitby, the Montessori school in Greenwich. Harry had a friend who was able to arrange an interview. When we arrived at the school for the interview, Andrew had to go to the bathroom, and he promptly locked himself in. I was so embarrassed because I wanted everything to go perfectly so he would be accepted. For what seemed like hours, we talked to Andrew through the bathroom door. Finally, they took the door off the hinges and got him out. He wasn't crying or screaming; he wasn't even upset. Whitby accepted him nonetheless, and he was enrolled there through tenth grade. Of all the children, Andrew spent the longest time at Whitby.

Andrew was considered old for Whitby because he was past all the early development tactile toys and teaching aids. As a child, Andrew was very mechanical—he was fantastic with his hands. Before he was eighteen months old, he would unscrew the cap of my parents' tiny brass hammer and take out the even tinier tools. He wasn't even walking and he was able to take everything out, put everything in. When he was four years old, he took apart his teacher's typewriter at Whitby. The teacher told

Andrew's first passport photo, May 20, 1970.

me she almost had a heart attack, but when she asked him if he could put it back together, he did so perfectly. From an early age, his hand-eye coordination was amazing.

One time, a friend told me that her son, who was a friend of Andrew's, had come home from school with a beautiful English Matchbox car. Her son told her that Andy had given it to him. I couldn't believe that Andrew had given it away—those Matchbox cars were expensive. When I asked him why he gave the car away, he told me he traded it for a Twinkie—forbidden fruit in our home.

I think Andrew was happiest during his twelve years at Whitby. When Harry and I transferred him and all his siblings to Rye Country Day, Andrew was a junior. He was plunged immediately into standardized test preparation. I picked him up from his test prep course one afternoon and he burst into tears. He put his head in his hands and said, "I'll never be anything but a garbage man." I was stunned. I had never seen Andrew so defeated. He excelled at so many things, but testing was not one of them.

Andrew got through the SATs and went to Villanova University. He was, by his own description, a terrible student. He used to help all his friends prepare for tests and they would end up with Bs and he would get a C-. After two and a half years at Villanova, Andrew

Andrew after his First Holy Communion, Five Chimneys, May 9, 1964.

called us one afternoon and said he wanted to leave college. He explained to us that he didn't want to waste our money or his teachers' time. He wanted to go to work. Harry told him that if he quit college, he could not live at home.

Looking back, we shouldn't have let him quit, but it was a very different era. If we had insisted, we would have felt out of step with the tenor of the times, which valued individual pursuits and passions. Back then, getting a college degree was not as important as it is today. Professionally, Andrew has done well for himself in the private wealth-management field, but he tells his children, Courtney, Caitlin, and Lily, "Don't do what I did. Finish college no matter what."

Andrew is very intelligent and extremely likable, like his father. He loves to travel and meet people, making connections and networking—he never forgets a face.

DEBBY

After Andrew was born, I was pregnant again quickly with Debby—they were born eighteen months apart. I gained a lot of weight during my pregnancy with Debby. The doctor had gotten my due date wrong, so I was never sure how far along I was.

Debby in a portrait by Hella Hammid, Five Chimneys,
Purchase, New York, September 1963.

Our elder daughter, Deborah Ann Malloy, was born on April 3,
1959. In those days, women were left alone in the labor room, and
nobody checked in on you unless you called. I think she was born
around 5:00 a.m. because I heard the bells ring at the chapel of the
College of New Rochelle nearby. Right after I heard the bells, I
had a big contraction and rang for the nurse. Soon after, Debby was
born on that beautiful morning.

Because Andrew was so gorgeous and perfect and handsome,
my mother worried that if I had a girl, she wouldn't be as beautiful
as Andrew was handsome. But Debby laid that worry to rest
quickly—she was adorable. Both children had blue eyes and fair
skin and very light hair.

Debby was also an angel. She had to be, because I would plunk
her outside in her pram and she would nap there. I would play with

Andrew while Debby napped, and when it was time to pick her up, she woke up and ate like clockwork. It was a cinch.

I was a bit naive and perhaps too trusting when I was a young wife and mother. I used to put the children down to nap in the pram in our front yard, because I remembered Didi having Eddie nap outside in the fresh air. One day my neighbor across the street warned me about the danger of leaving the babies there unattended. From then on, they were put down to nap on our screened-in porch, and they always slept soundly.

Debby walked a little sooner than Andrew, she talked a little sooner, and she went to Whitby a little sooner, at two and a half years old. She was always a bit independent, with a big, big heart, and she had limitless compassion for animals, especially horses.

Debby, along with all her siblings, took riding lessons at nearby Kenilworth Riding Club. She started riding at five years old and took to it immediately. Over the next four years, she continued to take lessons, spending as much time as possible with the horses. When the opportunity to half-lease a pony came up, I jumped at the chance. Pinocchio was cute but wicked, with lots of talent but many bad habits. Like many ponies, he had bounced from child rider to child rider, picking up tricks all along the way. Without a seasoned rider to break those bad habits, Pinocchio had developed a reputation for throwing riders off. He did not want to jump and had tossed many a rider by dropping a shoulder or stopping at the last minute just before takeoff.

No more than a week after Debby started riding Pinocchio, her trainer called me. "Mrs. Malloy, you should come see Debby. She can get Pinocchio to jump and no one else can." I came in to watch Debby ride. It was clear that Pinocchio had met his match, and it was then that I first sensed Debby's talent.

We made do with Pinocchio, but as Debby got taller, she began to outgrow him. The trainer suggested that we look at a nice medium pony that had just arrived at the barn. I'll never forget what he said, "Mrs., manners is writ all over her face." We had just met the pony we would name Special Edition, and that name couldn't have been more apropos. She did everything: pony club, fox hunts, horse shows, hunter paces. I even hitched her up to a governess cart and competed in harness classes. She was an unbelievable little pony, and she only cost $350. Today, she is buried at Edition Farm in Hyde Park.

We had Special until our youngest child, Vivi, outgrew her. At that point, we passed Special on to another family as a lesson pony. From there, Special was passed on to a local family with a son who was interested in riding. Unfortunately, his interest waned, and Debby found out that Special was not being cared for properly—standing in a dirty stall with no water or hay throughout most of the day. Though she was only thirteen at the time, Debby decided to rescue Special. She couldn't drive, so she enlisted a friend, who drove our horse van to go with her. The owner wouldn't allow Debby to take Special, but that didn't stop her. She contacted the ASPCA and complained. The ASPCA removed Special from her owner and we got her back. She spent many happy years at Edition Farm, pony clubbing and competing in horse shows until her retirement. But Special's retirement years were busy as well, because all my grandchildren had their first pony rides on her. She had a good life.

Through Debby's passion for riding and our increasing involvement with the horse world, I found out about Pony Club for the children. With its emphasis on all-around horse care and training young riders to become knowledgeable horsemen, Pony Club provided the experience that I was looking for: one that went beyond horse shows with their focus on competition and winning. I value an educational approach that prioritizes the horse over the blue ribbon. Pony Club was a good fit, as it aligned so perfectly with what we were doing at home. Throughout our years in Pony Club, I was very involved and learned alongside my children. I became the district commissioner of the Purchase Pony Club and co–district commissioner of the Greenwich Pony Club.

At the same time, Debby continued to compete in horse shows and win. When she was about ten years old, she began training with

Debby on Regal Edition at A Day in the Country Horse Show,
Greenwich, Connecticut, c. 1972.

Judy Richter and riding a pony named Regal Edition, Reggie for
short. Judy saw Debby's talent but didn't like Reggie at all. I had
bought Reggie because he was handsome and reminded me of
Blaze, the hero of the C. W. Anderson books. Bad idea. Judy saw
Reggie for what he was and told me, "He's a brat."

Judy Richter is a true horsewoman and a dear friend: forthright,
articulate, hardworking, and generous. She and Debby shared a
deep passion for and connection with horses. Judy pairs that deep
understanding with what I can only describe as good horse sense.
The environment at Judy's stable, Coker Farm, was perfect for
Debby, giving her the opportunity to ride and care for multiple
horses. Judy trusted Debby to groom and train horses independently, as she saw that Debby was extremely disciplined. She knew
that Debby understood horses on a similar level to her, and as a
rider, Debby could sense exactly what kind of input a horse needed
at any given time. There is no question that Debby's experience
with Judy changed the trajectory of her life with horses.

Judy found a wonderful first horse for Debby—Something Else,
a large junior hunter and equitation horse from upstate New York.

He and Debby were such a good fit; she ultimately rode him at the equitation finals and won the warm-up class at the Garden.

Given all the time she spent with the horses, it's a wonder she was able to keep up with her schoolwork. She was a good student and got good marks even though she was up early, mucking out in the morning and busy riding in the afternoon. She worked very hard, making time for homework during the school day or during car or van rides to and from the stable. She had also developed into a very talented skier, which took up time as well.

Debby and Kenneth were probably the most gifted skiers of all of our children. Debby rose to the top quickly and was a candidate for the U.S. development team. We drove up in the rain to the finals at Mad River Glen, in Vermont. We were in the parking lot when Debby greeted us, dressed in her ski clothes and a black plastic garbage bag, as it was still raining. She told us she was third—making her the third best female skier in the East—and we were so proud of her. She just said it quietly, but all of us knew: This was huge.

But Debby had to make a decision. There were shows and lessons in the winter for her riding career too, whereas the boys who golfed put their clubs aside until the courses opened in the spring. A few weekends later as she was strapping on her boots on the floor of the condo rec room, she said to me, "Mom, I can't do both. I can't do the horses and the skiing. I have made a decision. I can't talk to my skis. . . . I choose the horses." And that was it. She had a chance to shine in both disciplines, but horses and riding won out.

For the dedicated equestrian, it's a different world. Debby would get up at 4:00 a.m. and start her exercise regimen, which was stretching, plus the medicine ball and the treadmill. And then she came down and had a cup of coffee. By eight, she was on her first horse. She would finish in the barn sometimes seven at night.

She could be out there an hour, working out something on a horse. I asked her one day, "How do you know how to fix all the things, how do you know?"

She looked at me and said, "Mom, if I don't know it by this time . . ."

The trainer George Morris, whose students include many Olympic riders, said that Debby was one of the most talented riders he ever had, but she was not the best student. Debby was so used to riding on her own for so long that she always wanted to figure things out herself.

Competing in juniors, she would sit and watch the German team at 3:30 a.m. at Madison Square Garden, when they were allowed to practice in the ring and do their flat work. She would do her homework while watching all the teams. Then she'd go and look in their tack rooms and see what kind of bits they used, and what kind of feed the horses were fed. She has been a student of her craft forever.

During Debby's senior year at Rye Country Day School, she applied to several colleges, including my alma mater, Wellesley College. When asked about her top priority during her interview, she made it clear that it was riding. To our great disappointment, Debby did not get accepted to Wellesley, and I believe it was due to the fact that she prioritized riding over everything, including her college experience.

It was a huge disappointment for Debby. In those days, for Wellesley and other top colleges, if you were accepted, you had to have the school as your focal point, and nothing else. And of course with her, it was riding. Nowadays, a talented person who's on the A-rated show circuit, who's trained by George Morris, who's in the Olympics development group, is a prized admission. But not back then. It was very traumatic, and Debby never got over it.

Some years ago, I brought her to campus as my guest on an alumni weekend. We spent two days there and she met some classmates of mine, went to classes with me, and toured the campus. It was wonderful, and she said, "Someday before I die, Mom, I'm going to graduate from Wellesley." And I believe she would have.

She decided to attend Lafayette College in Pennsylvania, but during a visit to the campus she was told that freshmen were not allowed to have a car. This was a deal breaker for Debby, who had chosen Lafayette in large part due to its proximity to her trainer's stable in Hunterdon, New Jersey. She ultimately started her freshman year at Manhattanville College, which was just down the street from our home. After three months, however, she realized that she couldn't make both school and riding work. She had been living at home, helping out with our boarding barn, and giving lessons to young children, while continuing to compete on the A show circuit. It didn't take long for her to realize that she could not do both to her expectations.

"I can't do it, Mom. I can't do the horses and do college. I come back from shows exhausted, and I'm way behind in my classes. I can't keep up." She had just gotten home and was standing by the back door when she told me. What was I going to say? I should have insisted and found a way. I should have told her to forget the boarding, forget the lessons, but I didn't, and I still blame myself for that. To be honest, I needed her at Edition Farm, but I now worried that she would be sacrificing her intellectual growth for her athletic pursuits.

With Debby, riding has been a lifetime passion. She always said, "Some people like to ride, but I *have* to ride, that's the difference." Her passion for riding was inspiring, and I shared it. I had to! Spending hour upon hour in extreme cold or heat, at dawn or deep into the night, watching her ride. It was a lot of work, but we did it together. I have always thought that I should write a book and title it *Living with Talent*, about the experience of raising an exceptionally gifted child. It was a particular experience to parent such a focused and driven competitor with such innate talent.

One time, I was at a show with Debby and Vivi. Vivi had a mare, a filly, which had banged its knee in a class. We were about to compete in the next class, and Debby said, "What are you doing? Look at her knee!"

"Oh, it'll be fine," I said.

Debby said, "No, it won't." And she sat there on top of a bucket, hosing the horse's knee with cold water. "Mom, this horse is hurt. Nothing gets better on a horse; a horse gets worse. You can't show this horse anymore today." We were at a big show in Southampton, but Debby put the horse first.

She was so right and so wise. She's taught me a lot. She said to me once, "Never do anything, especially with a horse, because it's convenient. You'll make the wrong choice."

Another time, Debby was coming home very late from a horse show in Germany, in a big horse van with a big steel tack trunk, a highboy-type thing that sits on the floor in one of the front compartments where there is a bed for the groom. This van has a front ramp just for equipment, with a hook on it in the back and a remote control to open and close the ramp. There is also a hook that's used to secure the highboy.

As Debby and the grooms were unloading the horses, she started to put the ramp down, but the highboy hadn't been hooked properly, so the ramp came flying down fast. She said that she heard her grandfather Popi's voice saying, "Roll, Debby, roll!" And she rolled out of the way. It could have killed her.

Debby told me later that she heard Popi's voice loud and clear. She was very close to her grandparents, especially my father. She always said that he was always there in the form of an eagle. When she sees an eagle, that's Popi.

In 1981 Debby competed in Quebec City and won the Rothmans Grand Prix on her horse Plain Jane, a Thoroughbred. Meanwhile, on the show circuit she had met a New Zealand boy and fallen in love and wanted to follow him to New Zealand. Debby urged me to sell Jane and use the money for her sisters and brothers, whom she felt were wanting because of her expensive sport. She felt that she should leave and try to make it on her own, and this was her way out. Then, another horse, whom she loved and had hopes for a bright future as a show jumper, died in our little barn in Purchase one night. It was pretty horrible for all of us. That was it for Debby. She couldn't see a future for herself in the United States and left soon after that.

Debby went to New Zealand and then Australia for a period of five years. Those years when she was on the other side of the world were awful for me. We would visit her and see how she was managing on those borderline horses. I cried so much seeing her there, thinking about what she had left behind and the life she had chosen. I wanted to help her with the simplest things. I remember seeing her tack up a horse to ride, and she had hay twine that she was fashioning as draw reins. I was more than horrified; they were dangerous because they couldn't be adjusted easily and could chafe the horse and break. I said that I would send her some leather ones, and she said that it was fine and not to bother. There were other things that made me shudder, but she loved the wildness of the life—too raw for me to fathom. I would cry on the plane all the way home. Harry did not know what to do to soothe me. I was inconsolable.

Our first visit to that part of the world was to Palmerston North, in the southern part of New Zealand's North Island. When we arrived at the small airport, our luggage was nowhere to be found, and the airport staff told us they could not make a long-distance phone call to try to locate it. Harry was furious and said he was leaving on the first plane out of there. I told him that we had come halfway around the world to see our daughter and I was not going back now.

Things were so rudimentary and pathetic there. When Debby heard the dilemma we were in, she tore around the countryside finding cocktail onions for Harry's martini, wine for me, pajamas for him, nightgown for me, slippers. . . . She did everything to make us comfortable for what we hoped would be just one night without our baggage. In just a few hours, we were united with all of our worldly goods. It was a rough start in a strange land that had taken our little girl away.

Debby loved the wild aspects of life on a New Zealand sheep farm. She loved to tell us all the exciting and (to me) not-so-exciting things—like taking the show jumpers hunting and jumping them over sheep fences, which are wire! They would ride out on the same horses at night in a storm with feed bags tied to either side of the saddle to save the little lambs, which were always born then, it seems. They picked up the lambs, put them in the feed bags, and brought them into the sheds.

The sheds were for sheep shearing—there were no barns. The horses lived outside with New Zealand blankets as their shelter in bad weather. Sometimes it would rain, night and day, for ten days straight—no wonder the gardens are so lush! But the horses never saw the inside of any structure.

On the very rare times that Debby would fly home for the holidays, I would pick her up at the airport and she would be wearing one of those heavy woolen jackets everyone wore in New Zealand. The car would smell of wet sheep—a muttony smell. My son Mark once said that when it rains in New Zealand, the whole country smelled like a wet sweater. Debby said she never wanted to eat mutton or lamb stew again when she returned to the U.S.

Debby had gone to New Zealand and then Australia to ride better horses, but it never happened. When she rode for a show barn in Australia, the other rider, a young man, always got the better horses. We visited her in Perth and met her boss, the owner of the show barn. Debby begged him to let her ride one of his top horses, but he never gave her the chance. To see my daughter begging to ride one of his top horses broke my heart. Anyone could see that given a chance on one of them, she would have been his rider from then on.

Shortly after that visit, I met Debby's former trainer George Morris at the Madison Square Garden Horse Show. We were in the freight elevator in the back and he asked about Debby. I told him that she was still in Perth, and he said that he knew a couple who had just bought a show barn in Virginia. They were importing Irish jumpers and had told him that they needed a rider. This was a chance to get Debby home. I was thrilled. I called Debby immediately and she said she would think about it, but it did not take her long to pack up and go to Virginia.

It was at a riding clinic in Virginia that Debby met her future husband, Hans Günter Winkler. He was a great equestrian and show jumping rider who had won five Olympic gold medals, one silver, and four individual medals with the German team between 1956 and 1976. One of the most successful German Olympic athletes, he helped bring the nation's pride back after the war, when they were so beaten, bombed, and defeated. When he came to the United States, he beat riders from every single country in Madison Square Garden. So, Hans Günter Winkler was known to us long before we met him.

Debby was riding in Virginia and called me one day and said, "Mom, Hans Günter Winkler is going to give a clinic. . . . He's coming over to Morgan Park. But he's only taking three Olympic hopefuls, and I want to get in. I want to ride in this clinic, but I can't do it without a letter of recommendation. Who do you know who can help me out?" So, Mom to the rescue. I asked Michael Page from Old Salem Farm to write a letter, and Michael laughingly said, "She doesn't need a recommendation from anyone." But he graciously wrote the letter, and Debby got into the clinic.

At the clinic, Hans lined all the people up, as clinicians do, usually at the end of the first day. He asked them what they've been doing, where they've been riding, what their hopes were for the horse. When he came to Debby, he said, "Where have you ridden in your life?" And she told him that she rode in the U.S. and had also ridden in Europe and New Zealand and Australia.

"Would you like to go back to Europe someday?" he asked.

And Debby said, "Absolutely."

After the clinic, Hans asked people about Debby. What kind of girl was she? What kind of rider? What kind of a work ethic? He liked the American style of riding Thoroughbreds and was looking for somebody to come over from America to ride for him. The Germans were trying to get more Thoroughbred blood into their show jumpers so that they could introduce more speed into the bloodlines.

He had previously hired another American rider, who turned out to have personal issues, and got rid of her pretty quickly. After hearing all these good reports about Debby, he asked her if she would come over and ride for him. Debby was ready to pack up and leave immediately. I said, "You can't do that. You go over, you see what it's like, and then make a decision."

She went over to ride for him in 1986, and they were married in 1994. So, it took a while for them to establish a romantic relationship.

In Germany, Debby got better and better, riding very difficult horses but learning a different technique, because they weren't Thoroughbreds. She was used to approaching a jump and then she'd just balance the horse and he would go over it. The German horses would not just go; you had to send them. She had to work really hard to dominate them. Eventually, she worked with the lighter types, the Hanoverians and Trakehners. It didn't happen overnight, but she mastered the techniques and became a wonderful rider and teacher.

Hans, on the other hand, was always a great rider—a rider like Rodney Jenkins, the American rider who never had a formal lesson and was inducted into the Show Jumping Hall of Fame—a natural. They cannot teach their technique, because they don't know or understand what they do. It just comes to them. It's very hard for a student to decipher what, exactly, they do on a horse.

Debby had a lovely life in the charming town of Warendorf, which is the equestrian center of Germany. It was a nice world. She worked terribly hard with the horses, but she had a wonderful social life too. She could get herself all dressed up and put together and go out at night after a very, very hard day and charm them all. They all loved her—who wouldn't?

Debby loved her family but she was so far away that it was very hard for her to be part of it, and to understand the little nuances of things. She wanted to help, but it was hard with email or a telephone call, because you don't see the person's face.

Many years ago, when I spent several months in Cuba after college and before I was married, I decided to go to Varadero for the sun and beautiful sandy beaches. I stayed at a place we all frequented if we were not staying at a family-owned house. It was called the Kawama Club ("kawama," *caguama* in Spanish, is the word for turtle). The manager of the hotel had a lovely daughter who was about twelve years old at the time. She was an awesome swimmer, obviously a good athlete, and she dove into the sea from the long pier. She was tanned, with long blonde hair. I watched her and had this thought that haunts me still today:

I would love to have a little girl like that one day.

And then it happened . . . I had Debby. I got what I wished for.

Another day, many years later, I was with the family in Barbados, another paradise spot in the Caribbean where we spend vacations in the winter. Everyone looks forward to it; however, Debby and Hans rarely were able to join us because of the circuit in the international show jumping world. It is a complicated algorithm, but in order to qualify for the most important shows you have to garner points throughout the year. Missing a big show meant losing a chance to attend the final competitions as the year went on. Thus, in 2011 Debby and Hans were in Germany, not Barbados.

It was our first day on the island and I sat by the pool and soaked up the sun and swam and looked forward to these days with family around me . . . heaven. We went into the house for lunch, and Mark said he had taken our computers into the living room where the connections were better. After lunch I went to check the signal on my laptop. There was an email from Hans. It said, as far as I can remember, that Debby had had a fall and was in the hospital and gave me the number of the doctor to call. I started screaming, "Vivi! Vivi! Vivi. . . ." She came running, and I just pointed to the computer. My family went into emergency mode. Someone called our travel agent, Teresa, who made a miracle happen. She got Mark and me on a plane that night to England and then to Germany from there. It was prime vacation time on the island and to do this was amazing. I was not crying; I was kind of holding my breath from there on. Kenneth's wife, Jeryl, dear girl, was helping me pack and putting aside shorts and bathing suits and just leaving in what I traveled down in, plus necessities. I remember she gave me a long woolen red scarf, which I wore, slept in on the plane, and wrapped around me most of the days in cold, wintery Germany. The flight was awful for me, sandwiched between strangers and fearing that Debby was in pain. We knew nothing, only that she had had a bad fall. We were in the dark.

When we finally arrived at the Münster Airport, two girls, Hans's secretary and another girl I knew from his staff, greeted Mark and me. We drove right to the hospital. The girls said nothing. They had been told to do so, I am sure. We called the doctor again and he said that she was worse. All I could think of was worse than what? Had fever started, infection? The girls led us to the hospital floor and we were told to put on these plastic coats and maybe something on our feet too. I remember running down the hall and crying out, "Debby! Debby!" When we got to the room, she was on life support. I couldn't hug her, all I could do was kiss her and stroke her, with all the tubes and machinery in the way. I spoke in her ear and told her I loved her so much, so much. . . .

When Mark and I left Barbados, I had told the other children, Andrew, Kenneth, and Vivi, that we would go and get the lay of the land before they all went over. But even before Mark and I had left, they were making calls to fly to Germany too. Their trip was even more arduous, as the only way for them was to fly to Canada, then England, and then Germany. It seemed that they were there that same afternoon. But by now I had lost track of time. Throughout this, I kept thinking I had to keep myself together, to be an example to them, to the Germans, that Americans had discipline and concern for others—hospital staff, other patients—in the midst of what was to me, horror . . . my little girl.

The doctor in charge spoke fluent English, fortunately, and said he wanted to discuss the situation with all of us, my children and me. He said that Debby had broken her neck in the fall and that she had had two heart attacks, which were very painful, and she could have more. He intimated that we should speak with one another and that he would do whatever we decided. My memories about this are fuzzy and impressionistic; all I could think about at the time was that Debby was suffering.

I told Hans I wanted a priest to give her Extreme Unction, the Last Rites of the Church. Someone there in the room, maybe the nurse, said a minister had been there. I said I wanted a Roman Catholic priest. We did get one, but to this day I regret that I said she could not receive the Host. I was so scared she would choke. I spoke to a priest several months later and he said he had given Communion to many on life support. I felt awful, and still do, that I took that blessing away from her at her last moments on this Earth.

And then we all said goodbye to Debby. They asked us to leave the room while they took out the tubes, disconnected her from the machines, but I wouldn't and it was horrible, horrible. When they removed the breathing tube she coughed and gasped and she opened those beautiful blue eyes and looked at me, at us. To me, she seemed to be begging to live, but my children said that she would have been a paraplegic and on life support and that that was no life. We were doing the right thing for her, but . . .

We got through the funeral in Germany. It was held at the Olympic Center in Warendorf, in the big riding hall where Debby had spent so many hours perfecting her craft, practicing, practicing, practicing. There were amazing flower displays and hundreds of people present because she was Debby Malloy Winkler, and Hans was famous and respected in Germany and this was his hometown. Hans was very gracious to all of us, and we spent time in his base- ment looking at all of Debby's trophies in the beautiful display cases. Mark took photos of everything, and Hans said he would send them all to us if we wanted them, and of course I did. They are all in the farmhouse at Edition Farm.

Debby used to say that when you won a horse show in Germany there was always a big presentation ceremony. Whatever province or town the show was held in would have a procession of lovely girls in native costumes handing the winner the trophy, a big bouquet of flowers, and a big wheel of the local cheese, and then they had the

Victory Gallop and the cheese would be hitting the horse on the rump and it would start him bucking, and the rider would do all he or she could do to hold on! That's how Debby was—punctuating a story about winning trophies with self-deprecating humor.

People say, "Oh, at least she died doing what she loved." I think she was not happy when she died. The horse had spooked or done some silly thing and she was probably disciplining it and working hard in that moment. What the horse did was serious, dangerous, and she knew it. She was not loving that moment. We are pretty sure that the mare reared up, lost her balance while in the air on two legs instead of four, and toppled over on Debby. No, she was doing what she loved in her life, but not at that moment, not the way people describe it.

Last night, just by chance, I saw on television an interview by Anderson Cooper with his mother, Gloria Vanderbilt, a few years before she died. The details of her horrible loss are well known. She had a lot and a lot was taken from her. Her twenty-three-year-old son Carter, Anderson's older brother, jumped off her terrace in New York City in front of her. She said she went to bed and stayed there three weeks and just cried. She said she had no tears left after that.

I don't have any tears left either. Instead, I have the echo of a saying: "Be careful what you wish for. . . ."

That little girl diving off the pier in Varadero, who was so lovely and athletic and blonde and tan (a hard combination), the little girl I wished for, I got. And then I had to lose her. I had to lose Debby. For my joy and my wonderful life, I had to pay a price, and it was the thing that I had always wanted. So much was given to me in my lifetime. It was such a long shot to end up with the golden ring of the carousel. Because I received so much, I tried to earn it by being a loving child, obedient, smart enough to get into Wellesley and to find the perfect husband, and then blessed with five darling, gorgeous, healthy children. Something had to be given back. This is what I felt when Debby died and still feel to this day. That my life was too perfect . . . something was going to go. Be careful what you wish for.

KENNETH

Andrew and Debby, our two oldest, were easy babies and I thought that was the way all babies would be. Then I had Kenneth. Two weeks before my due date, I started having contractions, and Harry rushed me to the hospital. In the labor room the contractions were coming one minute apart, and then they stopped. By this time, dads-to-be were allowed to visit the labor room, so Harry came up and found me reading a magazine. He asked, "What the hell are you doing?"

I told him that the contractions had stopped and I didn't think the baby was coming. At that point the doctor came in, excused Harry, and examined me. He agreed. "You're not ready yet. You can go home." I was exhausted. I felt as if I hadn't produced anything— I had been down to the wire, but had nothing to show for it. No baby.

Two weeks later, I went into labor and it came on very quickly. I called Harry at work, and when he got home, my water broke. I made it into the bathroom upstairs just in time. As I was grabbing towels and getting ready to go, I yelled to him, "Did you plant the azalea bush?"

Harry had given me an azalea bush for Easter and I was furious that he had not yet planted it. He told me not to worry about it right now, but I knew this was my only chance, so I said—and this is absolutely true—"I'm not going to the hospital until you plant it."

So Harry, swearing a blue streak, grabbed his shovel, dug a hole where I wanted it, and threw the azalea in. He then ran upstairs to get my suitcase for the hospital, which wasn't quite closed. On the way down, he stepped on our little poodle Seamus, kicking him aside as the bag flew open and all the contents scattered.

Somehow, we managed to get to the hospital, Harry tearing down I-95. At first I said, "Honey, don't go so fast." Then I'd get a contraction and say, "Go faster!"

When we got to the hospital, Harry jumped out of the car and ran in shouting, "My wife is going to have a baby!" They came out and got me into a wheelchair and took me upstairs and into the delivery room.

The doctor said, "This time you mean it." Our third child, Kenneth Henry Malloy, was born extremely quickly on May 1, 1961.

Kenneth was everything our other babies had not been—he was never at rest. Where Andrew and Debby slept and napped on the clock, Kenneth didn't want to sleep. He required constant rocking to go to sleep, and as a newborn, he would crawl around in his bassinet. When he reached one end, I would turn him around and he would crawl to the other. I called the doctor and told him about this, and he suggested that I put Kenneth in a crib with bumpers and let him crawl all he wanted. So I did just that.

Though incredibly active and energetic, Kenneth suffered constant bad colds, viruses, and infections, and had very bad adenoids and tonsils. I remember our pediatrician, Dr. Seanor, making a house call when Kenneth was an infant and ill with a fever. As he tended to Kenneth, I told him, "I'm pregnant again."

"What?" he replied. "I haven't gotten this one out of the woods yet."

They didn't have the variety of antibiotics that they do today, so we would take Kenneth to Dr. Seanor for gamma globulin shots to build up his immune system. But even that didn't seem to work. Finally, when he was about eight years old, the doctors agreed to take out his tonsils. It changed his life, and mine too. Once they took his tonsils out, he suffered far fewer colds and they were much less severe. I could finally breathe a little easier.

Raising Kenneth required a lot of energy and attention because he was so full of energy himself. I remember his third birthday party, a simple gathering in the backyard with ice cream and cake, but when it was over, I was exhausted. I remember going up to the bedroom, collapsing on the bed, and saying to Harry, "We made it. We managed to get him through his third year."

Kenneth was smart and a real boy, through and through. On those rare occasions when I let the boys out to play in their good clothes while I got the girls ready for a holiday visit, Andrew would come back exactly as he left, clean and tidy, and Kenneth would come back dirty and disheveled, with a scraped knee and a big smile on his face. I'd say, "Kenneth, what did you do out there? What did you do to your clothes?"

He'd reply, "Mom, I'm the Tide kid!"

There was an old commercial for Tide detergent featuring a little boy who was always dirty and disheveled. His mother would use Tide in the wash, and he'd be spanking clean by the end.

My pet name for Kenneth is "Nooch." At some point in his life I started calling him "Ken-ooch," and then it became Nooch. Even now, his lovely wife, Jeryl, uses the same term of endearment.

Kenneth and I realized from the beginning that we were the most alike in many ways. In the living room at Five Chimneys, there was a portrait on the piano of me as a child, taken in Central Park. I was dressed in a very severe outfit—coat, leggings, and hat—and I looked like a boy. One day, Kenneth, who was very young at the time, toddled into the living room, pointed to the picture, and said, "Mommy, why did you dress me like a man?" He could already see the similarity for himself.

Years later, when I went to Italy to meet the Matacenas, my biological paternal family, for the first time, Harry and my son Mark accompanied me. I felt sure that my Italian family would consider Mark the most "Matacena." However, before they had even met Kenneth, they pointed to a picture of him that I had brought and said, "*Oh no, Vivien, questo. Questo figlio, Kenneth. È piu Matacena.*"

From the beginning, Kenneth had enormous athletic ability and great hand-eye coordination. When he was at Whitby, his Montessori teacher told me that while other children would need to pick up chips individually to replace them in their box, Kenneth could flip them back into their box in the correct order from a distance. She told me she'd never seen such coordination in such a young child.

Whitby was a godsend for Kenneth because he learned differently. For example, because students didn't need to sit at desks, Kenneth was able to move, which allowed him to learn best. His teacher would let him lie in her lap as she was teaching another student, and as he watched her teach, he absorbed it. His teacher told me that was the way he learned to read.

The adjustment to RCDS was most difficult for Kenneth and Vivi, but Kenneth was a good student and a great athlete, so he enjoyed all that RCDS had to offer. The hardest thing for Kenneth was the expectation that he "show his work." He never had to "prove" his answers at Whitby, so he did math in his head. Though frustrated at first, he persisted, getting used to the discipline of writing his work down, and he did well.

The athletic program at Rye Country Day was much more extensive than at Whitby, and Kenneth made the most of it. He was an excellent soccer player, and throughout his years at RCDS he developed strong relationships with his coaches, who loved him. I framed a handwritten letter one of his soccer coaches wrote to him, which said, "If the rest of the team played with your verve and heart, we would have won every soccer game." When Kenneth does something, he gives it his all.

Kenneth is also very social and fun to be with. He loves people and has always been very comfortable striking up conversations with anyone. He immediately puts people at ease.

Like Debby, Kenneth was an excellent skier, but he couldn't tolerate the cold. He would expend so much energy keeping warm on the way to the top of the mountain, that by the time he was halfway down the course, he had run out of gas. So his ski team coach, T. D. McCormick, recommended that Kenneth find a warm-weather sport.

Harry taught all the boys to play golf when they were young, and Kenneth became a very good golfer—so much so that when it came time for college, he focused on schools with good golf teams, with the hope of receiving a scholarship. Harry found out where the well-respected golf pros coached, and he and Kenneth toured those schools. They visited Duke University, the University of Texas, and Louisiana State University. LSU had a strong golf program and the coach was thrilled with Kenneth, so that's where he went.

As a member of the golf team, Kenneth lived in the athletic dorm as a freshman. His roommate was a handsome young man whose father was a famous golf pro. After about two months, he was expelled. Only after he left did Kenneth tell Harry that his roommate was a terrible drunk, coming back to the room late and throwing up frequently. No surprise, then, that he was asked to leave.

I called the dorm a few weeks later, and a young man with a very deep voice answered the phone. He said his name was *Fleur.* When Kenneth called me back, I asked him if I'd heard correctly: *Fleur?* Fleur, Kenneth's new roommate, was great—the top wrestler on the LSU Wrestling Team, weighing in at 350 pounds. I think he became a wrestler because his mother named him *Fleur.* He was charming, polite, and just a wonderful young man.

When Harry and I visited Kenneth at LSU, we were struck by the beauty of the campus. There were buildings with Spanish-tiled roofs and fountains in the middle of small courtyards. And the stadium was huge. At that time, it held 100,000 people. But one of Kenneth's favorite points of interest was his dorm cafeteria. One of the perks of living in the athletic dorm was that the cafeteria never closed. You could go at 3:00 a.m. and order whatever you wanted— even steak and eggs.

Kenneth had a great experience at LSU, and after he graduated he thought about becoming a golf pro. He discussed the idea with Harry, who asked him if he could shoot sixty-five for three days in a row. Kenneth admitted probably not, and Harry told him that being a golf pro wasn't in the cards. But knowing what a good player Kenneth was, Harry knew golf would be wonderful for his career. For clients, playing a game of golf is much more relaxing and enjoyable than having a lunch meeting or office visit, and they'll remember that when Kenneth calls for business. Harry's words turned out to be very true. Kenneth has been with Smith Barney (now Morgan Stanley) for years. He has many loyal clients who love to play golf, some of whom will fly him in to play with them.

Kenneth on the beach at Sandy Lane, Barbados, winter 1973.

I know from personal experience what a joy it is to play with Kenneth. Not only does he have the most beautiful swing, but he's easygoing, playing with such equanimity that you wouldn't know if he had a bad hole or a good hole. In many ways, Kenneth's approach to golf reflects his approach to life. He seems to take the good with the bad and is certainly a glass-half-full type of person. His friends and acquaintances would describe him as a cheerleader, always having an encouraging word. All that said, Kenneth is cautious, though not a pessimist—a good combination, given his profession as a financial advisor. His equanimity has served him well given the ups and downs of the financial markets in recent years. The good times are great, but the bad times . . . I watch the market all the time now. Harry once asked me why, since I don't have that many stocks. I monitor it because it gives me a feel for what my two sons are going through each day and what their days are like.

After graduating from LSU, Kenneth moved home and began working in Manhattan. He commuted by train from Rye to Grand Central Station. Over the course of a few weeks, Kenneth noticed a lovely young woman who took the same train. Eventually working up the nerve to introduce himself, he met his future wife, Jeryl.

Harry and I met Jeryl for the first time one evening at Five Chimneys. We had some friends over when Kenneth and this young woman came walking through the kitchen. Kenneth introduced

Kenneth with the "Guru of Golf" Harvey Penick, author of golf's famous *Little Red Book*, Austin, Texas, summer 1978.

Jeryl quickly as they walked through, without stopping or taking off their coats. Before we knew it, Kenneth said, "Okay, we've got to go. See you later," and out they went. I was left thinking, *Who is this Jeryl?* We were introduced to Kenneth's true love in typical Kenneth fashion, like a moving target.

A short time later, Kenneth asked that we all have dinner together, because he wanted to introduce Jeryl more formally to the family, not only to Harry and me, but to Mommy and Daddy as well. He also wanted us to have dinner with Jeryl's parents, Meg and Neil, whom we had known for years through Westchester Country Club. After meeting Jeryl, Mommy said, "She has the face of a Madonna." Jeryl does, indeed, have the face of a Madonna, but leave it to my mother to describe her beauty in such a lovely way.

Within a year, wedding bells were ringing. I'll never forget the moment at their wedding when Neil, Jeryl's father, said to me, "Did you feel some magic in that church today? There was a magic. This is a really, really good marriage." And he was right. It has definitely turned out to be a wonderful marriage.

Like Kenneth, Jeryl is close with her family and has many friends. She grew up in Rye, very near my parents' home, went to Sacred Heart Academy, and graduated from the University of Vermont. She shares Kenneth's passion for sports and is a great athlete and tennis player. Perhaps most importantly, she and Kenneth both look on the bright side and laugh together.

Kenneth and Jeryl are wonderful parents who have raised four great children—Conor, Maggie, Kenny Jr., and Shane—putting their family first from the beginning. When the children were little, Kenneth would come right home from work to play with them. Even now, though his children are adults, he remains very involved in their lives.

Kenneth is very emotional and, like me, will tear up at the drop of a hat. Simple things, like a song or a beautiful story can start the tears flowing. He is the family's "poet laureate," creating a poem or tribute for important occasions. He can have a hard time getting through them, because they reflect his deep feelings for family and friends, and his words get to him as much as they get to us. His religion is close to his heart, which makes me very, very happy.

MARK

Our third son, Mark Lawrence Malloy, was born September 29, 1962. During my pregnancy with Mark, I was sick to my stomach beyond the first four months, and I didn't want to eat much. It was a very uncomfortable pregnancy, although the initial labor was uneventful.

I had mild contractions but they were frequent, so we went to the hospital. I was alone in the labor room, and all of a sudden I felt a pulsing in my thigh. I looked down and the sheet was bloody. I rang for the nurse and when she saw the blood, she ran to get the doctor. I had placenta previa. The placenta had torn and they had to get the baby out. In 1962, there were no monitors on your stomach, so they had no indication that something was wrong until I started bleeding.

Our obstetrician was honest with me and told me right then and there that he might not be able to save the baby. Later, Harry told me that the doctor had gone to the waiting room and said to him and Mommy that he doubted he could save the baby and that he would try to save me.

In the labor room, he and the nurse went to work. "Vivien, you have to have this baby now. So push!" I would try to push but I had no push left. When he realized this, both he and the nurse pushed down on my stomach hard. It was horrible—they were pushing the baby out with all their strength.

Finally, Mark was born, and thank God, he was fine. He was long and slim and an absolute angel. We called him the first American pope. I could plunk him in the playpen and just leave him there, smiling. Thank God, because by that time, I had three others.

When Mark was two and a half years old, we brought him to the top pediatric neurologist at Columbia-Presbyterian Medical Center. We had noticed some differences in his speech and fine motor skills, and due to his difficult birth, we wanted to follow up. I'll never forget what I learned that day.

The doctor did a few simple tests and described what he found in this way: Due to the trauma at birth, some of the pathways from the brain to the muscles were damaged. He described them as railroad tracks and explained that every time Mark thinks of what he wants to do, he has to make a new "railroad track." He'll get it done, but he can't do it fast.

Like the other children, Mark went to Whitby and was going to transfer to Rye Country Day School. In preparation for the transition, he attended RCDS summer school. I remember swimming in the pool with Mark one afternoon that summer when he told me he couldn't go to Rye Country Day. When I asked him why, he said, "Everything is too fast and I'm cheating to pass all the tests."

Even at that early age, Mark knew himself so well and had a strong moral compass. I told him he didn't have to go to Rye Country Day, so he went instead to Salesian, a Catholic school for boys, then on to Harrison High School.

Mark's family and friends know that he is the kind of person on whom you can rely, no matter what. If I called him and said, "Mark, I need you right away," he would drop everything and get there. Debby said a million times that if she were really in a jam, she would call Mark, and Mark would be there. That's the kind of person he is: bighearted, quietly kind.

Mark never asked for or demanded anything. He was an angel in little boy's clothing. A good sport from an early age, he naturally shared easily and would try his best. In a large family full of energetic children, Mark didn't complain and went with the flow. I'll never forget one day when Mark and I were headed to a horse show, with his pony and Debby's horse in the trailer. Just as we pulled out of our driveway, there was a commotion in the back, forcing me to stop in the middle of a very dangerous curve. When Mark and I got the horses out, I realized that we couldn't ship them together safely. I told Mark he would need to take his pony, Apache, back to the stable and he would miss the show. "Okay, Mom." That was it. No arguments, no fuss. He was disappointed, but took it all in stride. Such an easygoing child.

Mark was the only son who rode horses, and he was a wonderful horseman. Horses loved him because he was quiet, gentle, and patient. He competed in hunters and equitation; equitation was his strong suit. I usually went to all the horse shows, but one afternoon, I was at the barn when Mark returned from a horse show riding a horse named Why Not bareback across the lawn.

I will never forget this wonderful sight. I only wish I had a photo of him that day. Mark was covered with ribbons: championships, reserve champions, and first-place blue ribbons. He had cleaned up. He was so happy, and they were such a perfectly matched rider and horse.

I'll also never forget 1979, when all three of my riding children qualified to compete in the National Horse Show at Madison Square Garden. Debby rode in the open jumper division, Vivi rode in the hunter division, and Mark rode in the Maclay Finals—the equitation division. The qualifying rounds were held in the morning, and the list of those who qualified for the finals that afternoon would be posted midday. I watched from the back of the crowd as Mark checked the list of qualifiers, and he raised his hand to let me know he had made it. I was ecstatic. If nothing else happened in his life, at that moment I was so proud of him. He was riding a borrowed horse, but he practiced and practiced, and he got to the top ten.

Top: Mark shoveling sawdust for bedding with Samson looking on, Edition Farm, 1976. Bottom: Mark taking a break from grooming while Vivi studies, Children's Services Horse Show, Farmington, Connecticut, 1975. (Photos by Jill Krementz.)

Not long after that, in the spring of 1980, Debby went to New Zealand, and she left a couple of her horses behind. Mark was seventeen and it was his last junior year competing, so we decided to let him ride her jumpers for the season. He did well and wore his success very quietly and gracefully.

When it came time for him to go to college, Mark chose New England College in New Hampshire. It was there that he discovered photography, the field that would become his profession. He has a bachelor of arts in visual arts with a concentration in photography, and he went on to earn his master's in media studies and film, as well as a teaching certificate in arts education.

In the spring of 1985, during Mark's senior year, Harry and I went to New England College for Mark's senior photography show. Somehow he had found strawberries in the middle of winter in rural New Hampshire and was serving them with champagne, all beautifully presented, with Mussorgsky's *Pictures at an Exhibition* playing in the background. It was a beautiful event, and we were so very proud of him.

A couple of years later, Mark introduced us to a beautiful girl who was also a photography major. Her name was Heather, and she was tall, blonde, and sweet. I thought, *If this is the one, she's a very lucky girl.*

After Mark graduated, he wanted to stay close to campus because Heather hadn't graduated yet. He became a ski bum for a while, photographing the ski racing on the local mountain, but then he ended up breaking his leg while running gates. His bindings were loose so he tightened them, and when he wiped out, his binding didn't release and he suffered a bad break. That was the end of being a ski bum. Harry called Heather his nurse, because she had to take care of him.

Heather is a very good photographer, and she has taken many trips to Africa to photograph refugees. She and Mark went to Africa on their honeymoon, and she fell in love with it. She has had a number of exhibits of her photographs and has published a book of them as well. (Mark and Heather have since separated, but they remain the very best of friends.)

Mark is a gifted teacher and has taught photography at the university level for the past ten years. He called me one morning and mentioned that he had a morning class and he was picking up coffee and doughnuts for the class. I couldn't believe it—I never had a teacher like that. He said he'd rather have them stay awake for his

8:00 a.m. classes. If there's a seminar or a workshop that he really feels is worthwhile and the kids can't afford travel expenses, he finds a way to get them there.

Jill Krementz, whom we met when she wrote and photographed *A Very Young Rider*, a story about Vivi and her pony, loved to photograph Mark as well. He was always quiet and he was really her favorite. Mark was planning a trip to New York City with his students, so I suggested that he give her a call. She was most gracious, inviting him to come to her home with his students. She spent three hours with the class, discussing photography and showing them her work.

A friend once told me that when she called our house and Mark answered, she knew she would get the information she needed. He was always aware of where everyone was and what they were doing. Mark continues to be the family historian—he has the best memory in the family. If not for Mark, we would forget so many family stories.

Mark is a person who makes the best of what life has dealt him. He's extremely intelligent and loving, a brilliant teacher, and a wonderful, sweet, caring person.

VIVI

We already had a large family of four children, but I still wanted another girl. When I got pregnant for the fifth time, Harry said, "This better damned well be a girl because this is it!"

I was exhausted for most of my last pregnancy, with four young children to take care of, and then we had a record-breaking heat wave during the last few weeks before the baby was born. In order to rest and cool down, I would routinely take a freezing-cold bath after feeding the children dinner. I'd have the air conditioner on in the bedroom and would lie on top of the sheets like a walrus, looking at my enormous stomach.

Our youngest child, Vivien Consuelo Malloy, was born on July 28, 1965. As they had done during my previous deliveries, my obstetrician administered a dose of gas, putting me into "twilight sleep." When I came to just after Vivi was born, I asked Dr. Gray, "What is it?"

He said, "It's a girl and she's beautiful."

"Thank God," I said, and went back to sleep.

When I woke up I was exhausted and very uncomfortable. When Dr. Gray came to check on me, I asked if I could have an extra day in the hospital. As he authorized this extended stay on my chart, I remember him saying, "Of course. I know what you're going back to." So, doctor's orders: an extra day in the hospital to recuperate and a martini from home, made by Harry.

Though I had always dreamed of having an even number of children, when I discussed having another child with my gynecologist a few months later, he cautioned me. I already had five healthy children and I was getting older. So Vivi would be the last.

Vivi was my youngest and a daughter, and I decided that if you only get one chance in your life to spoil a child, this was mine. Because Mark was three years older than Vivi, I was able to spend more time with her one-on-one, a chance I hadn't gotten with my four older children, who were all born within five years.

Vivi was beautiful, but when she was about two years old, I noticed she had what they called in those days a lazy eye. I took her to the ophthalmologist, who informed us that she would need surgery. She underwent successful eye surgery when she was two and a half and wore a patch on her eye for several weeks afterward. I did ocular exercises with her three or four times a day to strengthen her eye muscles, and even though she couldn't read yet, she knew her letters, so we would hold up flash cards with large letters and have her identify them. It was tough to see our little girl with a patch on her eye, but it didn't bother her.

One of my favorite stories about Vivi is also a wonderful illustration of the Montessori method. Of all my children, Vivi had the hardest time learning to tie her shoes. I tried to teach her at home, and her teacher worked with her in school as well. They even had a shoelace board in the classroom, but nothing worked. One morning, when I asked if she needed help tying her shoes, Vivi said no. She told me that her friend Nancy Mullins had taught her. What neither the teacher nor I nor the shoelace board could do, a peer did. Children listen to children, speaking the same language and understanding each other. Maria Montessori realized this and encouraged it.

Vivi was in fourth grade when all the children (except Mark) transferred from Whitby to Rye Country Day. She cried every day during her first two weeks there because everything was so different. Her teacher, Mrs. Goldfarb, told me that this type of transition is overwhelming at first, but assured me that Vivi was very bright and that she would be fine. She ended up taking honors math classes.

Vivi began riding at three years old, starting with Fifth Edition and graduating to our dear Special Edition. When she was eight, we bought Ready Penny, a half-Welsh, half-Arabian medium pony. They were a great fit. She was a lovely mover and jumper. Vivi had been riding Penny for about a year, when we were at a local horse show at Boulder Brook. On my way to the van, I noticed a woman with a camera talking to Vivi. When I asked Vivi about it, she said that the woman wanted to write a book about her and would call me.

The next day I got a call from Jill Krementz. Jill was a photographer who had written a series of books about young athletes, including *A Very Young Dancer*. She explained that she was interested in writing a book about a younger rider who was responsible for the care and keeping of her pony, and whose family was involved. After doing her research and observing at horse shows, she found out about our family and Edition Farm. When she asked whether we would be interested, I told her I would need to check in with Vivi and the family.

Vivi had one concern. She didn't want to be singled out for attention, especially at horse shows. Jill agreed to those parameters, and Vivi was the young girl featured in her classic book, *A Very Young Rider*. To research the book, Jill followed us for a year, taking pictures and conducting interviews. She chronicled every element of life at Edition Farm, from horse care to farm chores to competing at horse shows. Little did we know that this would be the last year Vivi would ride Penny due to Penny's career-ending injury.

The book was published in 1977, and at that time my cousin's husband was the producer of *Captain Kangaroo*, a children's TV program. He asked if Vivi could appear on the show, taped in New York City, with her pony.

There was no way that Penny would be able to make the appearance. She was too high-strung. So the challenge became getting our small pony, Fifth Edition (Fifi), to the studio on Columbus Avenue. I had injured my foot and was on crutches at the time, so we couldn't transport Fifi in the horse trailer. Our friend and trainer, Judy Richter, once again rode to the rescue. She offered her husband Max's business car, a two-door sedan, for transportation. We put newspapers on the floor, pushed the front seats all the way forward, and off we went, with Fifi standing in the back while Vivi rode in the front with me.

We got to the city, parked right outside the building, and unloaded Fifi onto the sidewalk. Vivi was dressed in her riding clothes with her Pony Club pin on her hat, and Fifi looked gorgeous (though she had pooped all over the newspaper).

When I asked the guard how to get to the *Captain Kangaroo* set, he directed us to the third floor via the stairs. I pointed to Fifi and asked if there was another way up. Luckily, there was a freight elevator, and Fifi rode up without blinking an eye.

Once we arrived on the set, Bob Keeshan (Captain Kangaroo) came over and introduced himself, asking Vivi about her pony and the book. He wanted Fifi right next to Vivi during their interview.

When it was time for them to go on, we walked Fifi onto the set for the segment, and she raised her tail to poop. I hobbled over on my crutches, put my hand on top of her tail, and pushed it down. Captain Kangaroo let out a big belly laugh and said, "Is that all it takes to stop it?"

"In an emergency, yes." I replied.

So the pony didn't poop on the set, and it was a really wonderful interview. Vivi was great, Fifi was a star, and everybody loved the show.

After the book was published, Vivi rode ponies for another year before graduating on to horses. Vivi had an easier time with riding, not because she had expensive horses, but because she benefitted from what I had learned with Debby—which was a lot. We got Vivi horses that suited her size and her ability. We bought her a nice junior jumper, Reilly, and a wonderful equitation horse, Wallflower.

My two girls were six years apart, so managing their riding careers was sometimes a challenge, to say the least. I often felt torn when the two of them were competing at the same show—Debby in the grand prix ring, while Vivi was riding medium ponies.

Ultimately, Vivi had the talent but not the passion and the enormous drive that Debby had to ride. When the time came for her to apply to college, Vivi did not face the same dilemma as Debby. She knew that she would continue on with school and finish her riding career once her junior years were over.

She chose to attend the University of Michigan, and her first term of freshman year coincided with the "finals," the national equitation competitions for which riders from all over the country had to qualify. As it was her last finals, Vivi shuttled back and forth from Michigan to compete in Pennsylvania, Washington, D.C., and New York City. She did very well, placing third in the U.S. Equitation Team (USET) finals at Hamilton Farm in Gladstone, New Jersey.

The University of Michigan, with a student body of 40,000, was a far cry from Rye Country Day, where there were eighty-five people in her graduating class. Vivi was, from the get-go, highly intelligent, but in such a different way from Debby.

Vivi met Rich Hanson, who would later become her husband, during her senior year at the University of Michigan. They met in a bookstore, one of her favorite places. They started to chat, he asked her out, and it went on from there.

A few weeks later, Harry and I went out to Ann Arbor for Vivi's graduation. After the three of us had dinner one evening, as we were walking along, I saw a young man crossing the street toward us. I remember looking at him and thinking, *I hope he's the one.* I just had this feeling. And I was right, of course.

Rich is wonderful—intelligent, tall, sweet, funny, and a loving husband and father. He adores his family and is a true romantic. I'm very, very fond of him. The only downside is that he's a Chicago boy, so Vivi transplanted to the Midwest. They have a home in a historic district of Chicago, where they have a lovely life with great friends and wonderful schools for the children. They're far away, and we don't see them as often as I would wish, but maybe they'll change their zip code someday.

After graduating from the University of Michigan with a bachelor's in art history, Vivi went on to earn her master's in social work, specializing in children and families. She had so many sad stories to share. Even before she would start to tell me one, I'd get some tissue. She loved it, though, and she was good at it.

Years later, she combined her love of horses and her clinical training when she discovered therapeutic riding. She had heard through the horse-world grapevine that a young woman she used to ride with had opened a therapeutic riding center, where horseback riding is used as a therapeutic tool to help children and adults with physical, cognitive, and emotional disorders. For people with limited mobility, riding stimulates the central nervous system in the same way as if they were walking, so they can exercise their muscles and nervous system. And for wheelchair-bound children or adults, they have the rare experience of being taller than everyone else.

Vivi loved that work, and after volunteering at a therapeutic riding program, she decided to pursue the field full-time and became a certified therapeutic riding instructor. She helped decide which horses were suitable for therapy sessions and would ride them to determine their rhythm, gait, and temperament. Therapy horses are saints: They have to learn to carry a rider whose weight can shift

Vivi on Advent, c. 1975. (Photo by Jules Geller.)

unpredictably, be able to handle unexpected changes, and stay calm and consistent through it all.

She practiced in the field for two years before starting her own family. Vivi and Rich have a son, Owen, and a daughter, Julia, both of whom are huge fans of racing. I've named racehorses after both of them, and they ask about them all the time. I had hoped the horses wouldn't turn out to be duds, and they didn't. Viva Julia won five races in New York, and Andale Julia was a winner in Barbados. Owen Rico, a racehorse and later a three-day competitor (dressage, cross-country, show jumping), is no slouch either.

Even though she was still "Vivi" to me and her father, after she moved to Chicago, she was Vivien. But she will always be my little Vivi.

I'm very proud of being a parent to all our children, and I remember each one with joy. They are all full of adventure and have turned out to be decent, loving, kind, and considerate human beings. I'm very proud of that.

Edition Farm, Hyde Park, New York. (Photo by Trisha Thompson.)

EDITION FARM

HORSES HAVE BEEN A LIFELONG PASSION, BUT IT WASN'T UNTIL I HAD children that I was able to fully realize my dream of having our own horses and stable. In 1971, we converted a tractor shed on the grounds of our home into a small barn. Basically, we moved the tractor out and put the pony in. At first, the shed could only accommodate a pony for the children, but over time, we expanded, bought some prefab sheds, and it became a real barn—primarily for the family, but with room for a few boarders too. And that was how Edition Farm was launched.

For the next ten years, I enjoyed the horses along with my daughters and son. We were active members of our local Pony Club, and we all participated in the hunt, hunter paces, and trail riding. My children competed at horse shows and Debby also taught lessons.

The children learned the patience and energy required to ride and care for our horses. I am still amazed at what we were able to accomplish on a shoestring budget—the secret was doing all the work ourselves. I drove the van or trailer myself and groomed at the

First Edition at Stratford Stables, Westchester, New York, 1969.

horse shows. We did the barn work. At one point, we had seventeen horses: ex-racehorses, ponies, and horses that no one else wanted or that we rescued. Several made it to Madison Square Garden as champions, no less.

Edition Farm's name goes back to my first horse, a Thorough-bred just off the track named A Bit Happy. Though beautiful, he was too much horse for me, and in the end I sold him, but not before changing his name. Thoroughbreds usually have names connected to their bloodlines, and once off the track, their new owners often rename them. I was not a fan of his name, and my friend Helen Bilby suggested that since he was my first horse, we name him First Edition. I liked the idea. Later, we acquired a pony and named her Little Edition. When we wanted to name our farm, Harry suggested Edition Farm in honor of those first two horses.

Once my children left for college, I had fun riding Wallflower, a wonderful horse that Vivi rode to third place in the USET finals. Every time we went to a show I was champion or reserve. But I still felt like an empty nester. One day I found myself sitting at the kitchen table, waiting for the mail to be delivered, and I thought, this is *not* for me. After ten years of working with horses, pony clubbing, horse shows, fox hunting, and hunter pacing, I had a lot of knowledge, desire, and feeling for horses. I couldn't let that go to waste.

My thoughts turned to breeding Thoroughbreds as the next phase in my life as a horsewoman. Through the years, I found myself attracted to the energy of Thoroughbreds; they are much like a race-car engine, always on a high idle.

A friend who was already involved in horse breeding promised to help me find a mare. I kept calling her, and a few months later, she finally told me she had found the perfect package—a broodmare named Roberta's Dream. They arrived at Edition Farm in 1981, and she was already in foal with a chestnut colt by her side. What a lucky start. I knew so little, but Roberta knew it all. She did everything by herself, including having her foals born unattended. We didn't know anything, but we somehow managed.

My first sale was Roberta's chestnut colt, whom we named Sprat's Dream. He sold in Kentucky as a yearling for the "amazing" price of $3,000. A trainer bought him, and sure enough, Pat Day, a Hall of Famer later in his career, rode him at Churchill Downs, winning by eight lengths. I showed Pat Day the photo when we were in the paddock at Saratoga some years later, and he said, "That's the way I like to win 'em! When you win by that much, there are no others horses in the photo."

Roberta's first foal for me, a filly named Dreamy Croissant, was initially unimpressive—ranking four out of a possible ten for confirmation by a senior sales staffer at Eaton Sales. We went on to race her anyway (she was my only racehorse at the time), and her first race happened to be in Saratoga. She got fourth place, and we couldn't have been more excited. In spite of the sales staff's opinion, Dreamy Croissant went on racing, winning more than $100,000 over her eleven-year racetrack career.

The sudden loss of Roberta to colic in 1984, five years after I bought her, resulted in a hiatus in my breeding activities. I knew I had to learn more. I went back to riding and showing for a while, and decided to look for a real farm property.

EDITION FARM

The search took almost two discouraging years. I would find some nice land with no house, or a great house with no land. I couldn't find the perfect combination. On an unlikely day—a freezing cold day in March—I visited a run-down property in Dutchess County, New York, that would become today's Edition Farm.

It was so cold that day, and I tried to hide my delight as I looked across the fields, but later my real estate agent told me that I had "neon lights" in my eyes when we arrived at the farm on Spooky Hollow Road. I knew this was it. The house was a mess, but toasty warm. The farm had belonged to an elderly woman who had raised and trained Standardbreds, trotting horses, on the property. She had died two years previously, and although the property had barely been maintained since her death, I loved the farm and could see lots of potential beyond the neglected buildings and grounds.

Harry negotiated the purchase, and I give him lots of credit for making it happen. I remember getting a phone call while I was riding at Old Salem Farm. They brought me the remote handset, and when I picked it up, Harry just said, "You got it." I was so excited! As usual, Harry was always there to help me fulfill my dreams.

The farm was a beautiful piece of property, everything I could have wanted for horses, but it was very run down. The fencing was terrible, the barns and stalls were usable but not great, and the barn aisles were dirt. Step one was fencing. Without that, I couldn't turn horses out properly. First, we fenced in the main part of the farm, then the eighty acres across the street, or what the staff calls *la ochenta*, or "the 80."

After the fencing was complete, I didn't have funds to do much else. I didn't do anything to the house—the heating was terrible and the radiators banged—but I didn't live there, so I focused on the barns. We made my first foaling stall by knocking down a wall between two existing stalls.

I learned quickly that you always have to have two foaling stalls, the main one and one that I call the *on-deck*. One night a mare was giving birth in the foaling stall when I heard a commotion in the next stall and went to look. There was Wallflower, a big mare, jammed into this tiny stall, lying down and trying to have a baby. Though we got through those dramatic moments, I realized that we needed more room and proper stalls to make this a safe and workable breeding farm.

After buying the farm in 1986, I started slowly, with a few mares. As the farm and its equine residents began to grow, so did the Edition Farm team. We tried to manage in the early days with a skeleton crew, but some unfortunate things happened due to my own and my staff's inexperience, and I learned the hard way.

In one terrible incident, a foal broke his leg because my staff didn't have the knowledge to help him through a difficult birth. Another time, I was in the barn and one of the grooms ran in and said that a yearling had broken his leg. I thought he meant that the yearling was lame, so I went out, and sure enough, the yearling was standing there dangling his leg. He had reared up and come down on hard ground.

I called the vet, who came immediately, driving directly into the field. One look at the yearling and he told me that we had to put him down. I hadn't realized that the yearling shouldn't have been walked on such hard, rocky ground. The writing was on the wall: If I wanted to really improve my stock and become a successful breeder, I had to switch gears. Instead of trying to do everything myself, I had to get good staff.

The Edition Farm tackroom at Lake Placid Horse Show, with Twinkie front and center, 1980. (Photo by Kym Ketcham.)

Around that time, I had one well-bred, beautiful yearling at our home. Bob Fierro, my bloodstock agent, saw him and thought he was magnificent, so I decided to prepare him for sale. After trying to prep him myself, I realized he needed more than I could provide. He was alone there and hadn't had the opportunity to play with any other yearlings, which I knew wasn't good for him.

Bob recommended sending him to Tilly Foster Farm, one of the first and best breeding farms in New York. I had heard of Tilly Foster Farm for years; it was well respected in the New York breeding community and nationwide.

When I drove up to see Tilly Foster, there was no one around, so I walked around the facility by myself, and I didn't like what I saw. The stalls were terrible, the barn ceilings were low, and the fences were falling down.

Clearly, Bob hadn't been there for a while. I told him I would never send a horse of mine to that place. I wouldn't even send a dog there.

But Bob convinced me. He assured me that my yearling would only be there for six weeks, and he had very good things to say about Annette Orlando, the manager at Tilly Foster. So my yearling went there and was sold at the Saratoga preferred sale for a lot of money. He was the highest-priced yearling by Distinctive Pro sold up to that point. What a thrill!

I told Bob that I wanted to offer Annette a job as my barn manager, but I didn't want to take a person away from another job. He assured me that Tilly Foster was "going to fold any minute" and advised me to speak to her. So Annette and I met at Friendly's, and I said, "I need somebody I can trust, somebody who knows how to foal out mares properly and how to raise foals too. And how's your Spanish?"

Annette's biggest reservation about taking the job was when I told her I would be a hands-on owner. I said, "If I'm not there at the farm, I'm going to be on the phone a lot." Annette said she wasn't sure she could work like that because her current bosses would call once every six months, ask how it was going, and when she said everything was fine, they'd hang up. However, we agreed to give it a shot. She had foaled out hundreds of horses, and if I was going to be a serious breeder, I needed someone with that experience to work with me.

After Annette, several people came on board over time, and this core group has been with Edition Farm since the 1990s. I love the team we've built at the farm. I feel more like a mother hen than an employer, and I think people here feel like it's a family too.

Quality in horsedom is so very important. As I learned more and more, I really began to aim seriously for that. As the firstborn in my family, I'm used to running things. I credit my hands-on nature partly to Daddy. No detail was too small for his attention and correction. This attention to detail has served me well. A farm can go downhill quickly if you don't attend to every little thing: fences, fields, barns. . . . I'm a maintenance freak. If any little thing is wrong, I have it fixed right away.

Although people tell me there's no symmetry in nature, there is in mine. Anyone walking around the pristine grounds of Edition Farm can see the order, neatness, and symmetry in my world, from the landscaping to the immaculate pastures and barns. Edition Farm's trademark colors—green and white, because I'm married to an Irishman and I have green eyes—are in evidence everywhere at the farm, which is home to upwards of fifty horses, belonging to me as well as to clients, at the peak of each breeding season.

All of our hard work choosing matings for our mares and raising the foals shows on the racecourse. I'm particularly proud of our track record, which, since we aren't a huge operation, is quite amazing. Some farms have two or three hundred mares, or have one wonderful horse that does all the winning. We are neither of those. Our small operation has built our reputation on the high percentage of horses we foal out and raise that go on to win at the racetrack. I think Edition Farm is just right—not too big, not too small. We've had some wonderful racing seasons, when my horses have shown their grit, their will to win, and above all, their heart.

From the start, I've told my team that our first priority is for each foal to learn to trust humans, and that begins with us. There are so many ways to build this trust and courage. "Foal first" is our mantra, meaning we always lead the foal in front of its mother, to build their courage and independence. We're preparing them not only for weaning, but also for their life beyond Edition Farm.

If a horse feels fearful, it will use its defenses—biting, kicking, and running away. When I see any horse exhibiting those behaviors, I know it hasn't learned to trust humans. Such a horse is hard to handle and, unfortunately, can have a very difficult life. I don't want that for any of our foals. Because of this careful preparation, when our yearlings go to the sale, they stand out for being calm, alert, beautifully prepared, and healthy. I'm very proud of that.

After all the planning, it's a thrill to see my horses on the track. Having had five children, I've been to innumerable soccer games, football games, and horse shows. But I couldn't really go crazy at those events, because I had to root for the team as well as for my own child, or else I'd be accused of being a "pushy" mother. At the track, I can be a pushy mother. No one will castigate me for cheering, clapping, screaming and yelling, and jumping up and down. Nobody cares what I'm doing because they're doing the same thing for their horses. It doesn't matter if you're a Vanderbilt or a John Doe, we're all the same at the track. And the horses usually come first. I once heard a story about Andrew Mellon that really struck a chord with me. Apparently, he told his secretary, "No matter how important the meeting, if my trainer's on the phone, I'll take the call!" To this day, if my trainer calls, I pick up.

Horse racing is the most beautiful sport, without a doubt, and I do my best to support it. When Jerry Nielsen, a breeder I admired so much, asked me to join the New York Thoroughbred Breeders' board, I accepted. Since then, I've been very active promoting and helping the sport in every way I can.

FARM KEEPING

There is a rhythm and routine to life at Edition Farm. In winter foals are born and mares are bred back. Spring begins the preparation for the sales of August and the fall. In autumn we start weaning and preparing for the Annual Open House. Meantime, there is mowing the fields, fixing the fences, and repairing and maintaining every building and shed out in the fields. Through it all is the continued excitement of watching for the entries of horses born on the farm—mine or my clients'—in the upcoming races. Some I have bred and sold in sales, and with every bit of purse money earned or black type garnered, the value of the family of that two- or three-year-old goes up. The mare gets kudos for her offspring, and all the brothers and sisters join in the fray. It is the perfect trickle-down theory in action.

In the early fall, we wean (separate the mares and foals). We do this by "fields"; our fields of mares and foals are grouped by the foals' birth dates, so the foals are similar in age, have grown up together, played together, and have become friends.

When weaning begins, we start by taking two mares at a time out of a field and moving them to the far end of the farm. Usually, their foals are playing or eating with their friends, so they might scream, but they don't get upset. They have the other foals and mares in the field that they know, so they feel safe. The new mares may have a more difficult time with separation, but the older mares just go quietly—nothing worries them.

The second day is the hardest on the foals because we put them in a stall by themselves for the first time. Then, the absence of their mother really seems to sink in. Some foals become very upset, while others manage this transition more easily.

As weanlings, colts and fillies are similar in temperament, but come spring, when the testosterone kicks in, the colts are definitely much more difficult to handle. That's when we separate the colts from the fillies, and also separate the colts from each other if they are sales yearlings, because their playing gets very rough and they can injure each other.

As we're weaning, I'm already thinking about which stallions we'd like to breed our mares to during the next breeding season. Others don't start thinking about it until the New Year, but I like to go down to Kentucky in November to look at the stallions. We do all of our pedigree homework in the fall, so by November we have a list of possible stallions for each mare. I know my mares well—their physical and breeding traits, and their racing records—so when I look at a stallion, I try to see how the mare will match.

Every month of the year is exciting in its own way. Winter is a quiet time because the sales are over and the yearlings have gone, but the foaling barn is busy. It's an exciting time for me, because I'm always thinking ahead and anticipating the next year. As soon as the foals are born, I begin to critique them. What did the mare produce? And how can I improve upon the choice of stallion for her next year?

Ultimately, it's unpredictable. You never know how many mares will get pregnant. Some people say that it's all right if a mare misses a year, but it isn't just a year—it could be three or four before you have any product to sell out of her. So you try to make sure your mare produces a foal every year. A client of mine once told me that he wanted to give his mare a year off, and I told him what my vet had said after I suggested that to him. He told me that the mare would take her own year off somewhere down the road herself.

I love thinking about the next breeding season. I always say, "I feel like God. I'm taking this stallion and this mare, and I'm making my own creation." And will I be successful? Will it work out the way I'd hoped?

One mare, a beautiful tall chestnut called Behrly Mine, was very "windswept" when she was born, meaning she had no power in her rear end at all. Yet she still made well over $150,000 on the racetrack and won five races. She had a huge heart, but she couldn't push out of the starting gate, so she loped along and just kept going when the others would start to tire. She didn't have what they call a "turn of foot"—she couldn't turn it on suddenly. She just had to keep her pace and wear the other horses down.

I always said that if she'd had that good rear end, she could have been a mighty horse. When I went to Kentucky to look at some of the mating choices, they brought out a stallion called Henny Hughes. I looked at him and said, "Behrly Mine!" because he had a rump, a wonderful rear end, and a lot of balance and muscle. When Behrly Mine's colt was born, he had that rear end. He has everything she has—the long neck, the long legs, which I love—and he has the power. So that worked out like a gem.

This January, I'm expecting about thirty-one foals to be born at the farm. Some mares will ship to Kentucky for breeding for the next year's crop. Kentucky really does have the best stallions in the world. When Vivi and I took a horse tour of Ireland, when she was about fifteen, I remember walking into a beautiful stud farm, pristine clean, called Kilfrush Stud. The farm manager showed us a field full of pregnant mares and started to tell us all about them. "This mare is in foal to Unbridled, and that mare is in foal to Seattle Slew, and that mare is in foal to . . ." In other words, they were all in foal to Kentucky stallions. They had been flown to Kentucky and then back to Ireland. That really impressed upon me, then and there, how strong our stallion population in Kentucky really is.

Once, one of my mares had a late appointment with a busy, popular stallion at a Kentucky farm. The van arrived at the stud farm shortly before the six o'clock appointment, and at six promptly, the stallion man came out. He had had a long, hard day, yet when he put the lead shank on my mare, he still took time to pat her and say, "She must be very special because she's going to a very special stallion. She must be a very special mare."

And I thought, *This is Kentucky. They understand.* He knew that yes, of course, she's very special—she was a great racehorse—and he realized the thought, the planning, and everything that went into why we chose that stallion.

At first, we owned Edition Farm with partners, but after two years or so, our partners lost interest, and Harry and I bought them out and now own the property outright. Our two-hundred-plus acres of land are our pride and joy. We get great personal satisfaction knowing that our horses graze in the best natural environment possible. The rolling terrain helps horses develop good bone and muscle just by the normal exercise of roaming freely.

After thirty years, I'm very proud of Edition Farm. My mind, my spirit, my physical being are dedicated to the farm and to how it's run. Just as I am a picky, neat homemaker, I'm a very picky, very neat barn owner. I see things that no one else notices and I take care of it right away.

It is the same with how I approach breeding. I look for quality—for exceptional mares and stallions—and I use patience to see it through. I'm not breeding for the Kentucky Derby, although I'd love to win it. I'm not breeding to win the Breeders' Cup, but I'd love to win that too. I am breeding to produce a horse who can run for many years, who has stamina and can either do the job on the track or in another discipline after racing. If I had a Derby or Breeders' Cup winner, that would be great. People tell me I am getting closer and closer, so if I live long enough, it might happen.

Vivien, thrilled with her first big win after the kids had left for school and jobs, and Wallflower, exhausted from the effort—a favorite photo. North Shore Horse Show, Long Island, July 1986.

Nine

A BREEDER'S EYE

THOROUGHBRED BREEDING IS AN ART FORM. WHILE BLOODLINES matter, I think the successful breeder has to have an instinct. They must imagine what they cannot yet see. In my family, there are artists and engineers, so imagination and a good eye are in my blood. I know my mares, so when I'm looking at stallions, I "morph" the mare onto the stallion—I put the mare's image onto the stallion. So much of successful breeding is like that; it's all in the mind's eye.

A breeder has to understand both the stallion and the mare individually and then try to visualize how they will complement each other. For example, many people think that if you breed a big-boned stallion to a lanky brood mare, you'll get a mix. Even I used to think that. But in reality, you get one or the other. So it's essential to study how both the stallion and the mare reproduce and stamp their foals. Does the mare reproduce herself no matter what, or does she allow the stallion his piece of the equation? The most "commercial" mares have foals that look like the stallions. People go to the sales and say, "Oh, did you look at that Quiet American colt of Vivien's? Did you

THE CASTLE FORBES STAKES
$35,000 Added

N.Y. Edition Farm's
Fancy Pan 2nd   **Mine Tonight**   Chris Antley up
Cougar Sue 3rd   M.H.Daggett Trainer
1 Mile~1:39   Dec. 5,1987
                                                  Turfotos

The Meadowlands
Trophy presented by Sal J.Marino

My future "Blue Hen" mare, Mine Tonight, wins the Castle
Forbes Stakes! The Meadowlands, New York, December 1987.

look at her Holy Bull filly?" I think that's what people look for when
they're buying. They want to recognize the stallion in the foal.

Owning a farm gave me the opportunity to study so many different combinations, both my own and those of my clients. Over
many years of careful observation, paired with my natural inquisi-
tiveness about horses, I began to gain a breeder's knowledge and
eye, which I'm still refining all the time.

I can see why some stallions are so exceptional. The first time I
saw Kingmambo, a masterful stallion of note, walk toward me, I
just said, "Of course." Of course he is a champion. Of course he
sires wonderful babies. I could see it immediately. Everything was

in complete balance—no one part was more dominant than any other. I knew that my inner eye was developing. To be a successful breeder, one must also have the courage of one's convictions. As my children always say, "You can't talk Mom into a horse, but you can't talk Mom out of one either."

THE BLUE HENS

Although my first actual broodmare was Roberta's Dream, my first major Thoroughbred mare was Mine Tonight. I had been looking to replace a baby of Roberta's Dream, London Valentine, and Mike Daggett, my trainer at that time, told me there was a sale coming up. Known as the "Broken Bones" sale, it was held in the parking lot of Belmont Park, although the actual bidding was held in the grandstand.

Mike and I usually saw eye to eye when it came to prospects. When we looked at a sales catalog, inevitably the same horses would appeal to us. That day, he brought Mine Tonight to my attention, but he thought she'd go for $50,000, which I couldn't afford. He suggested that we partner with another owner of his. Neither Harry nor I wanted a partner. Harry had always said, "If you can't do it yourself, don't do it." But I wanted Mine Tonight, so I felt we had no choice. Harry ended up being right, given how things turned out in the end.

It was my first sales experience, and my new partner and I each had a hard limit of $25,000. If Mine Tonight went for a penny over $50,000, we would lose her. When the bidding began, all I remember is praying that we'd get her. What a thrill to hear the auctioneer's gavel bang and have the spotter point to me—she was mine, Mine Tonight!

Mine Tonight was worth every penny. When we bought her, she hadn't yet won a race, but she went on to win races at all distances and on all surfaces, regardless of weather. She traveled to racetracks in New York, New Jersey, and Maryland, winning stakes along the way.

But nothing spoils a partnership more quickly than success. Our partner in Mine Tonight had a disagreement with our trainer, and as a result, he wanted to give Mine Tonight to another trainer. We were between a rock and a hard place. Mike had found Mine Tonight for us and trained her to her many victories, but our partner was adamant that we buy him out. Her worth had skyrocketed and we couldn't afford her, so he bought us out. After that, Mine Tonight never did well on the track again, so our former partner retired her and decided to breed her. Her foals went on to become stakes winners.

Meanwhile, I never got over losing her. I kept tabs on her whereabouts, and if I heard she was close by, I would visit her. A few years later, when she appeared in the Keeneland sale, I bought her back. She was no longer the $50,000 racehorse we had purchased years before, but she became my first Blue Hen mare. So named for its rarity, the Blue Hen mare is the foundation of a prolific producing family, generally producing multiple stakes horses. The stakes winners she had already produced made her pedigree wonderful. Mine Tonight provided the building block for my broodmare band.

A few years later, I went back to Keeneland to try to purchase another wonderful broodmare, Wake Up Kiss. Bred by John Hettinger, a top New York breeder and one of the founders of the New York breeding program, Wake Up Kiss was by Cure of the Blues out of a mare called Good Morning Smile. She was a stakes winner herself and was already in foal at the sale. That foal, A Shin Forward, went on to become an international champion and stakes winner. He became the second-highest money-earning New York bred, behind Funny Cide. She was a gorgeous gray mare who always presented herself like a champion in the front field of Edition Farm. With Mine Tonight and Wake Up Kiss, my first two Blue Hen mares, I was building a high-quality broodmare band and learning every step of the way.

At that point, I set my sights on claiming a racehorse as another way to expand my broodmare band. (A claiming race is one in which any horse can be bought.) Mike Daggett brought my attention to a filly named Legal Streak. I was nervous because it was my first claim. When we went to the paddock to see the filly, my first impression of her was not great: skinny with a dull coat. I worried that she might not be worth claiming, but we needed to make the decision fast. Mike was confident that we could improve on many things, so we decided to put in the claim.

Like her appearance, Legal Streak's performance in the race didn't inspire confidence. To me, it looked like something may have gone wrong, because she was "eased" during the race, which usually means something is wrong and the jockey slows her down to prevent injury. As it turns out, she wasn't hurt, but the track was muddy and slick, so her smart jockey slowed her down because she was slipping and sliding.

After I claimed her, I went back upstairs to meet Harry, embarrassed and worried that I had made a big—and expensive—mistake. Before I reached the table, a fellow member of the Turf and Field Club came up to me and told me how lucky I was. She was thrilled for me because she knew Legal Streak's bloodlines: Nodouble out of a Secretariat mare, a fantastic combination. Of course, in those days, I didn't know anything, and until she told me, I didn't realize what I had. Sure enough, Legal Streak was the start of the Vivaling family, becoming my third Blue Hen mare.

I always try to give my new broodmares the best shot, right out of the box. A friend of mine once asked me why I breed my unproven broodmares to quality stallions in Kentucky right from the start. My thinking is that any other approach takes too long. Why wait four of five years to find out what you've really got? In this equation, the broodmare is the mystery. If I breed her to a successful sire and she produces nothing of note, then I have some idea of her quality as a broodmare.

The first time we bred Legal Streak, we sent her down to Kentucky to be bred to Explodent, a half brother to Northern Dancer and a proven sire. Since Legal Streak, as they say, couldn't even walk in the mud, I wanted to breed her to a tough stallion who could run long, short, on dirt, and on turf. That was Explodent: He could run on broken glass and win.

But Legal Streak was not getting in foal. After the second unsuccessful try, the stallion manager told me that Explodent was getting old, yet they were still breeding him three times a day. He suggested that I ask his owners if they would allow him to rest for one day, and we could then breed him with Legal Streak later in the evening. They agreed to that, and I laughingly suggested setting a romantic mood with candles, a little wine, and some music. They agreed to everything else, and bingo! She got pregnant. As it turned out, that was the last foal that he sired. Explodent was retired soon after.

A few months later, Legal Streak had a filly. We named her Vivaling, after my daughter. Legal Streak turned out to be a terrible mother to all her babies. Unlike other mares, who stood over their babies to keep them in the shade, swishing their tails to keep the flies away, she would canter off from her sleeping foal, leaving them to run after her. Not surprisingly, Vivaling grew up very independent and strong, knowing that she couldn't rely on her mother for much other than the milk bar.

Two years later, Vivaling had her first race at Belmont. I'll never forget the sight of her coming into the paddock that day. A brilliant chestnut with a big blaze and beautiful eyes, she was glowing and looked ready for anything. I turned to my trainer, Mike, and said, "You know, this is enough for me." Just the fact that I was able to breed something this beautiful and raise her to become a healthy and happy horse good enough to run at Belmont was the fulfillment of a dream.

Any breeder will tell you that. You begin with a plan. Hopefully, the mare gets pregnant and she foals out. If you're lucky, that foal gets to the races, and when it comes down the stretch . . . for a very fortunate few, your horse wins. There is nothing like it. Of the thousands of Thoroughbred foals born each year, less than half get to the races, and of that number only about 3 percent win a race. To get Vivaling and my other horses even that far is itself an accomplishment for me.

Mommy had joined us at Belmont to watch Vivaling's first race. She was quite elderly at the time, so it meant a great deal to me that she had come. What a thrill that Vivaling went out and won! She broke her maiden (won her first race) the first time out in a very fast time of 58.3 seconds. I went to the winner's circle filled with pride, and when I returned to the club Mommy was crying. When I asked her why, she said, "I know how much it means to you, darling."

IT TAKES A VILLAGE

I have always learned best with my mouth shut. I listen and read constantly, and as a neophyte to the breeding world, I was keenly aware of what I didn't know. From the start, I surrounded myself with people who embody that which I value most: honesty, integrity, and knowledge of the sport. Frequently, that means someone who has grown up in the industry and who, like me, has horses in their blood. As I have refined my breeder's eye, my advisers have come to respect what I bring to the table, and I credit my support team with helping me learn how to build my band of mares. This trusted circle includes my bloodstock agent, Mike McMahon, my pedigree and biomechanical expert, Bob Fierro, and my consignor, Craig Bandoroff.

When I go to a sale, there may be thousands of horses to choose from. The Keeneland November breeding stock sale, for example, goes on for twelve days, because there are 5,000 horses for sale, many of which are broodmares. There is no way I can review them all, but my bloodstock agent can. Mike looks at every horse and creates a customized list for each client. He knows everyone's budget and chooses accordingly. Then he emails a preliminary list for review before the sale.

When I get to a sale, I've already shortened his preliminary list down to the mares I'm most interested in, and we tour the sales barns to look at them. Even when I knew very little about breeding, I liked a certain type. Throughout the years of educating myself and refining my eye, the type I like has remained the same: a classic Thoroughbred with an elegant head, long legs, and a long neck.

Over the years, Mike has learned not only what my type is, but also what it isn't. In the early days, he tried to convince me to look at a certain well-bred mare, but realized quickly that I will never go for a squat, bulky type, or a horse with an ugly head. These are deal breakers for me, regardless of pedigree.

Another essential part of my team of advisers are the vets. I've learned an immense amount from them, particularly John Jagar and John Steiner. I also have good vets down in Kentucky who speak to farm owners and broodmare managers there. They can find out important things about the mares that aren't printed in the sales catalog, like how easy a mare gets in foal.

One year at the Keeneland sales in Kentucky, I saw a broodmare by Seattle Slew—finally! My big chance to get a Seattle Slew mare. I asked John Steiner if he could find out about her, and as I was sitting in the sales pavilion, waiting to bid on the Seattle Slew mare, John sat beside me and told me not to bid on her. After doing some homework, he found out that the mare had a terrible breeding history: Either she couldn't get in foal or she would get in foal and lose the foal. Thank God for John, who saved me from making an expensive mistake.

When I first began looking for a consignor, a person who arranges the sales of horses at auction, I wanted to work with the best, and the people I respect all recommended Craig. They said that he was the most honest. I didn't know much about the sales ring at that point, so honesty was what I needed, and everything else would fall in place.

I had asked Craig if he would consign my two yearlings to the New York-bred preferred yearling sale in Saratoga, and he said, "Oh, I'm not staying for that. I'm leaving after this next sale, the select. I don't go to the New York-bred preferred sale; it's too expensive to keep my staff up there."

So then I went to my second choice, and the next year I asked Craig again, and he said he'd do it. Now, when I tell him the story that I begged him to stay for that sale, he laughs. He now has big consignments, and he's told me, "Vivien, I make more money at New York preferred than the select."

The realities of being a breeder mean that there comes a time when I need to decide to sell horses. When that time comes, I set realistic reserves on them. If they are not sold, that's when I have a decision to make. Should I sell for less than my reserve or race them myself? More often than not, I choose to keep them and race them myself. I have learned the hard way that selling a horse for less than my reserve can ultimately turn into buying it back at a higher price. What frequently happens is, although you start out as a breeder, you end up with a racing stable.

Craig and I have a good relationship, and he also has a good reputation and relationships with all the sales companies. That helps when they come and make their choices of the yearlings they will accept for the different sales.

Several years ago I found myself at the Saratoga yearling sale with a horse that I knew in my heart I didn't want to sell. A few hours before the sale, Craig came to discuss the reserve. He had his iPad with all the pertinent information: who had looked at her, how deep their pockets were, and how many times she had been vetted.

When I admitted that I didn't really want to sell her, Craig was annoyed. He suggested we scratch her, but I wanted her to go through the ring to show what my mare could produce.

"All right. What kind of reserve do you want to put on her? Fifty?" he asked.

And I said, "No."

"Seventy-five?"

Again I said, "No." I wanted to say one-fifty, but I thought he'd think I was crazy or I didn't know what I was doing.

So he said, "One hundred?"

And I said "yes," because I was scared to say one-fifty.

So Craig grumbled, "All right, putting her down, one hundred."

The evening went on, and she came into the ring. The announcer went into the pedigree, telling the crowd that her mother was a stakes winner and her grandmother was Mine Tonight. "Look at this beautiful filly," he said.

The first bid was $30,000. It went up quickly from there: $30,000, $50,000, $70,000, $80,000, $90,000.

I said, "God, I'm going to lose her! I should have said set the reserve at one-fifty."

Then, $95,0000 . . . $96,000 . . . $97,000. Finally, she was led out at $97,000. Another three thousand dollars and I would have lost her. Her name is Ouchy Night, and she's already stakes placed three times. She's won four races and over $200,000. So I was right to do what I did. And now her first foal is a stakes filly too, Wild About Harry. She followed in the footsteps of her dam.

The episode with Ouchy Night was the beginning of a new phase in my relationship with Craig. I believe that it was then that he began to respect me as a breeder and client.

I am blessed because I have a small but loyal group of clients who are not new to the horse world. They've all been breeding for a while, and they have racehorses too. So they're ready for those awful phone calls that you have to make sometimes.

I don't really like clients who are very new to the game. We've had some in the past, and it was very difficult. If their yearling didn't sell, they blamed us for everything. I had recommended Craig, my consignor, to them. He took me aside at the sale and said, "How the heck did you get me involved with that group?"

I said, "I'm so sorry, Craig. I had no idea."

Now, I try to avoid clients who don't understand breeding and selling and are suspicious about everything. Or those who've been through the wringer with other people and they think that the whole industry is corrupt.

My clients and I are in this together. I'm not just the owner of a farm; I have broodmares, foals, yearlings, and racehorses. I know how they feel when something bad happens and when something good happens. It's touch and go sometimes, until that foal gets to be a yearling, and everything is more stabilized.

Once, I took a share in a stallion called Williamstown. He stood in New York, and I got wonderful horses from every mare I bred to this stallion. One year, I wasn't going to use my season to Williamstown, so I called one of my clients and told him he was welcome to him. He said, "For nothing?"

I said, "Yes. It's my season. I want to give it to you, because I know you're looking for a stallion for Million Dollar Smile."

"Well, why would you do that, Vivien?"

"Because he's a good stallion and I love Million Dollar Smile. The pedigree fits. I just thought you might like to use it."

The client was thrilled, but I felt I was just doing the best thing for him and the horses. The foal that was born of that breeding won several races—one race by ten lengths. I am happy that it all worked out, and it gave me joy as a breeder to see that I could give someone else success too.

Left to right: Luca, Honey, Courtney, and Jaylo at Waccabuc, October 2008.
(Photo by Kathy Landman.)

DOG TALES

So much of my life was involved with the children and the horses. Our activities had a regular pace: Mondays were quiet; we rested the horses and focused on cleaning the tack, the tack trunks, and the trailer. Tuesdays, we'd ride the horses on the flat, and Wednesdays we'd drive two hours to Hunterdon, George Morris's stable in New Jersey, to practice jumping. On Thursday, we'd hack the horses, pack the tack trunks, and prepare the trailer. Then on Friday, we were off to the next horse show.

That tempo ruled our lives. I have always loved projects, particularly the discipline of preparation and keeping to a schedule. Every week was a project, preparing for the next horse show. My children have always said, "Give Mom a project and she's raring to go." We prepared and practiced, and schooled and showed all year with the goal of qualifying for the finals and the important horse shows in the fall.

When the children went away to college and Debby went off to New Zealand and Australia to ride, there was a gap in my life. For a while, I kept up that same tempo, competing in horse shows, but it wasn't to last because Wallflower, my daughter Vivi's wonderful equitation and a dream horse for me, had to be retired.

My focus turned to getting more involved in dog training because I'd always loved working with dogs, and clearly I love competition. When I was about twelve years old, the Westchester Kennel Club Dog Show was held on the polo field at Westchester Country Club. I didn't have a ticket, so I watched through the fence. I was fascinated as I watched the obedience class, the drills, and seeing what the dogs had to do.

So once the children were gone, I decided to start training my own dogs. I began by going to dog obedience classes at our local community center. Later, I found out about Kaye Reilly, a famous obedience teacher, who taught classes locally. Kaye was wonderful, but even though I trained with her and tried hard, I was not good at all.

The first dog I trained in obedience was our Rottweiler, Duke. When he was young, we had sent him to a training center in New Jersey, but it hadn't worked out well. Duke was miserable with the obedience training, so we tried another approach, *Schutzhund*, attack training. But, as we discovered, Duke was a mush—just like Ferdinand the bull—he didn't want to attack. So I told Harry, "Forget this!"

I kept at it with my new dog, Princeton, a beautiful German Shepherd. I showed him in several obedience trials, and I remember one such trial where I saw a handler with a leather collar on her dog. A leather collar is very gentle, yet her dog was paying absolute attention to her, heeling so beautifully. I asked her how she did it, and she simply replied, "Diane Bauman." When I asked her who Diane Bauman was, she said, "The best in the world." Well, I had brought my children to George Morris, who was the best equestrian trainer in the world, so I was used to seeking out the best, no matter who or where it is.

Soon after, I approached Diane at a dog show and asked her if she would help me with my dog. At that time, Princeton was getting titles but not winning. I saw for myself that we were just making it, and I wanted to improve. At my first lesson with Diane, I observed to her that she had many serious students, and I told her I wasn't sure whether I was that serious. She looked at me and told me no one comes to her who isn't serious. So I got serious.

I got serious because it's fascinating. As I've discovered, you have to work with your own dog. You can't send your dog to someone else to be trained and then try to take over—it doesn't work that way. You have to develop a bond and become partners—you and your dog are in it together, in lessons and in the ring.

The dog obedience world is a friendly one. All of your friends are fellow competitors, but they all clap for you and congratulate you. We call ourselves fellow sufferers, because we're all in it together. We've all been there: You've worked for years for that moment in the ring, and then there's a child eating a hot dog right outside the ring and you're helpless as you lose your dog's attention.

I remember taking my dog Honey, a bichon frise, to a dog show in a huge exhibition hall at the Eastern States Exposition in Springfield, Massachusetts. Honey and I had to do a signals exercise in which I had to give her signals to heel, stand, and then maintain her position while I walked all the way to the other end of the ring. Once there, the judge would tell me when to give her the signal to lie down, sit up, and to come. We had trained hours and hours for this exercise.

And then, there was a bird. I had walked all the way to the other end of the ring when I turned around and saw Honey growling softly. From way, way up in the top rafters, this bird came swooping down—right past Honey—with a little hay for its nest, before flying back up to the nest it was building.

I'm dead. I'm lost. There's no way, I thought. The judge gave me the "down" signal. Honey obeyed my down signal, and then the bird started its aerial acrobatics. Her eyes followed the bird, not once looking at me. The judge gave me the "sit" signal. When I gave Honey the signal, she didn't move. The judge said, "Exercise finished. Call your dog."

Another favorite: tiny dog and *huge* trophies. High Scoring
Novice Dog, Winner of the Novice Class, and High in Trial:
Honey (1995–2010) wins it all! First Company Governor's
Foot Guard Dog Show and Obedience Trials, Hartford State
Armory, Connecticut, 2000.

Even though we had been disqualified, everyone came over to
say how cute it was to see her, way out in the middle of the huge
ring, trying her best while being dive-bombed by a bird. As I always
say, you never know what's going to happen at a dog show.

Showing dogs fulfills my competitive drive. It's fun and exciting,
and sometimes nerve-racking. I told Debby once how nervous I became in the ring, and she said that she felt that same adrenaline
rush when she competed, but that it helped her and I should use it.

As with any pursuit, training is essential but not always enjoyable. Sometimes I don't feel like going out and training my dogs, but
once we're out there warming up and my dog is responding, it's so
heartwarming. If they have a bad day, it's not the end of the world.

I have been a member of the Port Chester Obedience Training Club since I started training. It has a wonderful indoor facility and offers practice sessions all year round. I go there religiously, because consistent practice, even in winter, is essential.

The obedience circuit is similar to the horse show world: getting up at four in the morning when it's pitch-dark, sometimes in the pouring rain or in freezing temperatures, to drive hours to the competition. Once there, the unloading and lugging of crates and putting the equipment into place resembles horse shows, where we set up stalls and tack rooms, always far from home. Harry asked me, "Aren't there any competitions that are local?"

My dogs also competed in agility trials, but due to how quickly the handler needs to move, I worked with a terrific young woman who ran the dogs for me. I did the agility training at home, where I have a course set up with several obstacles—tunnels, weave poles, A-frames, and a seesaw. The high point for me was when my Border collie, Courtney, was awarded the MACH (Master Agility Champion), the highest award obtainable.

I have had many different breeds that I showed in obedience and agility. I've even had strays that made wonderful obedience dogs. I once trained a stray that we kept—we called her Tippy because the tips of her feet were white—and she ended up winning her obedience class. As is typical of strays, one day she left, and we never saw her again.

A dog's temperament is also an important factor for showing. I had a corgi, Barnsley, who I showed in obedience early on. He was quite nimble—a wonderful heeler—but he made it impossible to enjoy showing because he was very aggressive with other dogs. I couldn't sit and talk to friends because he would be growling at their dogs. Though Barnsley would perform beautifully in the ring, I would have to carry him through the showgrounds to keep him away from other dogs.

I'll never forget one Open class where the dogs needed to complete both a long "sit" and a long "down." During the group exercise,

Twinkie (1978–1994) in her new bed, the day she came to us,
Purchase, New York, 1978.

Barnsley was lined up next to a Doberman pinscher, and I kept my
fingers crossed that he would stay focused, otherwise I was sure
there would be a horrible dog fight. Neither Dobies nor corgis have
tails, so they can't be pulled apart in the event of a fight.

The dogs made it through the long "sit" without incident, but during the long "down," the Dobie started to roll over toward Barnsley.
This dog was going to be DQ'd anyway for losing his position, but I
was petrified that he was about to start World War III. I stood there,
helpless, watching as Barnsley looked at the Dobie, his lip beginning
to curl. It was the longest five minutes of my life in the ring, but Barnsley held it together, got his third leg in open, and was awarded his
title, Companion Dog Excellence (CDX). But that was it. I didn't go
on to qualify him further because it wasn't pleasant. He was a time
bomb during group exercises and when he was outside of the ring.

It seems to me I've always had a German shepherd in my life, and I've trained two of them in obedience, Princeton and Luca. Though German shepherds are well suited to obedience, they are not as nimble—you rarely see them in agility as winners, and their size can make the handler's job harder. A big dog requires a bigger crate, bigger equipment, and sometimes, a stronger handler.

Luca was a wonderful obedience dog in the ring, but outside the ring he pulled a lot. On the grounds of a show, you could use a choke collar to control your dog, but not a pronged choke collar, which I needed to hold him back and walk with me. If you were seen using a pronged choke collar, you would be called before the American Kennel Club (AKC) and prohibited from showing permanently. Ultimately, I decided that we would stop competing in

Luca (2002–2014) at home in Waccabuc, fall 2006.

obedience trials once Luca got his Utility Dog title, as I didn't want to have to worry about controlling him outside the ring.

At one show, he won his Utility class and he qualified in his Open class. He got very low scores in both classes, so at the end of the show I went home without checking to see if he had won any other awards. The next day, a friend called to tell me that Luca had won the High Combined Award in the trial! I could see that ribbon in my mind: very long with a pink and green rosette and matching streamers.

I immediately called the show secretary, who told me that the ribbons get destroyed after the show, so I couldn't get Luca's. Next, I called the head of AKC Obedience, and she couldn't help me either. Poor Luca never got the ribbon he deserved.

I'll never forget when Luca finished his last Utility Dog leg. He had to complete an exercise called the Directed Retrieve, in which three gloves are placed across the ring, behind the dog and the handler's backs. Then the judge calls out the number of the glove to be retrieved and the handler must turn with the dog, face the correct glove, signal the dog to retrieve it, and the dog must return it to the handler. In our practice sessions, Luca was great at picking up the glove, but instead of returning with it right away, he would start playing with it, shaking it, trying to kill it. So we had worked and worked on getting him to bring it back directly.

The Directed Retrieve was the last exercise of the class at this show, the last thing that he needed to do. He had already completed every other exercise successfully. This was it.

I sent him out, he picked up the glove, and then started his usual routine, shaking it, throwing it up, and catching it in his mouth. If it had hit the ground, he would have been immediately disqualified. I stood there, helpless, watching him have fun, and finally, Luca looked at me. All of a sudden, remembering what he was supposed to do, he trotted back to me with the glove in his mouth and sat perfectly in front of me. I asked Luca for the glove, then he swung around and sat at perfect heel position.

Three-year-old Jaylo (2004–2015) gets her CD! Queensboro,
New York, October 2007.

"Congratulations. You qualified," said the judge, who then turned
to me and said, "You must have had a heart attack."

And I said, "You have no idea!"

My best dog was Honey, the bichon frise. Honey and I did so
many things together. She was a little thing, weighing in at only ten
pounds. Honey was pretty young when she started competing, but
from the start she had incredible focus, never taking her eyes off me
in the ring. Any trainer will tell you that a dog's attention is the key
to obedience. Even after she retired, for the rest of her life, Honey
would always have her eyes on me.

Honey was such a trooper and I could take her anywhere. One year I decided to take her to a bichon frise specialty show in Chicago. At first, I wasn't sure about traveling with her by plane, but Diane reassured me, telling me to go and have a good time. So off Harry and I went, and Honey got reserve champion. Sometime later, the dog who had been champion retired, so I figured, Honey's the champion now!

Honey proved to be a wonderful traveling companion. On the flight home from Chicago, she was in her dog carrier on the floor between my feet. She hadn't made a peep, so no one on the plane knew she was there until we landed. When I unzipped the top of her carryall and her little head came up, the other passengers were delighted, complimenting her on her wonderful manners. Of course, I felt like saying, she's an obedience dog, they're very good—that's what they do!

Harry shared my love of the dogs, especially Honey. If I didn't qualify with Honey, Harry would say, lovingly, "Did you f--- her up again?"

It was never Honey's fault. Ever. I had to agree, and I'd tell him, "Yep, that's what I did. I messed her up."

Now I have another project in my dog life. Her name is Celia, a Havanese, named after Celia Cruz, the Cuban singer. My first Havanese, Jaylo, who was a breed champion, was already named when I got her. Someone asked me how I could possibly name a Cuban dog after a Puerto Rican singer. So I picked a Cuban singer's name for my new Havanese. I asked several people who the most famous Cuban singer was, and they all said Celia Cruz, the Queen of Salsa.

When Diane Bauman met Celia, she said, "I like this dog, she has a lot of spirit." I hope I am worthy of such a good dog and can do her justice when we start competing.

Paul Pileckas (far right) and the rest of the crew at Popponesset Inn, Cape Cod, Massachusetts, summer 1949.

Harry Malloy in his Mamaroneck High School yearbook photo, 1949.

Paul Pileckas in his yearbook photo.

LEFT: Ensign Henry Malloy, in training at Treasure Island Naval Station, San Francisco, California, 1953. ABOVE: USS *McGowan* (DD-678).

USS *Lake Champlain* (CV-39), on maneuvers off Korea in 1954.

Harry and his sister-in-law, Cathy Malloy, September 1953.

Harry's sailboat, *Corsair*.

Nena (ABOVE) and Vivien and Andy
(BELOW) at the WCC beach club,
Rye, New York, 1950.

Vivien on her wedding day, with Nena,
January 12, 1957.

The house at 26 Mohawk Street, in Rye, home from 1958 to 1963.

Five Chimneys, in Purchase, home from 1963 to 1988.

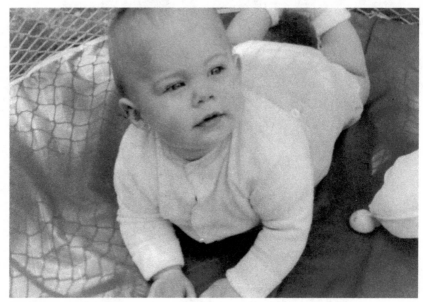

Debby in a playpen, 1959.

Andrew at three years old, trying out his new bike, Rye, New York, winter 1960.

Kenneth at one year old, May 1962.

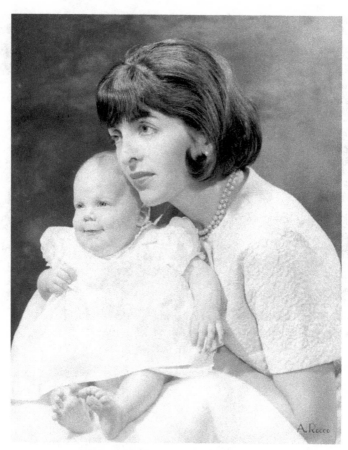

The two Vivis,
Rye, New York,
late 1965.

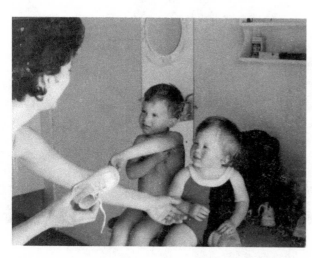

Vivien with Andrew
and Debby in the
cabana at WCC
beach club, Rye,
New York, 1960.

Andrew and Mark Morrell at Big Little Show, c. 1964.

Debby riding at Sakonnet, August 1963.

Originally married
by a judge thirty-
three years before,
Nena and Andy are
married by a priest
in the Church, at
St. Catherine of
Siena, Cos Cob,
Connecticut,
July 1968.

Harry and Vivien at the golf club, 1968.

Debby Malloy Winkler on a great jumper, early 1990s.

Debby on Pinocchio at Stratford Stables Horse Show, Purchase, New York, October 1968.

Debby and Mark, home with ribbons from Armonk Horse Show, Mark's first horse show, Five Chimneys, October 1968.

Vivien and friend at Kenilworth Riding Club, Rye, New York, 1947.

Debby on
Pinocchio at
Stratford Stables,
Purchase, New
York, December
1968.

Vivien on Toby at A Day in the Country Horse Show, 1970s.

Vivi at Hilltop Place, June 1967.

Left to right: Mark, Kenneth, Brian and Patrick Morgan, and Debby with Mother Superior Morgan (right) at Manhattanville College, Purchase, New York. Mother Morgan was a musical advisor to Richard Rodgers on *The Sound of Music*.

Debby at
Stratford Stables
Horse Show,
c. 1967.

Debby on
Pinocchio,
Stratford Stables,
December 1968.

Debby at Hilltop
Place, June 1967.

Left to right: Max Richter on Scherzo, Mark on Apache Edition, Vivien on Toby, and Debby on
Regal Edition at A Day in the Country Horse Show, Greenwich, Connecticut, 1972.

Mark on Apache Edition at the Purchase Horse Show, 1974.

Vivi on Special Edition at the Purchase Horse Show, 1974.

Vivi at Five
Chimneys, 1975.
(Photos on this
page and the
following two pages
by Hella Hammid.)

Debby and
Harry at Five
Chimneys.

Debby at Five
Chimneys.

Kenneth and Clipper at Five Chimneys.

Left to right: Debby, Vivi, Harry, Andrew, Vivien, Kenneth, and Mark at Five Chimneys, 1975.

Andrew at Five Chimneys.

Mark on Just In Case (a.k.a. Casey),
Edition Farm, Purchase, New York, 1975.

Left to right: Mark, Debby, Vivi, Kenneth, and Andrew in the garden at Five Chimneys, July 1976.

A Very Young Rider
(a.k.a. "The Book")
by Jill Krementz,
1977.

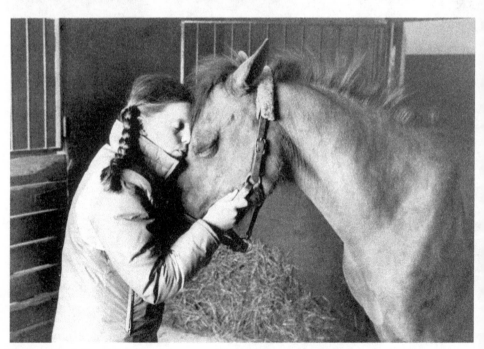

Vivi and Ready Penny in 1976. (Photos on this and facing page by Jill Krementz.)

Chores were part
of the deal.

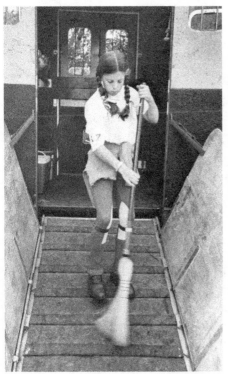

Left to right: Harry, Debby, Vivi (holding Twinkie), Vivien, Mark, Andrew, and Kenneth at Five Chimneys, c. summer 1974.

Vivi and Harvard Square win the Junior/Amateur Owner Hunter Classic at the Hampton Classic, Bridgehampton, New York, August 1983.

Mark studying the competition at Ocala Horse Show, winter 1977.

Debby watching Rodney Jenkins schooling for the big Grand Prix at the Devon Horse Show and Country Fair, Devon, Pennsylvania, May 1976. (Photo by Jill Krementz.)

Vivi on Ready Penny at Ox Ridge Horse Show, June 1976. (Photos on this and facing page by Jill Krementz.)

Vivi in the van with Ready Penny at Ox Ridge Horse Show, June 1976.

Vivi putting up her latest additions to the trophy room at Five Chimneys, fall 1976.

The two Vivis at the Devon Horse Show and Country Fair, Devon, Pennsylvania, May 1976.

"Hold . . . for . . . your . . . distance . . . Vivien!" George Morris with Jonathan Devine and Judy Richter at the Lake Placid Horse Show, July 1976. (Photos on this and facing page by Jill Krementz.)

George Morris and Debby at the Lake Placid Horse Show, July 1976.

Vivi and Rodney Jenkins, signing his autograph, at the Lake Placid Horse Show, July 1976.

Vivi and Ready
Penny at the Lake
Placid Horse Show,
July 1976.

Debby and
Something Else
at Edition Farm,
summer 1976.

239

Vivi setting
out the feed,
Edition Farm,
fall 1976.

Vivi and Debby
scrubbing
buckets at
Edition Farm,
fall 1976.

Vivi and Mark
in the van at
the Boulder
Brook Horse
Show, spring
1975.

LEFT: Andrew sleeping on top of his homework, Five Chimneys, c. 1976. RIGHT: Debby multitasking (during a rare moment indoors), Five Chimneys, c. fall 1976.

Vivi at Rye
Country Day
School, Rye,
New York,
fall 1982.

LEFT AND BELOW: The Royal Canadian Mounted Police troop performing at the National Horse Show at Madison Square Garden, fall 1976. (Photos by Jill Krementz.)

Mark and Apache Edition win at the Stratford Fall Horse Show, Stratford Stables, Purchase, New York, 1972.

Mark on Apple Core at Lake Placid Horse Show, July 1981.

Debby competing in Germany, early 1990s.

Debby and Only Oscar win the Amateur Owner Jumper Classic at the Hampton Classic, Bridgehampton, New York, August 1980.

Harry and Vivien at Sun Valley, Idaho, c. 1978.

Vivien at the
Tiger Balm
Gardens in
Singapore,
mid-1980s.

Harry and Vivien in Thailand, 1980s.

Left to right: Andrew, Debby, Vivien, Harry, Vivi, and Kenneth, c. 1984, standing beneath a portrait of Vivien by then-unknown, but soon-to-be-famous, artist Felix de Cossio, c. 1961. He was an early exile from Cuba after Castro's Revolution. Nena found him, and he painted her portrait too.

Clockwise from top left: Harry, Vivien, Kenneth, Vivi, and Mark in character for a Western studio portrait; what you do in Aspen when not skiing, 1979.

Left to right: Harry, Vivi, Mark, Kenneth, Vivien, Debby, and Andrew, Aspen, Colorado, 1980.

Shane Malloy on
Special Edition,
Waccabuc,
September 30,
1993.

Left to right: Grandchildren Courtney and Caitlin on April; Shane on Special Edition; Vivien kneeling; Kenny, Maggie, and Conor on Lovebug. Waccabuc, September 30, 1993.

Courtney and
Caitlin on April,
with their mother,
Kelsey Malloy, at
Waccabuc,
fall 1994.

Courtney,
Andrew, and
Caitlin at Sandy
Lane Beach,
Barbados.

Left to right: Vivi, Mark, Harry, Vivien, Kenneth, Debby, and Andy at WCC for Vivien and Harry's fortieth wedding anniversary party, January 1997.

Back row, left to right: Kenneth and Kenny, Jeryl, Kelsey, Andrew, Heather, and Mark. Middle row: Vivien, Nena, Debby, and Harry. Front row: Conor, Maggie, Courtney, Caitlin, and Twinkie, in Waccabuc, our Christmas card, 1993.

90 Spooky Hollow Road farmhouse before it became Edition Farm, c. 1940s.

90 Spooky Hollow Road after getting the initial Edition Farm treatment, 1989.

"Finally mine!" Ten acres of beautiful land to join Edition Farm, Hyde Park, New York, September 1990.

Left to right: Conor, Shane, Maggie, Kenny, Courtney, and Caitlin, Waccabuc, fall 1994.

Harry and High on the Bayou, September 1992.

Scottish Highland cattle at Edition Farm, October 2004.

Mares and foals in the front field at Edition Farm, fall 2004. (Photos by Kathy Landman.)

Vivaling breaks her maiden on her debut! Belmont Park, New York, May 26, 1993. The crew in the winner's circle included Mike Daggett, Harry, and Vivien (Nena was watching from the Turf and Field Club).

Belmont Park,N.Y. Purse $23,500 May 26,1993
N.Y.Edition Farm owner **VIVALING** Art Madrid,Jr.up
M.H.Daggett trainer 5 fur.time :58:3
Cynanite 2nd Like That 3rd

THE BROADWAY HANDICAP
Aqueduct, New York Purse $89,100 January 22, 1989
N.Y. Edition Farm owner **CLIFFIE** Richard Migliore up
M.H. Daggett trainer 1 mile & 70 yds. 1:43:1
Beru 2nd - pres. by Mrs. Diane Scherf - Joe's Tammie 3rd

Cliffie wins the Broadway Handicap! January 22, 1989, Aqueduct Racetrack.

A family affair for Malloys

Couple put heart, soul into business

By LEO WALDMAN

Special to Daily Racing Form

NEW YORK – They may not be the largest breeders in New York, but Harry and Vivien Malloy love horses and have dedicated themselves to breeding the good stakes winner by sending their four mares to good sires. Most importantly, their enthusiasm is for the game and visiting the track.

The Malloys reside at their 15-acre Edition Farm in Waccabuc. They have three horses in training with Mickey Daggett at Belmont and stand Bayou Blurr ($157,381), whose first foals are 2-year-olds, at Jim Edwards' Keane Stud in Amenia.

"You have to be careful how deep you get into racing," Harry Malloy said. "So many people just think of the initial investment, but they soon find out that's only peanuts. To enjoy the sport as we do, you stay within your means and watch your money. We are happy with a small farm, an eight-stall barn and four mares. We don't want to get any bigger and have pressure and large bills. You must stay comfortable."

Vivien Malloy has been involved with horses since she was 3, going the route of pony clubs and horse shows. She purchased her first broodmare in 1981 and her first racehorse in 1984 and tried to get her husband interested in riding, but he fell off both times he tried and retired from the saddle.

Over the years, Vivien Malloy has done everything around a barn – from mucking stalls to exercising horses to driving horse vans. She admires those who work on the backstretch for their loyalty and dedication to horses.

"Once you smell the manure, you never give it up," she said.

Vivien Malloy, who breeds mostly New York-breds, chaired the committee which selected 1995 New York broodmare of the year, Antilassa, dam of New York-bred millionaire Lottsa Talc and New York-bred 1990 sprint champion Appealing Guy. Other committee members were Sunny Westerman, Anne McMahon and Kate O'Connell.

The Malloys have a daughter, Debbie, who is married to German equestrian show-jumping rider Hans Gunther Winkler, winner of five Olympic gold medals and currently captain of the German Olympic equestrian team, which will compete in Atlanta.

The Malloys' broodmares include stakes-winning Mardi Gras Maid, dam of five stakes horses and who dropped a filly by Green Dancer this spring. The others are Legal Streak, a Nodouble mare who produced a filly by Distinctive Pro and is in foal to Affirmed; Vivaling, a 5-year-old Belmont allowance-winning daughter of Explodent out of Legal Streak in foal to millionaire Alwuhush; and Synful Maid (Synastry out of Mardi Gras Maid), another winning 5-year-old who has a colt by Cure the Blues and was bred back to Anjiz. All 1996 foals will be registered New York-breds except the Green Dancer filly.

❑ Three registered New York-breds ran in graded stakes last weekend, with the best performance being Victory Speech's second to favored Skip Away in Thistledown's Grade 2, $300,000 Ohio Derby. Owned by Michael Tabor and Susan Magnier and trained by D. Wayne Lukas, the son of Deputy Minister now has a record of 12-4-2-4 and earnings of $236,162.

Lottsa Talc competed in the

MALLOYS: Enthusiasm for game.

$150,000 Chicago Breeders' Cup at Arlington International, finishing fifth and picking up $5,150 for total earnings of $1,008,462, and Double Dee's was used up forcing the early pace in Belmont's Grade 1, $200,000 Mother Goose, finishing last.

❑ The New York Thoroughbred Breeders' monthly publication, the New York Thoroughbred Report, is being redesigned and will be distributed at Saratoga. Organization leaders are negotiating for a lease to move the office to Saratoga from its present location in Elmont.

❑ Grecian Flight, former New York-bred horse of the year and winner of $1,320,215, has produced her first winner, the Kentucky-bred 2-year-old filly Wingspread, who broke her maiden by five and a half lengths in :59 4/5 for five furlongs at Belmont.

By Gulch, Wingspread is owned by co-breeder Henry Lindh, who bred and raced Grecian Flight and bred Wingspread in partnership with G. Watts Humphrey.

Daily Racing Form article on Edition Farm, Sunday, June 30, 1996.

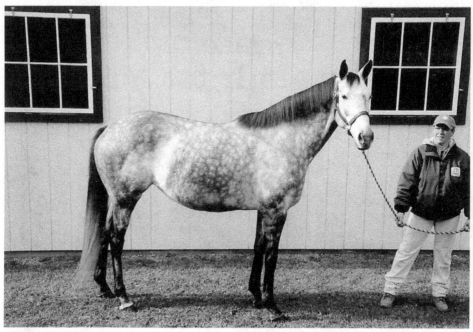

New York–bred Turf champion Wake Up Kiss, in foal to Forest Wildcat with a colt that will become the champion turf horse A Shin Forward, arrives at Edition Farm, November 2004.

Behrly Mine, born April 13, 2002, pictured in South Carolina to begin training, October 2003.

Princeton at SUNY Purchase Obedience Show, Purchase, New York, 1995.
(Photo by Mary Bloom.)

Honey and Princeton, Christmas card, 2000.

Courtney at play, Waccabuc, New York, 2005.

Honey wins High in Trial, February 2004.

Luca wins it all! Port Chester, New York, January 2005.

Seamus and Debby on her second birthday,
April 3, 1961, at Mohawk Street, Rye, New York.

Vivien and Luca at Waccabuc, July 2013.

Celia as a puppy, winter 2016. (Photo by Kathy Landman.)

Lello Matacena in Italy.

Eleven

FINDING MY FATHER

I NEVER DID FIND HIM. I HAVE TO START WITH THAT.

Under the terms of the custody settlement, my biological father, Lello, was not allowed to contact me in any way. He could not write, phone, or wire. While he had let me go, he was still curious about me and wanted to see me. He had a friend in Manhattan, a dentist, who had an office in the apartment building where we lived. When Lello was in New York—on the trip connected with his suit for custody—he approached the building's doorman and asked him to point me out.

Years later, I asked Mommy why she didn't let me see him. "I was afraid that he wouldn't let you come back, and I didn't have the money to fight him. I didn't want Andy to worry," she explained.

All my life I was scared to ask my mother about him. Minkie said Mommy told her I looked like him, but she never told me that. Whenever I would screw up the courage to ask her, she would shush me if she heard Daddy approach. She did not want to mention Lello in front of Daddy, who had given me so much and had made Mommy

263

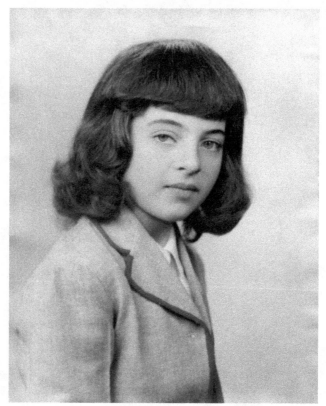

Vivien at age ten, looking like Lello.

so happy. She did not want to rock the boat, and my questions would be a sign that I was ungrateful and would get me in trouble. At least that is what my young mind thought. So I basically shut up.

However, once Daddy died, in 1993, I thought, *All bets are off. I am now going to have that conversation. I am going to find out more.* But there was never that long afternoon together talking about how everything occurred. So I have to be content with the bits and pieces I garnered from aunts, cousins, and Mommy herself.

To start the search, I asked my brother, Eddie, if he could help. He had worked for an English firm and had many connections in Europe. After almost sixty years of waiting, it took him twenty-four hours. I remember Eddie's words, "We found your father."

It seems Lello had been living on the volcanic island of Ischia,

Portrait of Lello Matacena.

renting part of a house, for the past several years. My brother wanted me to be careful, advising that I "verify, verify," but I was so happy. Harry and I went to our favorite Italian restaurant under the El in Queens, ordered a bottle of wine from Ischia, and made plans to visit my Papa. I had it all staged in my head. . . . I would run up to him and hug him and probably cry my eyes out with happiness.

But it wasn't to be. The next evening, I received a phone call from the office of Eddie's business associate. The woman asked if I was Vivien Malloy and said, "I am sorry to tell you, but your father died two years ago, at the age of ninety."

I think I cried by myself out by the pond for hours, looking at the night sky. I had come so close to my reunion. I wanted him to see me, to be proud of me. I had always tried to be good—to be the best I could be—without his knowing how much I longed for him. I knew I had to be like him because, although I was like my mother, there was a part of me that belonged to him, that was like him.

The next step for me was contacting my Italian family, and that assuaged my sadness. Harry, Mark, and I went to Naples in 1994. From the moment I saw my sweet uncle Elio at the airport in Naples, wearing a red boutonniere so that I would know him, I was surrounded by so much love and affection. All these years they knew that Lello had a child—a daughter whom they were not allowed to contact—and they were as curious to meet me as I was to meet them. What a happy discovery! To them I was the ghost of their Lello back amongst them. They looked at me with such love. They said I walked like him, that I ate like him, that I had his charm, his beauty . . . it was so heartwarming for me.

The Matacenas are an amazing family. Poets, screenwriters, set designers, antique restoration architects, naval architects . . . it goes on and on. They are learned, surrounding themselves with art, sculpture, and history. They speak of the fifteenth century like we speak of the daily news. Naples, the city that is their home, is a part of them and a point of pride. They've guided us on tours underneath the streets of modern Naples, showing us the excavation sites of earlier cities buried for centuries and have made ancient history come alive for us.

My father came alive to me from my conversations with Uncle Elio and the other members of the family and the photographs they shared. I don't think Lello ever recovered from the loss of my mother. He had a lot of other women in his life—he was so handsome and charming—but no more real romances. In his seventies, my father married his companion, but he had no other children. He retired to the island of Ischia, renting a house overlooking the bay. He was a robust man, and he didn't need a cane until the last year of his life. He walked every day. I believe that he loved Nena, and only Nena, until the very end.

I learned my aunt Giulia, Lello's sister-in-law, was with him when he died. When she and I met, she gave me photos that he had kept of Nena and him in Cuba. The photos had been kept in an envelope with the directions *"bruciare"*—"burn this"—written on it. Fortunately, she did not burn them. Other than the religious medal from his First Communion and two small dishes that he kept on his bureau, those photos are all I have of my father.

I also visited Ischia in 1994, and went to the house where he lived. His name was still engraved on a stone post outside, with the notation "eng," for engineer. I met an elderly gentleman who lived a few doors away, who remembered Lello's daily walks, what a kind and elegant man he was, and how he would admire his neighbor's garden.

Despite the large age difference, my father and his youngest brother, Elio, were very close. After I had finally connected with my Neapolitan family, Elio came to New York to meet Mommy. He brought her a bunch of violets. "These are from Lello," he said.

Elio told me that after Lello returned to Italy, he never wanted possessions. He lived in rented houses and would either sell or give his siblings any objects he inherited. I believe he did this because he'd lost what was most precious to him—my mother and me—and he never wanted to be so attached to anyone or anything ever again. You may call it romantic dreaming, but my aunt Giulia hinted that this was the case.

Lello Matacena and I would never meet. However, he never forgot his daughter, his only child. In fact, he left me a small legacy in his will.

ELLIS ISLAND

My past came back to me a few years ago when my daughter Vivi and I took her son, Owen, to Ellis Island. Owen was studying immigration at school, and Vivi thought it would be wonderful to go to Ellis Island and try to find some information on Lello.

We went during their Christmas visit, on a freezing winter day. The Hudson was rough, and as we stood in line waiting to board the ferry, the *Miss Liberty*, we could see the boat going up and down, up and down. We felt like immigrants ourselves, as the crew shouted instructions to us. "Don't go back! Don't go back, go forward! Go in the far door! *Go, go, go, go!* Step up, step up, keep going, keep going!"

Somehow we got on a bench and sat down, and then finally the boat started moving and the ride smoothed out. It was the most perfectly beautiful day; it was so clear. I was looking at the skyline, but everybody was on the other side of the boat, looking at the Statue of Liberty.

We arrived at Ellis Island and went inside. The ground-floor displays of suitcases and trunks that had been left behind and the silhouettes of immigrants designating the arrival statistics were very moving. Owen loves statistics, and we marveled at how many immigrants had come through this small island to start a new life in America, including my mother and me. Then we went up the stairs to the room where all the immigrants used to wait for their names to be called. As soon as I got to the top of the stairs, I saw the benches and the white tile and things started to look familiar.

I was especially moved by the fact that all these young people—teenagers, young children—were so respectful in this place. Nobody was laughing or talking. Nobody was yelling. Everybody was quiet. I could feel the immensity of the idea that this room held so many who came to America with hope and that many were turned back.

Sitting there on the bench in the big room, I remembered my own journey. When Mommy and Daddy married, Mommy and I had to enter the country through Ellis Island. Mommy was still officially a Spanish citizen, and I was born in Cuba to a Spanish citizen and an Italian citizen. I remember sitting at a bench—it might not have been in that room, but I'm sure that I was in the big room for a short period of time. Mommy told me that Daddy had a half-dozen lawyers with papers and documents to facilitate getting us off the island quickly.

It was September when Mommy and I arrived, and it was chilly. I had never had a sweater on, let alone a coat. My new grandparents,

Grandpa and Grandma Goodman, had bought me a coat, and it was brought to Ellis Island. But I didn't want to wear it, saying, "No, no! It itches me. It's hot!" All of this spoken in Spanish, of course.

Mommy asked me if I was thirsty, and she bought a bottle of orange pop for me with a straw in it. I had never had a straw; I didn't know what to do with it. She put the straw in the bottle and instead of sucking on the straw, I blew into it! Orange soda came spraying out all over the immigration documents and all over Daddy's lawyers. It's a miracle I ever got off that island at all.

At Ellis Island today, there are kiosks with computer screens where you can input your relative's name and see if he or she is in the records. I tried inputting my father's name, but nothing happened. The kiosk wasn't working. I didn't want to give up, though, and I went to the information desk.

Happily, for a small five-dollar fee, a volunteer helped me find information. She looked up my father's name and, sure enough, found the manifest of a ship, the *Lorraine*, from France. And there he was: name, height, eye color, weight. With further investigation, we also discovered that he had sailed between the U.S. and Europe at least three times.

We also discovered that my biological father was never actually on Ellis Island. As the volunteer told us, "He's top of the heap, he's *'primo parte,'*" meaning that he stayed on the ship and the immigration officials went to him.

The records also showed that he was going on to Havana, Cuba, to visit his uncle Orestes Ferrara. It was all there. All the stories that Mommy had told me were confirmed in the Ellis Island records.

Lello sitting on his mother's lap with relatives and his nanny (in back), Public Gardens, Naples, 1902.

Lello in Naples, 1902.

Lello as a toreador, Naples, 1903.

Lello sitting on a wall in Nice, France, 1905.

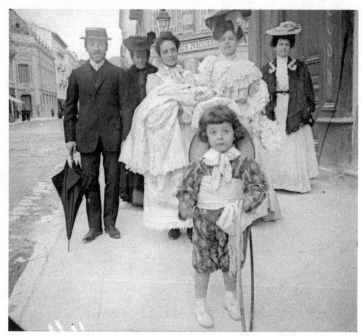

Lello playing with a hoop in front of his mother, Filomena; a nurse holding his sister Clara; and a French friend of theirs. Nice, France, 1905, the day of Clara's baptism.

Lello astride a horse in Naples, 1910.

Lello with his mother and sisters. Left to right: Clara, Filomena, Wanda, and Lello holding shotgun, Portici, 1910.

Left to right: Lello, Wanda, and Clara, Portici, 1910.

Lello at home with his sisters Clara (center) and Wanda (right) and their nanny, holding his baby sister, Amadea.

Lello standing with shotgun, Portici, 1910.

Lello at the races with his parents, Agnano Hippodrome, Naples, 1911.

Left to right: Wanda, Lello, and Clara, the day of their First Holy Communion, Naples, 1916.

Lello on the day of his First Holy Communion, Naples, 1916.

Lello and friends, Agnano Hippodrome, Naples, 1926.

Lello enjoying
an event in
Naples,
c. 1926.

Lello and his brother Elio Matacena at the beach in Lucrino, Italy, 1927.

Lello with his sister Clara and friends, Agnano Hippodrome, Naples, 1926.

Lello joking around with a friend, Naples, c. 1926.

Lello with Filomena and a friend of theirs, Venice, 1929.

Lello and a
friend with a
motorcycle at
Via Caracciolo,
Naples, 1938.

Left to right: Lello; two friends; his sisters, Wanda and Clara; and his brother
Amedeo, in front. At the beach in Lucrino, 1939.

Back to front:
Lello, Elio, and
Amedeo, aboard a
yacht in the Gulf
of Naples, 1938.

Lello with Gennaro and Gabriella's eldest son, Lorenzo, Public Gardens, Naples, 1977.

Harry and Vivien in the town square (TOP), and in front of the town hall (BOTTOM), Tembleque, Spain, 1997.

Tembleque street scene.

Plaque on exterior wall of building in Tembleque, Spain,
honoring Jorge Mañach.

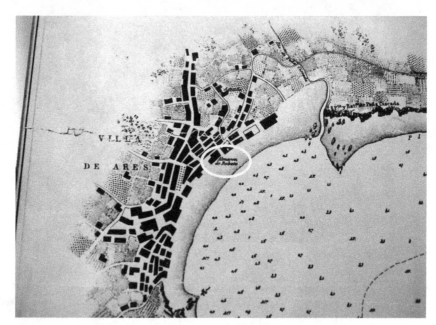

Antique map of Ares, Spain (Galicia), including the Bay of Ares. Circled is the notation, "Almacen de Robatto," the "Robatto Warehouse."

Vivien and her cousin Jose Antonio Robatto near Ares, Spain, 1994.

The Robatto family home, Ares, Spain, 1994.

Harry and Vivien in Ares, Spain, in front of the Robatto family home.

Jose Antonio Robatto and Gabriella Matacena inside the Robatto family home, Ares, La Coruña, Spain, 1997.

Gennaro Matacena, Jose Antonio Robatto, and Gabriella Matacena on the veranda of the Robatto family home, with the present owners, Ares, La Coruña, Spain, 1997.

Gennaro Matacena, Jose Antonio Robatto, and Gabriella Matacena inside the Robatto family house, with the present owners, Ares, La Coruña, Spain, 1997.

Francisco Robatto and his family in Madrid, Spain, c. 1994.

Harry and Vivien in Galicia, Spain, 1994.

Left to right: Pepe Robatto, Vivien, Emilia Robatto, and Harry in front of the Hostal de los Reyes Catolicos, Santiago de Compostela, Galicia, Spain, 1994.

Vivien with her cousin Gennaro (left) and uncle Elio (right) at Elio and Giulia's house in Posillipo, Naples, March 1994.

Left to right: Mark, Mr. Savarese, Vivien, Mrs. Violetta Savarese, Gennaro, Gabriella, Giulia, Elio, and Harry at Giulia and Elio's house in Posillipo, Naples.

Harry in his tam-o'-shanter, September 1953.

Twelve

SOME FINAL MEMORIES OF HARRY

December 20, 2010

It's a chilly December afternoon in Waccabuc, almost two months since Harry passed away, on October 22, 2010. I am thinking of one of the many ironies of life, in that one can be faced with a great loss and a great joy within just a short period of time.

Within forty-eight hours of losing Harry, on the morning of the 24th of October, the phone rang. The caller said, "How does it feel to be the breeder of a Grade 1 winner?"

I, of course, was ecstatic. After I saw the video of A Shin Forward's win, I felt that Harry had been there with his arms around the horse in the stretch—the run that the horse made was so incredibly fantastic. Harry would have been thrilled, to finally realize our goal. You can't get better than a Grade 1 win. This one was in Japan!

A friend of mine told me that the breeder of a winner is very honored in Japan, which would go along with the whole Asian view of the sanctity of elders. If I had been in Japan when my horse won there, my house and office would be full of orchids sent to me to celebrate this success.

It's so hard for me not to share this success with Harry, but on the other hand, it was like a gift from above from him. A Grade 1 win is a goal of every breeder, and I hope to do it again in my lifetime. If I don't get that far again, that's fine, but it remains a goal. Next time, I'd like it to happen in America—we'll have to breed a Derby horse! Harry wanted to win the Derby. Everybody, of course, wants to win the Kentucky Derby.

A Shin Forward won the Mile Championship in Japan, breaking the track record in the process, which still stands today. In the weeks after the funeral, as I read letters of sympathy, I received many emails offering congratulations on the win. It was extraordinary, to say the least, to go from one to the other.

During the last year of his life, Harry struggled to live, but he never complained. He didn't want to leave us. He started showing innocuous symptoms, like having trouble swallowing his vitamins, and so we had to break them in half.

He loved peanuts and always had peanuts beside his chair. Yet, suddenly, he was choking on peanuts! "Honey, you've got to chew them," I'd say. Then he would put his arms up, and he'd start coughing. It began to happen frequently, getting worse and worse.

One day, we went for a late lunch at Bacio, and all was well. We were talking, and the waiter brought our meals. Harry had something soft and easy to digest; I think it was either chicken or veal Marsala, very soft. He never took big bites and was always a slow, careful eater.

He began to eat, then looked at me and took a sip of wine. He put his head way back, as if trying to swallow, but he couldn't. Then he vomited everything onto the plate in front of him, and I put my napkin over it, and the busboy came with another plate to cover it all, and took it away.

I said, "Honey, this is it. Something is wrong and you've got to go to the doctor." I think that what had happened scared us both. I told him that I would be home after I did some quick errands, and he said, "I'll be home in a bit."

When he came home, we didn't discuss what had happened at lunch. But after that, the progression of the illness went very quickly. His regular doctor, Frank Kessler, initially said he had acid reflux and prescribed Nexium for five days. At first, we thought that helped, but it didn't. By the fifth day, there was no improvement. So Dr. Kessler sent him to his gastrointestinal specialist for an endoscopy. Kenneth and I were with Harry in the recovery room when the specialist came to report on the test.

"It's cancer of the esophagus," he said. "It's a tumor—not long, but wide." I thought, *Good, it's not long, no big deal.* But of course I was upset and worried. The specialist suggested a medical group at Northern Westchester Hospital that had trained at Sloan Kettering Cancer Center and used their treatment protocols. We met with those doctors and Harry started chemo.

He was already weak because he hadn't been eating well at all, and he also had diabetes with neuropathy in his limbs. Everyone else going into the infusion center walked right in, carrying books, tapes, and iPods, but Harry needed a walker by that time. He looked so much worse than anybody else, like he had already had five months of chemo when he hadn't even started yet.

I initially thought that it would be simple. You go in, you sit there for a while with an IV drip, and then you go home. Not quite. There are several different steps to the process. For instance, every time Harry got one chemo drug, they would have to flush it with a bag that looked as big as an IV bag that would be given to one of my horses. It was huge. The whole process was almost five hours every single time. Harry would fall asleep a little bit, but it wasn't fun.

When the sessions were finished, Harry was feeling so weak and looking so terrible, I insisted that he go back to his internist, Dr. Kessler. When Frank saw Harry, he said, "Harry you look like shit.

You've got to stop the chemo—it's killing you." The oncologist agreed to stop the chemo, and we had a break for several weeks before he started radiation.

Radiation was five days a week, but thankfully, the treatment itself was quick. Every morning, Kenneth was already there to meet us and help Harry out of the car and stay with us. First, they had to tattoo Harry, to outline the area for treatment and make sure they weren't radiating any other organs.

They kept saying that it was tricky. Tricky? Everything is—and risky too. I didn't really concern myself that it was so terribly dangerous, but it was because his tumor was very close to his voice box. Ultimately, the treatments paralyzed his larynx. He couldn't swallow. He couldn't cough. And toward the end, he couldn't speak. Because he couldn't swallow, Harry was fed with a feeding tube. At first, he was fed 24/7 in the hospital, with liquid food. The stuff smelled horrible and looked horrible.

Then we came home and had to learn how to give him the food. We had to learn about pumps and the home version of the hospital equipment, which was battery operated and turned out to be unreliable. Alarms went off all the time and it was like the Keystone Cops around the house. We did the best we could with all the wires and tubes. One night, the medical equipment company rep had to come with a new pump, and I asked him how many clients did this feeding at home. He said, "At home? None. Our clients are all in nursing homes."

I can see why. It was difficult to manage. Harry kept asking if we knew what we were doing. "Oh, yes! Sure, hon. No problem," I replied. If I saw air in a line I'd call the medical equipment company in a panic. And they said not to worry. Well, they're professionals—they don't worry. However, I didn't know anything, and I worried about everything. If he coughed in the night, I didn't know if there was a problem or not!

One night, Harry woke me up and said, "I think we have a problem. I'm leaking all over the place." The feeding tube had come loose. My darling housekeeper Eva was gone overnight, and someone else was helping me. We tried to fix it on our own. We tried to plug the leak and changed the connection. Nothing worked. We couldn't reach any of the nurses, so I called 911.

The ambulance came and we went to the hospital. The feeding tube had come out. That was the first of three times it happened. Usually, it only happens with dementia patients, who pull the tubes out. Harry needed an operation to insert a permanent tube. However, the so-called "permanent" tube came out after ten days! They kept putting it back in. My theory is that Harry's diabetes prevented the incisions from healing properly and closing around the tube.

We visited the oncologist every few weeks. At first, the news was good. The tumor was gone, but Harry was still weak, and getting weaker. He couldn't stand up by himself or do anything for himself. He was losing weight, down to about 140 pounds. The cancer was gone, but Harry was in very poor condition. I found these doctors' appointments very frustrating. I felt they were useless. Thankfully, we had wonderful nurses at home. They cared for Harry when I went out for a bit and at night so I could sleep.

It went on this way until the end of August. He continued to get weaker, and we made trips to the hospital for various things— usually tubes falling out. Harry quickly learned the hospital routine. One time, he said, "I'm going to ring for the nurse."

And I said, "Honey, what do you want? I'll get it for you."

He said, "No, no, it's all right."

He rang for the nurse, once, twice, and finally, they answered. "What do you need, Mr. Malloy?"

"Bathroom," he said. Then he laughed. "It's the only way I can get people in here. If I say 'bathroom,' they come running." Of course, the reason they came running is because if someone had an accident, then they'd have to clean it up. But Harry had figured it out as usual.

At one point, he had to go into a nursing home because he was so weak. I found the best one in upper Westchester. It was beautifully appointed, everybody was very kind and smiling . . . but it was still the most depressing, horrible place I have ever been in my life. There were no private rooms, and it was horrible for Harry, but at least the staff was very kind. He wanted the TVG network so he could watch the horse races, and they got that all set up. Harry's room became the most popular room in the nursing home. Finally, he left the nursing home, but he couldn't leave in a car. We had to follow protocol and get an ambulance to bring him home.

There's a lot to learn when someone is seriously ill. You have to know what you're getting into and you have to learn the drill. For instance, visiting nurses can't give IVs at home, even if they're registered nurses. You can't get morphine for a dying person except through the hospice nurses. I didn't need a hospice nurse. I didn't need a shoulder to cry on. I just needed their drugs for Harry, and I told them that.

I remember one night when Harry was in the hospital, walking up and down the hall outside his room. We had private nurses with him, but the hospital nurse is the only one who can give the pain-killers. I felt empowered by Shirley MacLaine's character in the movie *Terms of Endearment* who goes out to the nurses' station and starts screaming at them to give her daughter the pain medication she needs. The nurses say, "Not yet. She has to wait twenty minutes." And then Shirley becomes a screaming meemie. "Give her the drugs!"

I wasn't a screaming meemie, but I just stayed at that nurses' station and kept repeating my requests. "Mr. Malloy needs such and such. Mr. Malloy needs such and such." You just have to continually insist.

I learned that if you call the ambulance and there is a crisis in the vehicle, even if you have a living will or DNR order in place, they will resuscitate anyway. Once they resuscitate somebody in the ambulance and you get to the hospital, then it's a legal matter, and almost impossible to follow the wishes of your beloved.

All of these things are little, until they become major. Even if you do everything right—sign all the papers, the releases, the forms—it doesn't seem to matter, especially when things go up in smoke. Anyway, we got Harry home, finally, and he was as comfortable as we could make him.

All of us were there, except Debby, who was on her way from Germany. Harry kept saying, "There's one missing." He held on and wouldn't take his morphine until Debby arrived. Once there, she never left his side and slept right beside him in a chair.

We had music on and the children were laughing, telling stories about themselves with their father. Harry was smiling; he heard everything. They say that the last senses to fail are hearing and touch. Those are the two senses that remain active, even if you're unconscious or semiconscious. I've heard of people who waken after twenty years in a coma, and they all say that they could hear everything around them. Even when Harry was semiconscious, we talked to him.

A few days later, before he passed away, the priest gave him the sacrament of Extreme Unction. We all said the prayers together. My children said they had never heard of some of the saints mentioned in the last rites, which is a beautiful sacrament. I think we prayed to twenty saints.

Harry's faith helped him, I know. When he was very, very ill, kind of semiconscious, he'd try to bring his hands together, to pray, but the nurses would pull his hands apart. They wanted him to rest his hands. I told them, "Don't touch his hands. He's trying to pray." He told me he wasn't afraid to die.

Harry always smoothed the way in life for me, for himself, and for the children. He knew how to placate people, how to charm people. I learned a lot from Harry. He just had a wonderful quality of making life smooth, making life the way anybody would want it. It's not that we didn't have sad things happen and bad things happen—though not many in our life, thank God—but when the unexpected happened, we'd call it "the Vivien and Harry show," and we would get through it.

One day, near the end, he was so, so bad, I just lost it in front of him. That's the only time that happened. I said, "Honey, I can't stand to see you so sick. I can't stand it." I started crying. He took my hand and he said, "Viv, we're going to make it." And I believed him.

This letter from Jim Henry, our neighbor, an attorney and a dear friend, sums up how people felt about Harry.

Dear Vivien and family,

Harry would certainly have enjoyed the send-off that you all provided for him. I wish to say that I cannot remember a service that impressed me so deeply, and I find myself becoming somewhat of an authority on these events as more of my pals run out the clock.

The diverse profundity, sensitivity, and humor of the kids and kid brother created a terrific profile of Harry for the rest of us. The Irish flavor of the event and all those Malloys were simply great.

And of course, the Mass, the church, and the club were, well, classy. It was the real Harry. And the best part of it all was that the event shined a big light and provided more insight on a very lovable person.

I left with some learning and I suspect that Harry's service had some kind of impact on everyone there. That is not the normal outcome of funerals I've attended. I confess that it sort of blew me away.

I know that such events do not just happen. You, with your quality of perfection, and your family made that special day take place at a difficult time in your lives, with very difficult tasks well executed. Trust me, it was worth it.

I enjoyed my own personal insight into Harry. During these recent years, we were often very heavy drinking buddies. In the course of an afternoon he would demolish as much as a glass of wine and I, after nine holes, a single small beer, always elegantly presented by one Ray Mentagrasso (that's the bartender at the club).

Ray and I expressed disappointment that he failed to—but never did say he wouldn't—let us in on the real insider stuff when Vivien's horses were running. He just didn't.

We also sought an invitation to Barbados several times. He never declined, but he just neglected to give us the exact date so we could book our flight.

I supposed this parable according to the gospel of Harry illustrates the limited need to be negative. I love you all.

Respectfully,
James Henry

I just think that's so sweet and shows why so many people are "Wild About Harry."

Harry and Pop Malloy with the Packard in the background, at home on Edgewood Ave., Larchmont, New York, c. 1953.

Harry with Joe Murphy at Harry's graduation from Villanova, May 1953.

Harry and Pop Malloy at home in
Larchmont, c. winter 1954.

Pop and his "Sainted Mother Mary," at home
in Chicopee, Massachusetts, 1924.

The three Malloy
boys: Harry, Pop,
and Jack at Harry's
Confirmation, 1943.

Above, left: Jack and Harry Malloy at Harry's graduation from Villanova, May 1953. Above, right: Conor and Harry at Waccabuc with CV and Nick looking on, September 30, 1993. Left: Ensign Harry Malloy at home on Edgewood Ave., Larchmont, New York, September 1953.

Vivien and Harry arrive at their wedding reception, Westchester Country Club, Rye, New York, January 12, 1957.

Edelmira "Puchie" Sampedro y Robato, Countess of Covadonga, and her husband, Prince Alfonso, Count of Covadonga, with Abuelita and Vivien, Havana, Cuba, c. 1934.

Thirteen

YOU ARE A CUBAN

ALL I WANTED TO DO WAS TO ACCOMPANY VIVI AND HER HUSBAND, Rich, and my two grandchildren on a trip to Cuba to try and show them the Cuba I remembered. We planned a trip for the Christmas holidays in December 2016.

My last trip to Cuba was with Harry in July 1959, after the Revolution, which took place in January of that year. Everything looked and felt the same still, but there was an aura of resentment against Americans. I had always been apprehensive about returning.

I always told people that my United States passport said that I was born in Havana, Cuba, and if Castro and whomever was the U.S. president at the time had an argument, borders would be closed, planes would be grounded—not for the tourists, but for me. I had no legal reason for thinking this . . . just a feeling and a memory.

Years earlier, I had met a Russian ballerina who had been a prima ballerina with the Bolshoi. She told me that when she was in London to dance in an opera in which Maria Callas was singing, she defected. I asked her why, after all these years, she had not returned to Russia. After all, I said, she was now an Italian citizen and traveled freely all over the world. She told me that no matter what happens in diplomatic circles, when you go through passport control, that official has control over your fate. If you are on a list of some sort—in her case, people who had defected years before—they could perhaps let her in but not let her out again. Despite my misgivings, we planned the trip to Cuba that my family was so eager to take.

And so it came to pass that I was in Havana at José Martí Airport at nine in the morning, moving through passport control, with Vivi and her children, Owen and Julia, ahead of me and Rich behind me. When it was my turn to hand over my passport, I placed it on the counter, and the officer looked at it and said, "You are a Cuban."

"No," I said. "I am an American with a United States passport."

"No, you are a *Cuban*, you were born in Cuba," she replied. She mentioned some law that Castro had passed in 1971 that said if you were born in Cuba, you would need a special visa to enter and leave the country.

I was told to stand aside, and Rich and I went over to two chairs at the end of this big empty room and waited. Another officer came over and asked me, "Why did you leave?"

I said in Spanish that I was three years old in 1935 and my mother took me by the hand and said, "We are going to New York." That is why I left.

All of my fears and trepidations about coming back to Cuba were vindicated. People had told me not to be silly, that tourists were coming in droves, that Obama had opened up all these doors of communication. Really? Well, *not* for Cubans. Born in Cuba, I was going to be treated like a Cuban. No rights, no freedoms, no participation in my status, and Cuban officials now had my passport. I could not go anywhere. I was a woman without a country.

Our cell phones didn't work, so we couldn't communicate with Vivi on the other side of the doors. She had no idea why Rich and I were being delayed. It was a myth that Cuba was opening up—all the warnings of my Cuban friends and family had come true. Everything I had always told people about why I was afraid to go back was happening. I told Rich to go on and join Vivi and the children and continue the trip, and I would just go back home. But he insisted on staying with me. Of course, my luggage was on the other side of the doors, and so were Vivi and the children. I was dying to show them the Havana I remembered, and Varadero, the most beautiful beach in the world. I did not want them to see all this through the lens of a Castro-directed guide. It looked like none of this would ever happen.

They delayed me for about two and a half hours, and then they said they would let me in but I would need a special permit from the Cuban Embassy in Washington, D.C., as I didn't have a certain visa for people born in Cuba. It was like the Roach Motel—you could go in, but no one got out. I went through the door, and there were Vivi and the children. We got our luggage and left the airport.

Our trip would continue, and I did not want to bother my family with my concern, but I wanted to make sure to get *out*. The travel agent staff reassured me that they would find out about the special permit I would need to return to the U.S., but they were in no hurry. The "mañana syndrome" had raised its ugly head, but I was on tenterhooks.

The next morning, we visited Old Havana and the beautiful Cathedral Square. The Catedral de La Habana is a massive Cuban Baroque structure. It was closed, so we could not go in. Surrounding the square were the dilapidated buildings of Old Havana, a section that was once so noble and grand.

We went on to Saint Francis of Assisi Square and I said a prayer to one of my favorite saints. "Lord, make me an instrument of thy peace" is the opening, and I have always tried to do that in my life. We walked through the narrow, cobbled streets of Old Havana, which were full of music from open-air bars and street musicians. It was lively and people were dancing in place quietly to a rhumba rhythm like true Cubans do. I knew my way down that lovely memory lane. The children, Vivi, and Rich loved it all, but I was anxious to show them the houses and the addresses I still had in my head.

I had one address in Vedado, a beautiful, quiet section of Havana with tree-lined streets and parks on almost every other block, where I lived until I was three. We found Calle D no. 60—it was not Abuelita's house, where Mommy and I had lived, but it was close. It had once been the home of Tia Cuca, the most beautiful of my aunts, the sweet one who was an incredible seamstress. When I saw it . . . oh my, oh dear. What can I tell you? To me it was now a slum dwelling. No elegant wrought-iron fence and gate. More like barbed wire and chicken wire. No lovely garden in the front. No view through to the *tras* patio.

The house had been changed into a myriad of apartments, or rather rooms—whole families in a room. They kept things the best they could; this is how people lived now. I tried to make the best of it, smiling for the nice lady who lived on the first floor. She was cooking a meal for her family, who were still at work. Our tour guide explained that I thought this was my aunt's house. We took pictures. I gave her a little money as a thank-you, and we left.

The sea was just a couple of blocks from Tia Cuca's house, but now there were cement-block buildings between no. 60 and any view of the sea. The sea breezes were now blocked, and the view was destroyed. All the beauty was gone. It was so sad for me.

We returned to our hotel. It was modern and looked like Miami in the fifties, but things worked, and that's why we chose it instead of the Saratoga or Hotel Nacional, which were gorgeous and charming but more like tourist traps with no amenities. I had heard from friends that nothing worked in these hotels—not the phones, plumbing, or air-conditioning (it was either on or off).

We went to Miramar, an area near the harbor for a lovely, promptly served dinner, and our tour guide greeted us with the news that the next morning we would go to the immigration office for the permit. But we needed a stamp from the post office, which was closed that day, so I was still a woman without a country until tomorrow—hopefully. I still felt in limbo, a place between heaven and hell, with a little bit of both.

The morning dawned and our tour guide met us at the hotel, we had a quick cup of strong Cuban decaf coffee (was it really decaf?), and then Vivi and I went with him to immigration, where we were supposed to meet another member of the travel service with the precious stamp in hand.

The office was on a dowdy street, an almost open-air combination of parts of a house with pieces of tin over some of it. It certainly did not look like any government building or office I had ever seen. We saw some chairs and went to sit down when we were waved in by an officer to another part of the room. I handed him my passport. By now I knew that they did not want to see the tourist visa I had anyway, so I kept that apart. He opened it up and said the now-familiar refrain, "You are a Cuban." And we started to go down that rabbit hole again. Then he said something about Washington, D.C., and we were off and running. I felt hopeless and helpless and, yes, a tad bit angry. But in a situation like this, I kept cool and dignified, acknowledging that what they said was true. I was born in Havana, Cuba, was now visiting the land of my birth as an American citizen, and just wanted to be able to go back home with my family when my trip was over.

This was too much for him to digest, and we were brought into another area, almost open-air. (Just some practical observations: What does immigration do when it rains . . . stop functioning? What happens to all the paperwork and the computers . . . don't they get wet?) Most of the conversation with the very kind official who was handed my documents was in Spanish. The tour guide was there to help with my stumbling efforts in my mother tongue. The stamp was adhered to the permit, some more questions, some information was recorded in the computer, and I was given a bit of a lecture. One: Fidel wrote and passed (of course) a law in 1971. Two: Hadn't I been back since the Revolution? I said no and that the last time I had been in Cuba was in early 1959. Three: Had I been back before that? I told her that I had been back many times as a young child and woman.

I didn't want to add that I had lived with my uncle Jorge Mañach for five months in 1955. That would have opened up another perhaps political discussion, which I was ready to have, but would have kept me with this woman longer than I wanted. I guess it seemed ridiculous to them that I would have left the land of the glorious revolution and gone to live in a capitalist nation. But I did, and I was going to return again if they would just stamp the paperwork and let me go. She was very kind, and I thanked her and we left. Whew!

While Vivi and I were at the immigration office, Rich and the children went for a ride in the now-classic cars. We met up and continued our tour. I was anxious to see if I could find the homes of my other aunts. I asked the tour guide to take us to the "country club" section. We drove out of the city, and things got a little better. All the dilapidated buildings were left behind as we entered a more suburban enclave. We passed the Habana Yacht Club, which looked decrepit, with empty shells for windows. It was, as my guide noted quite often, "under repair." It looked like it had not been maintained since the Revolution. It was, of course, a place where the elite would go, and our guide said that it was now being used as a club for different groups—the electricians, plumbers, etc. I told him that it was then still elite, still a club of sorts, and no different from what it had been before. That went over his head, and he did not comment.

We finally arrived at the address we had for my aunts, who lived next door to each other. Their two lovely homes, now residences of foreign ambassadors, were behind wrought-iron fences, gates, and foliage. Now, to make sure no one could see anything from the street, pieces of plywood painted green had been placed behind the fences and in front of the foliage. I explained to the guard at the gate that this house and the one next door had been the homes of my aunts, and perhaps I could just look at them from the outside. He said that might be possible, and told us to come back the next day around 9:30. I was getting closer.

We came back the next day. We couldn't go into the houses, but we walked around the gardens, and all of my memories came flooding back. At least they were cared for, although the gardens were not as lush as I remembered them.

Rich is a student of history, bar none, and he had heard or read that there was a museum in Havana where some wealthy Cuban had a Napoleonic collection. Of course, it was a beautiful house, a mansion really. We were told it had been the home of Orestes Ferrara. . . . Wait! Vivi and I looked at each other . . . was it possible? We had just stumbled, thanks to Rich, on the place where my father had stayed when he was in Cuba, and where my mother had been invited for lunch or dinner and had met my father.

Everything was coming together. Those pages in the log at Ellis Island that said where my father was going when he left the United States and whom he was visiting. The uncle who was the Cuban ambassador to the United States—Orestes Ferrara. Only Vivi and I knew the significance of where we were. It was amazing. The Napoleonic exhibit was truly amazing too. Death masks, letters, swords, uniforms, hair. It was as complete a collection as any other probably in the world. Here in Havana. Who would have guessed it? Was this fate? The home was incredible, and of course, Fidel made sure he saved it. It had marble up the yin yang, a dining room with a Baccarat chandelier, and beautiful china service. The rug was Savonnerie, and the furniture looked like it had come from Versailles. Mommy met Daddy here. I was sure of it.

Then we went on to the museum that had been the home of my aunt Edelmira. She was the mother of Puchie, Mommy's first cousin who had married Prince Alfonso, son of King Alfonso XIII of Spain. Of course, Vivi's daughter, Julia, asked if she was related to the countesses, wasn't she then a princess? We let her know that she was a distant relative of the king of Spain, but not a princess. She was fine with that.

Again, the home was magnificent. There were photos of the parties in the fifties that I looked at carefully—I must have been to one of them. So many of the girls could have been me or Minkie, and we were often in Cuba during the holidays. There was a photograph of one of Fidel's men with a metal detector in the basement or a storeroom that had been outfitted with shelves full of silver and crystal and then boarded over with stucco. Fidel found it all and saved some for the museum and the rest he probably sold.

The Cubans who fled after the Revolution thought they would be back. Everyone thought that once it was over, they would come back, reclaim their homes and property, and it would all be like a bad dream. Turns out, it was a bad dream that never ended. They never came back, because all they had was gone.

The next day was all my idea. I wanted the children and Vivi and Rich to see Varadero, the most beautiful beach in the world. But it had all gone up in smoke. Where were all the beautiful homes right on the beach? Why was the new hotel we were staying at on the very tip of the peninsula where the sea and the inland waterway or marina met and the wind was whirling like a hurricane *all* the time? Where was the du Pont property and mansion (the Castle, we called it), with its amazing collection of all the flora and fauna native to the island? Almost gone? Of course, Castro saved the golf club and the course, but the protected preserve around the property was now scrub pine and miserable small palms trying to survive in this windy piece of sand at the tip of the peninsula.

I was ready for some of this, as I had been warned that Varadero as I remembered it and as the world knew and loved it was gone. But I figured they can't change the sea or the sand, so I dragged the family out over dismal roads for hours trying to get to it. Vivi and I left Rich and the children, who were fine in front of the hotel's beach, and went searching. We got a cab and asked him to take us to Old Varadero. He did not seem to understand. I said please take us to where all the houses used to be and the Kawama Club. He took us to a ramshackle wooden building, half boarded up, and said that this was what was left.

One of the last times Harry and I were in Cuba was in 1959, after

Debby was born. There's a photo of us at the Kawama Club with my aunt Gladys Mañach and a family friend, Jose Ignacio Macia, and his wife. When and where I met Jose Ignacio is not in my memory bank, but suffice to say that there were gatherings of family and friends all the time. I know he was related to the Barraques, through my *tia* Clara, who had married Chago Barraque.

When I was in Cuba after college and living with my uncle Jorge and his wife, Margot, I went to Varadero and stayed in a little cabana or cottage from time to time. After all, I was a free spirit, surrounded by loving family on the island of my birth with no commitments, no idea of what the rest of my life would be like. . . . I was in a beautiful limbo.

Jose Ignacio was a prestigious deep-sea fisherman, and although being on board a ship was not my forte due to my suffering from sea sickness, when he asked me if I wanted to go fishing off Varadero at 5:00 a.m. one morning, I accepted.

We set out with his boatman, and they gave me gloves and a long wire—the hook and bait were at the end of it—and we trolled for mackerel. They are a great fighting fish, and it was a test of strength and patience as we slowly slipped through the calm, beautiful waters. Yes, I caught my share. Then Jose Ignacio, with a spear and goggles, dove into the water to free dive and catch some other delicious fish, a grouper as I remember. He was down there for what seemed like so long—no tank for oxygen, just free diving. I heard later that he was renowned for how long he could stay underwater, swimming and spearfishing. His lung power was tremendous.

I fell in love. He was an athlete, handsome, Cuban . . . 'nuff said. He knew I had a crush on him, but he never encouraged me, he never touched me. It was love from afar for me, and the man was married with wonderful sons and a beautiful wife. My aunts were horrified. One by one they came to speak to me when I was back in Havana, Clara and Elsie, but mostly Clara, the smart one, as Mommy always called her.

Eventually, I went back to New York and I heard Jose Ignacio and some friends were coming to the city. I was invited to meet them at the St. Regis. It was so strange, but when I met him that afternoon with a "bunch of Cubans," as Mommy used to say . . . it was over. In my milieu, he didn't fit. I don't know, but it was like a light switch: My crush was deflated. I met and married Harry and we started a family. Little did I know that the vacation to Cuba in 1959 would be the last time I would see Jose Ignacio.

Fast-forward several years. It is April 17, 1961, and I am pregnant (again) and living in Rye. Mommy was very active in the Westchester adoption service with her friend Ruth Draddy. They had fixed up a little house as an office in White Plains, with a darling reception room where the adopting parents would meet their new baby, all dressed in lovely clothes or sleeping in a beautiful bassinet—all of which Ruth and Mommy had designed and decorated. From time to time, if there was more than one baby to be baptized, Mommy would call me to help bring them to the rectory. On this day, I was handed my charge, a boy, who was obviously Hispanic, unhappy and tense in his body. I could not comfort him, and I thought that, probably in utero, he had suffered the trauma his mother was going through emotionally. At least that is what I surmised from just holding him in my arms.

When we arrived at the rectory, the priest, as he always did, read the story of the child that was on a sheet pinned to the diaper of each baby. When he came to my charge, he just shook his head and said, *tsk, tsk.* It must have been an awful story, but I am sure priests have heard them all. Sometimes on the sheet was a name chosen by the mother who gave up the baby, but in this case the priest said, "What name do you want to give this child, as there is none here?" And now comes the strange part. I had not thought of my crush on Jose Ignacio, the handsome Cuban, or of the fishing trips in the mornings in Varadero for years. Yet, I looked down at this little scrawny baby and said, "Father, I would like his name to be Jose Ignacio." And so he was baptized as such in my arms.

Later that day, Mommy telephoned me, very excited. "Vivi, turn on the radio or the TV. They are invading Cuba!" I was thrilled to hear someone was going to kick the monster off that beautiful island. Maybe we could all go back again, and my family could reclaim their property and live in their homes. Oh, joy! But the news became worse and worse. By the next day, we realized it was a fiasco. The invading force of Cuban exiles, many from families that I knew, had been devastated by Castro's forces at the Bay of Pigs. All had been killed or taken prisoner.

From one of the leading families of Cuba, Jose Ignacio had gone to Nicaragua to train and was the head of one of the battalions that had tried to invade Cuba. He was not killed outright but had a flesh wound. He was put with hundreds of others in a huge refrigerator-type truck with no windows, and they took off for Havana, which, at the time, was an eight-hour trip in the hot sun. Then the captain decided to stop for lunch with his men, and the prisoners in the truck endured more time in the heat, with no air, no water. There were a few survivors of this trip, who reported to Jose Ignacio's family that he took his belt buckle and scratched and scratched the metal side of the truck to make a tiny pin hole. He was tall, taller than most in his battalion, and he would lift one man after another so they could take a short breath of air. This was a man who could free dive for many minutes on one breath, and yet when they reached Havana and opened the back of the truck, a river of sweat with dead bodies flowed out. Jose Ignacio's was one of them. He died trying to save his men.

To me, God replaced one Jose Ignacio with another on that same day. I wonder where that baby is now. I hope someday he will realize that he was named after a hero.

After the Revolution of 1959, it became clear to the Cubans that Castro would be educating the children to be Communists, as was evidenced from the new ABC books in the lower grades: F is for Fidel, R is for revolution, Y is for yanqui. . . . Many parents wanted to get their children out of the country, but by that time, it was only possible by escaping in tubes and small boats—a perilous journey. There was only one other way: by air to Florida to family already there.

Later, between 1960 and 1962, the well-organized group Operation Peter Pan provided air transportation to the United States for unaccompanied Cuban minors, but there was a woman, a dear friend of my family, who knew all Havana society and did it herself. She was a one-woman rescue mission.

Her name was Lillian Ramirez and she was an interior decorator who had a shop in Havana and imported French Louis XV and XVI furniture, which was all the rage in the beautiful homes there. Everyone knew Lillian. She was joyful, funny, and loved the world and everyone in it, from the garage mechanic to the sugar baron. I loved her a lot.

People began approaching her to take their children to family abroad. In the beginning, Lillian made trips herself with the children, two or three at a time, but then Castro's noose tightened and passports became hard to get. No problem. Lillian falsified some and kept up the trips, sending the children alone to avoid suspicion. They were going to visit an aunt or a cousin or grandparents. Just getting them out of Cuba was the goal.

One day, Lillian got a phone call from a doctor who said he had heard about what she was doing and wanted to help with funds for tickets or in any other way he could be of aid. He asked her to meet him that night on a lonely section of beach so he could give her some money. She immediately called people she knew to ask about him—was he on the up and up, was it safe to meet him and accept his help, etc. She was no fool, and in Castro's Cuba everyone was suspect, unfortunately. There were spies all over, the typical modus operandi of the Karl Marx playbook.

The people she called gave him a glowing report, so she went to the appointed spot at the appointed hour. When the doctor appeared, he said that he wanted to contribute to her work to help the children escape, and he handed her a packet of money. Immediately, from behind some bushes, a group of *Barbudos*, Castro's soldiers, appeared. They grabbed Lillian and took her to prison, but the story does not end there.

Lillian told me of the "trial," laughing as she later described it. She was brought in front of a judge who asked her if she had committed the crimes for which she was charged. When she said yes, she was sentenced to jail and forced labor for fourteen years. She was at least sixty years old at the time.

The *Barbudos* sent Lillian to work in the fields in the hot sun. There was little food, and she became weaker and weaker, so they put her to work in the kitchen instead, where she stood over huge pots and stirred and stirred the awful mess that was their food with a paddle.

In the early days of her imprisonment, we were able to send her birthday and Christmas cards. She had developed a heart condition, and we carefully taped her heart pills to the inside of the cards. Every year my Christmas card had a picture of my children, sometimes with Harry and me too, which she taped to the wall of her cell. The women prisoners would ask if they could just come and look at the pictures for a few minutes. They had left everything behind, and it made them happy and hopeful to see the children. They were all political prisoners, opponents of the Castro regime—not criminals.

Lillian's case was our cause. Many people who knew her wrote letters to the American government asking them for amnesty for her and to plead for her release. Amnesty International became involved too. Finally, Castro realized that Lillian was so sick and was not able to work for the Revolution as everyone was supposed to do. They granted her house arrest for the remainder of her sentence. Her heart condition worsened, as she was not getting any medicine for it, of course. We could not send her pills. The prisoners were no longer permitted to have any mail, especially from the United States, so we couldn't send her pills anymore. She finished out her sentence in a tiny room in Havana. After many negotiations, her freedom was granted, and she flew, now in a wheelchair, to Florida.

She found a job as a manager of a building where she was also given a room. She described her boss as an angel. She was beloved by all again, and she got stronger now that she was able to have her heart medication again, along with good food and fresh air. She visited all my aunts and cousins, and my last memory of her is a gem.

Vivi was competing in a horse show in Florida, and my aunts Elsie and Puchie wanted to come and see me. Lillian was visiting and she came too. Vivi got a fourth in the first class. I gave the ribbon to Lillian, and she proudly pinned it to her dress and wore it the whole day. I was on one side of the ring, and Lillian had gone over to speak to Vivi, who was on her horse in the large schooling area on the other side. Lillian saw me, and with the fourth-place ribbon waving in the wind on her dress, she crossed the schooling area with all the commotion of horses and riders around her as if it was a quiet country lane. She was not afraid of anything and she continued on her mission with all hell exploding around her. I gave her a big hug as we sat and watched the show. Lillian applauded mightily when Vivi's nice round was over. It was as if all that she had done, all that she had risked for the children, all the days in jail, were never going to daunt her spirit. She was a hero again, but an innocent one this time.

Those who knew her will read this story with a smile, knowing nothing could stop Lillian from whatever she wanted to do. God bless you, my dear friend and hero.

After the cab driver dropped us off at Varadero, I took Vivi's hand and said, "Let's just sneak past the bar and that 'house' and get a feel of the sand and a view of the sea."

We walked until we were clear of all the ramshackle remains and looked down the length of the beach. I picked up some of that incredible sand and let it sift through my fingers. I told Vivi to do the same and to tell me what she thought. . . . "Amazing, Mom."

I stood there and imagined all the days past that I had spent in Varadero, as a child, as a young woman, and then with Harry after we were married . . . and I shed some tears of regret. My family would never know what a paradise it had been.

I was determined to find something old. We turned and went back to the cab and said to please take us back to the hotel. But then I saw an old church. I told Vivi I wanted to see if it was open. We asked the cab to wait and went to the front door. . . . Locked. Then around the corner was another door with a knocker of sorts and we used it. The priest came to the door and I explained that I was visiting from the United States and was born in Cuba. Then he asked me when I left, and I told him my story. He asked where I was born. When I said that I was born in Havana, he looked at me and said, "*Destruida*" . . . destroyed.

I said, "Yes, *destruida*."

Some other people came and he let us into the church. It was sweet, and I felt at peace there. I told Vivi to make three wishes, as there is a legend that if you visit a church that you have never been to, your wishes will be answered. I didn't make any wishes because, although I could not remember this church, I might have gone to Mass there. I remember that most of the time a priest would come to the Kawama Club and we would go to Mass in a thatched-roof structure looking out at the sea. All my family and cousins dressed up for Mass, even though we were at the beach. But Mass is Mass, so the men were in their guayaberas and the ladies had their heads covered with mantillas. Varadero might have been paradise on Earth, but you still had to get into the one in heaven, and so no one missed Mass—beach or not.

In spite of the dire warnings of my family—especially "don't go to Varadero"—I could never have imagined how Castro could destroy the sea and the sand of the most beautiful beach in the world, but he had. I could find nothing from the past until I entered the modest walls of the small church. There I closed my eyes and dwelled on the memories I had that no destroyer could take away. We said our prayers and felt blessed for the rest of our time on the lovely island of Cuba.

Edelmira "Puchie"
Sampedro y Robato
in studio portrait.

Nena, Abuelita, unknown friends, and Lello, Cuba, 1931.

Botanical Gardens, Havana, Cuba.

Left to right: Edelmira "Puchie" Sampedro y Robato and her husband, Prince Alfonso, Count of Covadonga, with Abuelita, Havana, Cuba, c. 1934.

REFLECTIONS

ANDREW ON MOM

(written in 2009)

I THINK THE EARLIEST MEMORY I HAVE OF MY MOTHER IS IN THE little house on Mohawk Street, in Indian Village in Rye, New York. We lived in this little neighborhood, about a half dozen or so streets, all named after Indian tribes. I can remember being around Mom and my grandmother, and they were both speaking Spanish. Of course, as you get older, it's sometimes hard to remember what's a real memory and what's been told to you, but that memory is clear to me.

My mom and grandmother were very close. We were always over at my grandparents' house, especially in the summer. At the time, this would be the sixties, my grandparents probably had one of the few private swimming pools around.

Our grandmother was known to us as "Dita," and I'm the one who christened her with that name. The Spanish word for "grand-mother" is *abuelita*, but I couldn't pronounce it, and I started calling her "Dita." Well, the name stuck, and all of us children called her "Dita." It became her nickname in the whole family. I also dubbed my grandfather "Popi," and that stuck too.

I guess more of my memories start at around age three or four. I recall being in a little playpen in Rye, and a neighbor kid threw a rock over the fence. I got hit and required stitches, believe it or not! I still have a little scar.

Our house was always very hectic, as you can imagine, with five children born in a seven-year span. I remember our household as very busy, with maids running around, always "hot and cold running help." Some of them were with us for thirty-five or forty years.

That's how I picked up the Spanish language. I'm not fluent, but I've still retained some of it. I was in Mexico recently with my son, and I was able to order entire meals in restaurants in Spanish. My son was amazed.

Our house in Purchase, of course, looms large in my memories. I especially recall the riding and horses in Purchase. I guess we moved there when I was about four years old. It was a big Stanford White house. When we moved there, it had a single-stall barn, really an old tractor shed. That was the original Edition Farm. Then, Mom expanded it to two stalls, then four, and it got bigger from there.

We all had our chores. As the oldest, I had to blaze the trail for the others. I had a lot of chores! My parents were stricter with me. By the time Kenneth came along, we kids didn't have to do everything, but we all still had little chores.

I wasn't a rider, though. I was a skier and played some golf. I gave up golf for a long time after losing to Kenneth in a tournament, but I took it up again in my twenties.

Mom was very much into riding, and horses have been her passion for a long time. She shared that with Debby, Vivi, and Mark. I rode a little. (I remember Dad saying that riding was not for boys!)

My riding career ended on a horse named Swannie. I think a mouse scared the horse, it took off, and I fell off. I decided then to end my nascent riding career, but I still loved being around horses. I made money at horse shows braiding and cleaning horses and caring for them for the rich girls.

I remember Christmas gifts. I remember getting a BB gun one Christmas. Can you imagine? No one would get such a gift nowadays. I would always take my toys apart and put them back together. Mom instilled that in me, that curiosity. I still like to take things apart.

We were lucky children. Life revolved around skiing, golf, and horses. Dad organized the trips. Mom was always busy with horse shows. Dad took the boys golfing; Mom did the horse stuff.

Many wonderful trips, especially the Barbados trips with my grandparents, stand out in my memories. These trips continue today, with my siblings and their families. We still go to Barbados.

My grandparents "discovered" Barbados in the sixties. Dita was from Cuba and she was always searching for a place like that. My grandparents had leased a yacht—named *Nepenthe* or something like that—and they sailed the Caribbean, starting from Trinidad and Tobago on up through the islands. They invited family members at different islands—Saint Lucia, Guadalupe, Saint Kitts. That was a really cool trip. They settled on Barbados as "their" island, and the family has been going there ever since.

I remember my first trip away from home, when I was sent to Great Oaks Camp in Portland, Maine. With both my mom and my dad, I was the "test kid"; as the oldest child, everything was tested on me. For instance, I'm the only one who actually went to camp, a real old-fashioned sleepaway camp with a uniform.

The other trips that stand out are the many trips to Vermont to ski. My parents did so much! Every Friday night, two cars left Rye, loaded with five kids and two Newfoundland dogs, and we drove to Vermont. Then, it was up early on Saturday mornings for ski races and other activities. I have to admit that my parents really went above and beyond to give us a lot of opportunities; most parents today—including me—don't do nearly as much.

Another trip that stands out in my mind is the trip I made to Spain, in 1967 or '68, alone. I went to visit my cousins from Dita's side of the family. The family's father, Celestino Joaristi, was a

prominent banker in Madrid. I stayed for a few weeks, saw Barce-
lona and the Costa Brava. What a wonderful opportunity. I was
embedded in Spanish culture and also had fun snorkeling, scuba
diving, and spearfishing. I had a ball. Mom had organized it all. And
when I went to Spain, Mom had one of the Spanish cousins come
to the U.S., our own exchange program.

She's a great mom. Organizing that trip is just one of a million
things she did for all of us. She loves her offspring fiercely. I'd say
that, even today, 90 percent of her energy is thrown into her kids.
She's a Mama Bear who says, "Don't mess with my kids!"

She is set apart by her fortitude and her drive. She is not like a
lot of women. I've known many successful women. She is very much
like a Hillary Clinton or a Charlotte Beers or a Martha Stewart in
terms of dedication to building something. Her horse business is
very successful. She doesn't make the same kind of money many of
her competitors do, but for a relatively small operation, she has produced some amazing results.

She's that kind of person. She is also very youthful, still very
beautiful. She has her act together. She knows what she wants. She
has always been a perfectionist, less so now than she was years ago,
but still, with my mom, everything is done a certain way. Everything is always in the right place.

I think she brought up good kids. We have good manners, without even thinking about it. We open car doors; we stand up when a
lady leaves the dining table. On early dates with my wife, a French
Canadian, I'd stand up when she left the table . . . and she thought
we were leaving the restaurant! She'd never seen that before.

We Malloy boys are hardwired with good manners . . . because
we will still feel the "hair pull" if we don't do it. We had that training
every day. We used to have family dinners on Wednesdays in the
formal dining room, and we had to wear a blazer and tie, use the
right utensils. We were taught how to eat Brussels sprouts and arti-
chokes correctly. Mom and Dad would lead conversation around
the table. All very proper.

I went to dancing class too—dressed up in a tie and white gloves—at the Greenwich Country Club. Again, as the oldest, Debby and I had to do some things—like dancing class—that my siblings didn't. My bed had to be made military style, so tight that you could bounce a quarter off of it. By the time Vivi arrived, her room could look like a hurricane hit it and nobody minded. These habits have stuck with me though. I could come home at 4:00 a.m. and I'll still take the time to hang up my suit. I can't leave stuff around.

Mom certainly provided a lot of practical guidance when I was growing up. I also recall, by the way, going to my grandfather, Popi, for business advice. I loved spending time with him and I had the perception that he was a successful NYC business guy, which he certainly was. Of course, I got guidance from Dad too!

Mom always talked a lot about the importance of spending time with one's children. I think there has been some frustration on her part on that score, regarding the time I was able to spend with my older daughters. When they were young, it was hard for me to do that! I was living in Rye, carrying a mortgage, getting on a 5:30 a.m. train to go to Wall Street, going to school at night. It was a blur. My grandparents and parents had more options in that regard, and I'm not sure my parents really understood that part of my life and responsibilities.

I understood and agreed with Mom's advice, but it was harder for me to do than for her. My wife also worked and traveled a lot. I knew the advice was good, and I appreciated it and wanted to heed it, but it was impossible.

Both parents gave me a strong work ethic, maybe too much. I never felt entitled. I remember working at Bergdorf's in the summers, in the mail- and stockrooms. I didn't resent it. I was seventeen years old, sitting in the back of a truck, which must have been about 120 degrees in the summer, taking inventory from New York City to White Plains.

Mom made all of us earn our allowances. She gave me a quarter each week to muck out stalls; my kids don't believe it! My grandparents, on the other hand, would sometimes invite me upstairs—over the store—for lunch when I was working there. They would linger over lunch for two or three hours, a meal that would put you to sleep! Very fancy.

Dita would look at me in wonder and ask, "Why are you working on a Friday?" She reminded me of that scene in the movie *Arthur*, in which Arthur, faced with the loss of his fortune, says, "None of our family ever rode the subway!" Dita marveled that some members of our family worked so hard. I wish I grew up in my grandparents' time, more interesting and more romantic. No computers or cell phones. And time for leisurely lunches!

However, my parents' more practical approach to life has better served me for the last twenty-five years, I will admit.

They are great parents to us all . . . and great partners to each other. Most of their friends have divorced, at least once. My parents rode through the bumps and stayed together. Today, if people don't get what they want from their job or marriage, they move on. I had to do that, and learned from it. My divorce even made me look at business relationships in a different way.

Because my parents stuck it out, I think I stayed in my failed marriage longer than I might have. So, their relationship certainly affected me, and I think positively. And when I say "stuck it out," I'm not saying they were unhappy, I'm just noting that they rode out the bumps successfully.

Now that they are older, they are even closer. Sticking together, for richer, for poorer, better or worse—but never for lunch, as the saying goes—worked for them. One of the reasons why, I think, is that they always each had a life. They would come to our sporting events in two cars all the time, because they lived different lives often. Even when we went to Vermont, they took different cars. I think that's healthy and they were way ahead of their time.

It's been tough with Dad right now, but I've never seen so much love between them. Mom is supporting Dad a lot; it feels good.

A while ago Dad had a stroke. Fifteen years ago? I was there when it happened. He was already in the hospital for another reason, and it was very scary to see. I remember a point where Mom was struggling with this development; she was taken off guard by the prospect of caring for an invalid. She was scared herself. But she worked through it and supported Dad, then and now.

Because Mom feels that people should stick together no matter what, the last decade has been bumpy at times for Mom and me. Mom supported my ex-wife, to a degree, out of concern for my daughters. That did affect my relationship with Mom.

We are closer now than in the recent past. I call and ask how she's doing as well as how Dad's doing. We have long conversations about what to do. I've been flying back and forth a lot.

Lately, I'm happy to say, things have been better, partly because of my dad's situation. Mom's a tough lady, and these last developments have scared her again. However, she will be fine; she is her own person. She never walked in the shadow of my father, or anyone.

DEBBY ON MOM

(written in 2008)

I'VE BEEN TRYING TO THINK OF MY FIRST, EARLIEST MEMORY OF MY mom, but no one memory springs to mind. The more I think about it, she was always in every part of my life, somewhere behind my right shoulder.

She was always there, supportive and very, very disciplinary. She had to be! She had five children, with only about a year's gap between births. That's not easy. I think we were pretty crazy. Everyone was healthy and we were rambunctious, with lots of energy. So, if there hadn't been this sense of discipline in the family, I think we would have been unmanageable.

I also remember her calmness, her composure. One of the most enduring memories I have—which has helped me throughout my entire life—involves a drive back from a lesson with George Morris. I had just had a lesson, and I think we had two horses in the van. Mom was driving me as always, my supporter and sponsor, and frequently my groom too!

We were driving downhill on a cold, wet day, on a curvy country road. All of a sudden, something happened, and I saw the steering wheel spin out of control and Mom couldn't hold it. Scary! Yet, she was very calm. I knew she wasn't really feeling calm, but she acted calm, trying to grab the steering wheel, and she did.

I remember thinking, Gosh, she really handled the situation phenomenally! It was impressive to see her handle this pretty nasty situation in a truck, which could have been a terrible accident. She got the truck under control. We stopped on the side of the road for maybe two or three minutes, she got her thoughts together, and then we drove on. What strength. What a wonderful example for me.

I think about that episode a lot, because I drive a horse truck now all the time in Germany. She always used to say, "Always turn early going into a turn or coming out of a turn with a truck." It's funny what sticks with you.

Mom is calm and perfect, no matter what she's doing. When she goes out, she's always dressed just perfectly. If the occasion calls for high socks, warm corduroys, and hiking boots, she's got them. No matter what she's wearing, she looks great. Always elegant. The dresses she wore to all of our weddings were always perfect.

She's loved by many people, not only by friends and social contacts, but also, on a smaller scale, political connections. In the county, she's always supporting something good.

I'll never forget her involvement with the trails in Bedford, working to keep the bridle trails open. I thought, Who cares? Who the hell cares about these trails, horses, and ponies? We go to horse shows. We don't do this stuff. Yet, she put her time and effort into it, because it was for the greater good.

I was eighteen when I left home. I went to New Zealand and Australia for five years, and then I was in Virginia for one year, and then I went off to Germany. So I wasn't home a lot as a young adult. I missed the early stages of becoming more of a friend to my mother. I finished growing up elsewhere.

Even before I left home, I was so focused on horses that I didn't have a lot of time for girlfriends my own age or family relationships. With horses, there's no question of boys or boyfriends or going out. Horses were everything to me.

I didn't have a lot of friends in high school because I was hardly ever there; my world was somewhere else. I remember thinking, when I heard the girls at lunchtime talking about boys or diets, that these problems didn't affect me whatsoever.

I was too focused on my own riding to see my mom as something other than the driving force behind my right shoulder. She was always there, and I appreciated her, but I never vocalized that, really. Then I left home. I think I had a very different experience with Mom than my sister had.

I have other early memories that are vivid. For some reason, I see her very clearly watering the pachysandra. I don't know where she found the time. Some women have one or two kids and can't manage anything else. Mom had five children. She took care of us during the day, and at night was still able to sew name labels into all of our school clothes or water the pachysandra. I guess she sorted her thoughts while she was doing that.

How did she juggle it all? How did she organize so well? We were on Alpine ski racing teams or riding or golfing. How did she manage all that? She was such a smooth organizer that we didn't really even know that we were being organized.

Every Friday, we'd be driving up to Vermont for skiing, and the car was always packed and ready with clothes, equipment, and food. I don't know how those boxes got into the back of the car, but it was Mom and her invisible logistics. We didn't have to worry about that. We had our chores at the barn with the horses or dogs or whatever. But we never really had to worry about anything.

I have two dogs, and we have ten horses in the stable. That's it for me. I wouldn't be able to manage kids as well! Yet Mom was able to throw that whole thing together and socialize to boot. Amazing. Mom had discipline and rules, including a lot of unspoken, unwritten rules.

For instance, we all had lunch boxes and Mom didn't fuss a lot with the lunches. We had a sandwich and maybe a banana, but I can't remember having cupcakes or Twinkies or good stuff.

It was a good lunch, but by the time we got home from school at 4:30 or 5:00 p.m., we were always starving. We would draw straws to decide which of us would go into the house first, to see what kind of mood Mom was in . . . and whether we could get a snack!

If Mom was in a good mood, we could all go in and have some cold cereal. We'd get something in a bowl and watch *Let's Make a Deal.* That I remember. And then, of course, we'd have to go out and do our chores.

We used to make Mark go into the house first, most of the time, since he was the youngest at that point. Mark would go in the back door; we'd shove him in. We didn't even get onto the back porch. We would just stand out there with our lunch boxes, a tribe of hungry kids, standing, waiting to find out Mom's mood.

If Mark came back out shaking his head, we knew that it wasn't a good day for cereal and *Let's Make a Deal.* On those days, we'd grab a couple of cookies and chew on those on the way out to the stables to do our chores.

Mom would make any of our visiting friends do chores too! Andrew and Kenneth would have friends over, and Mom would say, "Isn't that great! We can do a chore." There was always something to do.

I remember fun times, but also remember getting punished sometimes. If we'd done something wrong, there was no discussion. It was immediate punishment. There were a couple of times when I knew there was a good explanation for some transgression, when it really wasn't my fault or my brothers' fault, but explanations usually came later!

One time, we really got it. I think I was four or five, and Andrew was five or six. We had ducklings at home, and we weren't allowed to take the ducklings out of the cage. But we did! We took all these ducklings out of the house—there must have been ten—and put them in this little red wagon.

We took them to visit a neighbor boy. He was a rather stupid boy, I thought, with really curly hair, and he was a little bit heavyset.

He took one of these ducklings, and he said, "Can they fly yet?" Andrew and I tried to say, "No, we don't think so." But the boy threw it up in the air, and this little ducking came down on the driveway with a thud.

We thought, *Well, obviously he can't fly.* So we picked him up and tucked him back into our wagon. I certainly didn't think he was dead; he just couldn't fly. All the other ducklings knew he was dying, though; they were hysterical and trying to huddle into the other corner of the wagon.

When we got home, Mom cried, "What have you done?" I don't remember seeing her, but I remember her voice that day very well. We knew we shouldn't have taken the ducklings out of the cage, but we had thought, *We'll put them back in the cage, and all the ducklings would be fine.*

However, that one duckling died, and we got in loads of trouble. I got sent up to my room. Andrew got spanked with "the Belt."

Kenneth used to call it "tough love." It certainly didn't hurt us in any way. Our discipline was not pleasant, but I don't think that people should avoid discipline. It was good for us, and appropriate.

I think every kid, every horse, every foal, knows what's right and what's wrong, and they push the line. As soon as they know what's not allowed, then they don't push the line anymore. They don't go in that direction anymore. They might go in another direction, and push that line, but they won't push the same one anymore.

On the basic rules, I think my parents had it right. As a child, it's difficult after being reprimanded to turn around and love the person who just walloped you. Afterward, as an adult, you can appreciate what they've done for you.

I remember Mom's stories about discipline from long ago, of course. I remember her telling us about the time the nursemaid put Mom's hand in the oven. I'm still learning new things about my mother, even now, which is one of the reasons I'm glad she's putting her memories on paper. For instance, all of a sudden, she'd mention that a good friend of hers died—Frannie Santangelo—with whom she'd been on the swimming team. We never knew that. We knew she could swim, but we didn't know she was on the swimming team.

I wish she had talked more when I was home, but of course, I left at such a young age. I wish she had told me more about the family, good and bad.

There was a lot of alcoholism in the family, but I didn't know about it for a long time. After I had returned from New Zealand and Australia, I found out that many cousins and aunts, uncles, even Granddad, had been afflicted with it and some had died of it. Then I thought, I could have become a drinker!

She told me that my father's mother was an alcoholic, and died of it, and also that his stepmother was. I guess I can understand not talking about it when they were alive, but I would have liked to have known sooner, as a warning to myself.

I missed connecting with my mother as a young adult, with all my travel. After I was in New Zealand almost two years, I went directly to Australia. I was there almost two years. So I was gone almost five years. Then I went to Virginia for a year and then went off to Germany.

I've been gone for thirty-something years, since I was eighteen. So there's just a completely different relationship between Mom and me compared to, for instance, my sister and brothers.

But I'm a lot like Mom, I think, in my focus on horses and competition. Her legacy is with me. We both take care of the people we love, but we also place great importance on our passions.

For instance, my dad is ill right now, and he feels bad enough without also feeling guilty that she's giving too much of her time to him. He knows just how dedicated she is to her horses. She, at the same time, is very caring and devoted to him, but she doesn't want to give up that part of her life either. Thankfully, she doesn't have to.

We had a guy working for us who had seen his brother murdered by Serbians. He was hiding in a cabinet and saw his brother's throat cut, right in front of his eyes.

He fled the war zone and came to work for us in Germany. I believe our work routine at the stable kept him sane. He would come every morning to work at 7:30 and stop promptly at 12:30 p.m., even if he had a little more work to do to finish a chore. Routine and rules kept his tragedy from overwhelming him.

Similarly, I understand why Mom's routine is important now, not only to her, but also to Dad. She's holding on to her life and its routines for her sanity, because this is not a nice situation for Dad.

So, I think she's going through a bit of a conflict now, because she doesn't want to give up on her many activities. She's very worried about Dad, but nobody—especially Dad—wants her to give up her horse activities.

Mom and I both have a kind of selfishness. If we have a goal or if there is something we want to do, we won't climb over bodies to get it, but we will not allow very much to get in our way.

Even my husband teases me that you've got to be a dog or a horse to get my attention; otherwise, you can forget it! Dad always says that he prays every day to be reincarnated as a horse in my stable.

Mom's love is deep and real, and a little bit tough love. We wanted for nothing, but there was never anything that we had that we didn't deserve, that we didn't work for. We weren't spoiled brats.

Mom and I are both demanding of the people and animals around us, but we are also demanding of ourselves. Mom is harder on herself than on anybody else. When I read that in one of her memoir chapters, I realized that I am that way too.

I never realized that about myself, but since I read that, I've tried to be reminded not to be too tough on everyone, to be more mindful of the feelings of others.

Mom is a perfectionist, no question! An example of this, and another early memory of mine, is what we would call Mom's "party panic." She and Dad gave a big party three or four times a year. "Party panic" was our term for the frenzy that would commence two days before the party, because everything had to look fantastic.

One time, George Morris was one of the guests, and we had cleaned the barn until it sparkled. The day of the party, Mark came home late from school and went to ride. He rode and, mindful of the party, cleaned up after himself. The horse was put back and looking great. The stable was beautiful for the guests' arrival.

Except . . . as Mom and her guests were walking back, George said, "By the way, Vivien, there's a brush on the post outside." Mark had groomed the horse outside, so as not to get the stable dirty, and had forgotten the brush on the post.

I remember when George said that, my hair stood up! I had gotten goose pimples. I thought, *Oh my God, Mark's going to get crucified, crucified!* I think he lost TV privileges for a week or something! I remember those kinds of things, because she was so proud of the place. And now, I appreciate why. I'm a perfectionist too, as is my husband.

More and more, as I get older, I think I am like my mother. I look like her. Hans, my husband, will comment "You're just like your mother!"

Mom and Dad were complementary in their approach to parenting. Mom was, as I've mentioned, organized and by the rules. Dad was, let's say, a little more relaxed about everything.

For instance, he would say, "Let's go to church." We always wanted to go with him, because he would arrive late and slip in at Communion time. We'd join the line, go to Communion, and we'd come back into the corner of the church, genuflect, say prayers. I'd say max two minutes!

He would park illegally, sometimes in the handicapped parking spot . . . and then he'd do this horrible limp on the way out! But we'd be in and out of church in no time, then on our way to the bakery before the crowd arrived! Mom, on the other hand, would arrive early and stay to the bitter end of the service.

I think part of Mom's determination with the horses now is because she put Dad and us first for so many years. She is still getting comfortable with putting herself first. I remember a few years ago, she was agonizing over the purchase of a good racehorse mare. She had actually sold the mare earlier; the mare was up for sale again, and she wanted to buy it back. I always tell her she should have called her place Boomerang Farm, as she's sold horses, and even the farm itself, and then bought them back!

I said, "What are you saving your money for, for us? If it makes you happy, go for it! Enjoy yourself now!" But having said that, I don't think she ever didn't do something she wanted to do.

She and Dad lived their lives as a couple as well as with the family group. They both wanted a family, but they still went on trips and did things together. She and Dad have been great, supportive parents.

Mom achieved a balance in her life—with five kids—that many women would envy today. We were a huge part of her life but we weren't her entire life, which I think was fantastic.

She's always seemed so cool and calm, so organized. I sometimes wonder if she was always trying to be like her mother. She has a great deal of admiration for her mother.

She may still be looking for her mother's approval. The physical, maternal nearness was not there for her, because she was brought up by nannies. Dita (that's what we children called my mom's mom) always said, "I love my children. They have everything. They have good doctors, good health. But I was devoted to Andrew." That was her love, her husband. My mother was more balanced. She gave her husband and her children her devotion, and herself as well.

She came from a family with no horses whatsoever. They were city people. But Mom adored horses. She had to make it happen for herself. She took the reins and held on. I think that took a tremendous amount of guts. She had no support from her parents as far as horses were concerned.

I had all of her support; it was easy for me. But when Mom was a young rider, she was going completely against the grain. We have a saying in Germany, "She had to dance at many different wed-dings." She had to be the daughter of Mr. and Mrs. Andrew Good-man: Be social, go to a good college, dress well. That was one of the big things with my grandmother; you had to dress well always. Later on, she had to be a good wife and mother.

And then on the other side, horses. Mom had to work to fit that into her life, and she didn't give it up. I really admire that.

Mom didn't have a great deal of support from her sisters or brothers either. They had little experience with horses, and there-fore did not understand what the hell she was doing.

I think there is a great deal in my mother's family history that makes her what she is today. I think she was always conscious of the fact that she was a half sister to her siblings. I think she regrets never meeting her biological father. I think that was really sad for her not to have met him. On the other hand, maybe it's better that they never met. It would have been difficult for him to explain why he never had a relationship with her.

These issues have made family very, very important to my mother. She gets angry at my brother Andrew, because she thinks he's abandoned his two girls. It's been hard for him to deal with his ex-wife and communicate with the girls. She was very insistent with Andrew, to the point where I talked to her about it. I said, "Look, Mom, I don't want to say this, but your dad did exactly the same and you grew up just fine." Her feelings about her father were affecting her relationship with Andrew.

We are all affected by our upbringing, certainly. In spite of all her advantages, Mom felt like she had to fight for herself. I think she was consistently fighting for her position in her own family, with her own siblings. It was a different world. She was aware of the background, but in those days, you didn't advertise that you were adopted and that your father abandoned your mother when she was pregnant in 1931.

I think she was afraid that she might be sent away. My grand-father's needs came before everyone else's. And so, she was constantly a little bit on edge her entire life. I think she was—and perhaps still is—trying to prove that she's "good enough."

When she won the breeder of the year, I was so proud. She called me and sent me an article about it, and I sent the article to her brother and sisters. I wanted them to appreciate all of her work and her accomplishments, her national recognition.

Her passion gives her strength. And I think it's more important than ever for her to hold on to the horses, even as she is dealing with my dad's illness. It's the best therapy for her at this time!

Thank God she has the horses and the races and the training. You can get, and keep, your balance a hell of a lot easier if you're holding on to something that you are passionate about. And that's something that she needs now.

I've never seen her very weak. Just once or twice. One time was when Jack Kennedy died. I remember her crying in front of the television set. Seeing her cry made me feel like my world was crumbling, because Mom just doesn't cry.

The other time was when she came back from a consultation with a priest. She had just had Vivi, and her doctor told her to go on birth control, because the doctor felt that she was getting older and shouldn't have any more children.

So she went to her priest and said she had to be on birth control for health reasons. She said the man was very nice, but told Mom that if she took birth control pills, she couldn't receive Communion. Afterward, she told me that was one of the worst moments of her life.

Those are the only two times I really saw my mom in distress. She's tough.

Yet, no one feels more emotion on behalf of others than my mother. She helped me in ways that her own parents didn't help her. I didn't have to fight for my position in the family, as she did.

I have so many wonderful memories of both my parents.

KENNETH ON MOM

(written in 2009)

THE EARLIEST MEMORY OF MY MOTHER THAT I RECALL IS SITTING AT the foot of her ottoman, watching TV in her master bedroom. And she's behind me, sitting in her chair, needlepointing one of her many pillows or little rugs.

I love this earliest memory of my mother, the closeness and quietness of it. I don't know how old I was, maybe seven or eight years old. It illustrates one of the many things that I feel are so cool about Mom, that she was always active, even when she was at ease—watching television with one of her children—she was needlepointing, doing something, never just idle.

She was, and still is, the antithesis of a couch potato. She just can't be one, even when she is in resting mode, she is actively resting! When she gets horizontal, she falls asleep. She makes the most of each day and night. Bedtime was quite early for most of my childhood, and the wake-up calls were kind of early too.

So that's my first memory of Mom, needlepoint and the sense that Mom was always there, always active. She has an insatiable desire to learn. She took Italian lessons and piano lessons after she was seventy. I mean, she just doesn't stop.

My childhood was a happy one. I was an optimistic child and athletic. I never considered myself smart in my early years. I took advantage of a Montessori school that let us learn at our own pace, and my pace was awfully slow.

But I enjoyed my sports and participation in them immensely. We had a lot of fun, but I also recall that work and chores were an important part of growing up in our household. Feeding the dogs and cats, taking care of the horses whenever help was required. We definitely had a divided family in terms of weekend activities. There were the horse people, and then there were the golfers, and I fell in the golfers' segment.

One story I still love to tell involves friends from school, who I had invited to visit at Five Chimneys to play some baseball and stuff like that. I remember bringing these kids home one time, I think I had two friends over. We had ten acres; we were blessed. It was a great place to live. And so, here we were, talking baseball, and my mom sees us. "Ken, come on down to the barn. I need your help."

And I said, "Oh, jeez."

"Bring your friends," Mom said, "I'm sure they'd love to help too."

And so we went down and we had to muck out the stalls, shoveling the manure into this little wagon, which was then hooked up to a small tractor and taken to the other end of the property to be dumped.

Needless to say, my friends were not too excited about mucking out stalls, standing in the back of this manure-laden wagon, and helping me dump the manure. It was nothing that you wanted to be around. I'm sure it smelled like the essence of perfume to Mom, but to us, it was not quite as pleasant.

That's another little story that tells you a lot about Mom. She never assumed that somebody didn't want to get involved. She knew that what she was doing was fun and just assumed that everybody else would feel the same way. Her attitude was "Hey, everybody, come on in! You'll love it too!" Even if it's mucking out stalls.

I was the middle child. And now, I have four kids myself. I remember my mother ascribing traits to each child as we were born, telling us what to expect from the first child, the second child. She would always acknowledge that each is an individual, but then give you the briefing regarding your birth-order position and what it meant.

Supposedly, the oldest paves the way, the youngest is coddled. I was able to roll with it. I had a great childhood, and perhaps as the middle, I was able to observe different relationships within the family from a unique perspective. I could see all the dynamics: younger brother, younger sister, older brother, and older sister. I don't think that anybody can tell me anything about sibling relationships—other than twins—that I don't know.

I think some kids roll with it a little bit better than others, don't fight things, and just go along. I think I fell into this position within the family. I just felt very at ease with whatever was going on.

We had an interesting time as children. We each had our activities, overseen by a mother with a passion for us, but also an unbelievable passion for horses, the extent of which I really didn't appreciate at the time.

I knew we had horses. I knew Mom and the riders in the family often got up at the crack of dawn to go to a horse show. People came over to teach them, or they went to New Jersey or Greenwich to be trained.

I was your standard football, basketball, baseball, soccer, anything-with-a-ball kid. I liked those kinds of hand-eye sports. And golf on the weekends. My dad loved golf.

My dad was not very interested in the horses in the early stages; always supportive of my mother, but not actively. As I said, we had the horsey people and the golfers. There was a little bit of us/them. Andrew was a golfer, I was a golfer. Mark was a rider. Debby and Vivi were riders. So it was a divided household, but everybody supported everybody in their efforts. And we had one sport we all loved: skiing.

The skiing was such a unifying thing. I respect the heck out of my parents for the efforts they put into our skiing weekends. I think they bought the condo in '68 or '66. Before that, we were renting at Stratton. Once they bought the condo, we were up there every weekend.

In '68, I was seven years old. We learned to ski, and we raced until we were about thirteen or so. Up until age thirteen, it was competitive but mostly just for fun. At age thirteen, you had to make a decision to either focus on racing or enjoy skiing on a non-competitive basis.

Consider what my parents did every weekend. They took five kids, three dogs, food, and equipment in two cars, driving four hours on Friday night to a nine-hundred-square-foot condo. And as we were in the racing program, Mom and Dad had to get the whole family up and out early on the weekend mornings so we could get to the Stratton Mountain base lodge for the 7:00 a.m. drop-off for the ski team.

Then, we'd meet at "rack 10 at noon." That was the mantra: Rack 10 at noon. My mother would make sandwiches and have snacks like pepperoni sticks, all in this wooden, woven Austrian-looking picnic basket. I can see it now. She would stow it under the staircase at Stratton Mountain base lodge in the morning, go skiing, and it would be there at noon. We'd get it and all have lunch at the base lodge, usually on the second floor, telling stories about our morning as we ate. Then we'd all go out and ski for the afternoon.

In the early years, Mom made all those lunch baskets herself. Later on, when we were older and hanging out with friends, we started to get money to buy our lunches, but in the early years, Mom made all the meals!

It was fun, those ski weekends. It was fresh air, dynamic. We had controlled independence, in the sense that Mom and Dad knew we were all on the mountain somewhere. When we were older, we could also go back to the condo on our own, via the shuttle buses.

All that was so good in shaping responsibility while having fun and freedom. You had to be somewhere at this hour, somewhere at that hour, and over time, it was up to us to manage ourselves. Good training. So wholesome.

I put my older kids into ski school early and hard. I got a little softer with the other two, and it shows. The younger two don't have the real dynamic skiing attitude that the older kids have. Conor is a ripper. He's taken trips out west with his friends. He absolutely loves it. Maggie is an absolute ripper; she can carry speed.

Kenny likes the bumps, but he doesn't necessarily have the technique to handle the speed. Shane is still developing, still pretty conservative.

At the time in my childhood when we were skiing as a family, the late sixties and seventies, my mother was in her mid-thirties through her forties. She was a graceful skier. She looked good. She wasn't a ski bunny in the least bit. She put warmth first, but she still had a sense of fashion.

She skied like the classic skiers, feet always were together. She even did some racing as a hoot, because her kids were involved. She also participated as a gatekeeper in our kids' races, watching to be sure the kids got through the gates correctly.

Think about standing at a gate for four hours on a cold day, with a pad of paper and a pen, making sure that the kids get through the gate. If they didn't get through, you'd mark them down and they get DQ'd. And this is in southern Vermont in December and January— not pleasant. She would also act as a timekeeper.

So, she was graceful and she was very fashionable. I think she enjoyed the sight of her family skiing the most. She enjoyed the sport itself too. Mom and Dad took trips to Austria. She really had a good time with skiing, but I think skiing for Mom and Dad meant family cohesiveness, a chance to spend time together as a family.

I always described her as a lioness. She would do anything for her cubs. That love was never, ever questioned.

We also had Wednesday night dinner, at the big table. Dinner at the big table was a big deal. We had a beautiful dining room that wasn't used often, but we used it on Wednesday nights.

Mom and Dad sat at each end of the table, with the kids seated on each side, and we had a proper dinner. Other nights, we frequently had the evening meal in the kitchen, but Dad wouldn't be there most of the time when we ate in the kitchen.

But on Wednesdays, we all ate at the big table. We all told stories about that week. Each child would tell a little bit about what was going on in his or her life. It was a great little interaction, a great tradition—something that my wife really got on me for not instilling in our kids, because I really do think it's neat, looking back on it.

So much about my mother is impressive, but I'm most impressed with my mother's passion. It is the character trait that has driven her entire life. What makes Mom special in this regard is that she has been able to pursue her passions her whole life—without question, a life that is very enviable.

She is passionate about horses—that's without question too—but she also has a passion for teaching and instructing. She pursued that with her dogs, for instance, focusing on each one being the best dog it can be in a specific class in agility or obedience.

If you look at my mother, she has always been an obedience-focused person, as a way to get the best out of a person or animal. That goes from education selection for her children to the teaching and coaches chosen for the riders and horses. Obedience was always a big part of my growing up.

And it was old-fashioned obedience! My son Shane loves to hear stories about our childhood, because he sees his grandparents in a certain way, and we, as children, saw them as parents and thought of them as parents, which is a totally different experience. Most of the stories we tell Shane and the other grandchildren are about obedience and making sure that we did the right thing. Mom liked to pull hair as one of her disciplinary obedience tactics. Shane just can't believe it. She's strong too. She's got a good grip and . . . discussion over!

Another time, Debby was trying to get into the house through a locked glass back door. I had a friend with me or something and I started teasing her, trying to act cool. I was making her say "pretty please" and the whole thing. And she got mad and banged on the glass door . . . and she put her hand right through the glass.

Dad had an issue with that one! So we tell Shane about how Dad took the wooden cutting board and hustled me outside. I was wearing a bathing suit, by the way. And he told me to bend over—wearing that bathing suit that was nice and wet—and he gave me a couple of memorable whacks with that thing. I had two big white blisters on my butt for a little while after that. Shane can never believe that his grandpa, "Hoo-Ray," did that.

I tell these stories because they're just classically great stories about kids who need to get put back into the right lane. That was the time in which we lived, and that was the right thing to do. I think that obedience and discipline were part of being in that household; you were expected to act a certain way.

There was a lot of freedom, but there were a lot of expectations too. So, when I look at Mom, much of her approach to us is based on the belief that obedience is a good thing. Command/reaction is a good thing; I say this, you do that. I say sit, dog sits. I say do your homework, you do your homework.

So is that a good thing? I think it's great, as far as I'm concerned. I think the way they did it with us, the way Mom did it, the way Dad did it, was just so lathered with love.

I see now how hard it is to discipline the children you love. And the benefit of these acts done doesn't hit you when you're thirteen. They don't hit you when you're fifteen. They hit you when you leave home. That's when you start to appreciate the moral compass that your parents tried to embed.

And you know, if you can set it, the children will always know where true north is, no matter where they are.

I believe in that kind of discipline, but I'm the softy in the family. Wouldn't think I would be, but I am. I remember years ago, when my kids were younger—they are twenty-three, twenty-one, nineteen, and seventeen now—I used to say to my wife all the time, "They may not love me but they'll respect me." Sometimes, you need to be a bit tough to ensure that your children grow up strong. You have to have a certain relationship with kids at certain times, and that relationship changes and grows.

No matter what stage of our lives, Mom's always "had my back," which is a phrase that I use when describing support for someone. That support ranged from emotional to financial and everywhere in between.

I love that she can have dirt on her fingernails during one part of the day and yet have the finest dinner with wonderful manners and etiquette later that evening. She never was pretentious. She was always a great example of hard work and staying incredibly fit.

She drove for hours for the horses and riders and for the family ski weekends every weekend of the winter. The family ski weekends were something that exemplifies our childhood as a family. We were together in our condo with five children, three dogs, up early to compete in the ski races, and my parents would be involved in the race as timers or gatekeepers. If there was no race, and it was just training, then we would all meet at rack 10 at Stratton Mountain for lunch at noon.

Her guidance extends to the raising of my children. She was adamant that they had the best education available to them, so much so that she said she would be happy to pay for their private education. That's the gift that keeps on giving. She values learning and education so much that she not only ensured the best for her children, but was active in pursuing the best for her grandchildren as well.

Our town has a good public school system, but my mother was not satisfied that the system was good enough. And my wife has always been very adamant about having kids in a school that fits them, not fitting the kid to the school.

So, bottom line, between my wife and my mother, our children went to Brunswick, Iona Prep, and Sacred Heart—each a well-thought-out decision—and it's worked well.

And we certainly can't thank her enough for that. Sometimes having four kids in four different schools was tough. . . . Vacations were not necessarily the easiest thing to arrange, nor were the pickups and the drop-offs. But my wife worked it out, and I give her a boatload of credit for that.

All marriages are a wild ride, but for my parents, it seems like their sustained level of mutual love and respect conquered all. A good marriage is a lot of luck too. You go into it with the attitude that you're there until death do you part. There's a lot of dumb luck in just picking the right partner. Some of us are blessed with finding the right person. Certainly, my parents were prime examples.

Love and luck made for a happy marriage for my parents, even though they lived very separate lives when you think about it in terms of their interests. But they supported each other through thick and thin and the ups and downs.

They also had many blessings that contribute to a happy life. No health problems until recently, but also, they were able to afford things that have allowed them to live a passion-filled life.

I see more lessons in marriage in Popi and Dita: my grandmother, divorced when divorce was a no-no. Then meeting Popi, marrying him, and finding a new father for my mother. That's luck and love again.

Even with that divorce, my family overall respects marriage as an institution. I think they showed that they respected it. So, I look at my parents as being blessed first and foremost, and also as people respectful of and committed to marriage.

Marriages have their up and downs, but I don't think there's a better way of going through life than with the sound foundation that comes from a happy home and happily married parents. When you have this—it's almost like an engine of a car, if you will—you turn it on. It idles; it's nice, just sitting there. How do you go through life not knowing whether it's going to work when you turn the key? It's nice to know that it's there and it's working. You can have excitement in a marriage and have surprises and great times and spontaneity, but the engine of the marriage is this ability to work together so that it just idles, this nice little thing, and I think that takes two to tango. And certainly I see that in Mom and Dad.

What I see more clearly in Mom over the years is her drive. She's driven to be the best that she can be, if you look at everything that she does. I call her home a walk through Shangri-la. It's just exquisite. But Heaven forbid you go over there when she's throwing a party. Unbelievably crazy. When she's going to throw a party, she throws a party.

Look at Edition Farm—it's just unbelievable. A showplace. There isn't a piece of hay out of place. And this barn is totally green. She put a lot of money into solar.

She's as traditional and disciplined as she can be. There's kind of this wonderful mixture of characteristics that basically allows something like an Edition Farm to blossom, allows a Waccabuc to look as it looks. She spares no expense. She notices everything. She works tirelessly.

She considers it a reflection of her, of her integrity and hard work. She's so proud of it. Every day she's basically putting herself out there for review. And she doesn't want to disappoint. So, I think that's part of what makes her special to me. She has my back, that lioness attitude. I never was really a kid who was out of line, so I think my relationship with Mom has always been kind of a steady one.

I see new things lately, vulnerability linked to what's going on with Dad. It's interesting to see the way she's reacted to my dad's health. I don't think she likes to admit or show that she is afraid.

When you're in a foxhole together, you learn a little bit more about people. And with Mom right now, she's in a foxhole in terms of her relationship with her husband. There's a new mortality aspect, a frailness. There's a change of expectations of the golden years. Some of that tinged with sadness. Some of that tinged with anger, frustration. There are all sorts of different dynamics.

I've always said she's less Florence Nightingale than she is Nurse Ratched. She is not necessarily the one that is going to take care of every little bedpan and do other stuff. That's just not the way she is with her husband. She may give a shot to a horse. She may do all sorts of things for a horse, but for her husband, it's a different story. It's a very different dynamic.

You see these things as they manifested themselves in the last eighteen months. She needs to live her life, for her identity, for her emotional well-being, for her health, for her zest. She needs that.

And then on the other hand, you have the husband, the ailing husband who has issues getting around and all sorts of things that demand time: needs, physical needs, presence—not just calls, but you need to be there physically.

And that is not something that is easy to do for a non-sedentary, very active, constantly-pursuing-a-passion person. It just doesn't happen. And watching that dynamic take place is interesting.

I've always said, until you walk a mile in their shoes, you can't judge. And I think that whole scenario adds a very, very interesting dynamic to Mom's life and how she is facing one of the truly scariest periods ever for her.

MARK ON MOM

(written in 2019)

MY EARLIEST MEMORY OF MY MOM, PREDICTABLY, INVOLVED A HORSE. I can only assume it was someone's birthday party, and there was a pony present for pony rides. I have only the vaguest memory of it, but it was in the circle in front of Dita and Popi's house at Hilltop Place, in Rye. It was a white pony, though to me it looked more like a giant horse. I was very young, likely in my early "Nordic" days, when my hair was white blond. I was wearing a red coat and had on galoshes (welly-type boots). I remember Mom lifting me up and onto the horse and telling me to hold on to the saddle. I don't know if it was a western saddle, but that might've made sense for children's pony rides.

Memories of Mom were mostly moments, usually stills. One of the earliest I remember was when we watched Apollo 11 lift off from Cape Kennedy, and even more vividly was the blastoff from the lunar lander later that month (however, looking through You-Tube, the video image that matches my mental memory is that of the Apollo 17).

My earliest memory of my dad was in the late summer of 1968; it was at the house we were renting on Long Island, and Dad kissed me goodbye as he left for work in the city. I remember The Beatles playing on the radio, and I was sitting on the floor playing with blocks of some sort. (Mom and Dad had rented the house at Five Chimneys to a production company for several months that summer, for the filming of *Goodbye, Columbus*.)

Mom was always doing things with us and for us. The only times I remember otherwise were the rare trips Mom and Dad took early on in their years of family life, mainly skiing vacations in the late 1960s and early 1970s, and those were in the months before or after the New England ski season. I distinctly remember them going away to someplace called Zermatt.

But the vast majority of my memories of Mom were (and, to this day, continue to be) about horses. Either helping us practice and prepare for horse shows, travel to and from horse shows, or doing everything under the sun during the horse shows. I also remember most fondly when Mom would take us to the movies. Because we were all athletes, and because the horses are a 24/7 commitment, going to a movie was a rare treat. But even there, Mom would teach. With the exception of the annual holiday tradition of a movie at Radio City Music Hall followed by the Christmas Spectacular, Mom wouldn't take us to mindless popular movies. She'd take us to what today we'd call small independent and "art house" films. The earliest of these I remember was *Walkabout*. Not your standard kids' movie, but the fact that to this day I can picture the girl and her young brother crossing the Australian outback with the help of an aboriginal man is testament to the impact it had on me. Mom's love of movies led my brother Andy and I to get into the movie industry ourselves.

I'll never forget the trips home from horse shows, which invariably were at night. One especially memorable one was coming home from the Pennsylvania National Horse Show in Harrisburg. It was after the AHSA Medal National Finals, a class that started around 5:00 a.m. that morning. We left for home in the van at around 6:00 p.m., Mom driving, me helping her stay awake. So that I could help her, I closed my eyes as we were pulling out of the show grounds. Mom immediately said, "Time to wake up."

"I wasn't sleeping," I said, "I only just closed my eyes! What's wrong?"

"We're home!"

I think Mom's most impressive characteristic is one that likely came from Dita and Popi; that no matter what, everything must look neat and clean and well maintained. While many, if not most, would see this as some sort of neat-freak complex, it's actually more practical: If it's clean and well presented, it's far less likely to fail due to neglect. This goes for everything from the barn to the tack to the horses themselves. Our horses were some of the best looking and well presented coming off the truck, in the stall, in the barn, and of course up at the ring. The reasoning was simple: If the horse is clean, it's going to be more comfortable and any underlying health issues will be easier to spot.

I'm sure many have thought of this as her being a perfectionist, but Mom has never been a perfectionist. She always said the same as Dad: "Just go out there and do your absolute best. If you do that, then it doesn't matter if you don't win, you'll still know you did all you could on that day."

Mom was always there for us, no matter what, unconditionally. Later in life that unconditional support came with more direct expression of her opinions and desires, and to the faint of heart that may have seemed to be more of a my-way-or-the-highway stance. Rather, she'd tell you in no uncertain terms what she felt about your situation, mainly if she didn't agree with it. But so long as you accepted her right to feel the way she did, that never kept her from being there to support you, even if it seemed contradictory to her own opinions. This reality, I think, has helped me and my siblings grow as adults and as parents, and we are all the better for her example.

I honestly can't think of any bad advice I received from Mom or Dad. What I remember most are the times when I did things contrary to Mom and Dad's advice that proved the correctness of their advice. "Never overtighten your bindings." That's a piece of advice I willfully disregarded one Saturday just after college. Having had my ski come off the two previous races due to racing through rough, rutted gates, I was determined not to "chatter out" of my bindings on that day. So I cranked my bindings as tight as they would go. When I fell after hooking a gate with my right ski, my bindings did release, but not before my leg broke in five places. Lesson (re)learned!

Mom and Dad certainly didn't have an Ozzie and Harriet relationship, because they were both strong-willed people, but it was that mutual strength of will that kept them together while some of their friends began to divorce (a serious no-no in their minds). Having observed Mom and Dad's marriage, as well as my aunts and uncles and my grandparents, Dita and Popi, I knew that the most important part of a marriage is the friendship at its core, rather than the outward appearance of stability and strength. I married my best friend, Heather, after nearly eleven years dating. Ten years after we married I had to make the hardest of decisions—to maintain the marriage at the cost of the friendship or to sacrifice the marriage in order to stay friends. To me it was a no-brainer. I love Heather to death, always have and always will, and I was not willing to lose that relationship just to keep a marriage together. Heather and I decided to separate, and though we both regret it not working out, our relationship is closer and stronger than ever. While I can't say I'll never remarry, I don't see myself ever meeting someone as special as Heather ever again.

My relationship with Mom nowadays revolves mostly around the horses. I'm happy to help her out there, because the hours are much better than they were when I was a kid taking care of show horses, and because most of my help now is more of the technical-support type, which I'm comfortable with. I also love hanging with Mom at the track and at the sales ground, as I continue to learn about both the racing and breeding aspects. As was the case with Dad, I love handicapping the racehorses, and continually face the limitations of my knowledge. One thing I have learned for sure (and have proven this twice in discreet experiments) is that I'm a "cooler" when it comes to racehorses. That means that no matter how likely a particular horse is to win a race, if I were to place a bet on that horse, it wouldn't pay off on that bet. Hence, I find I make the most money when I pick horses but don't place bets on those picks. Of course, it doesn't help that my main criteria for picking a horse is if I like the name or if the horse is a gray (there are few gray racehorses, but they seem to do well far more often than the other colors).

Mom and I are able to stay close because after Dad and Debby's deaths, I chose not to look for a full-time classroom teaching position, so I could be available to travel back to New York on a moment's notice if Mom needed me. In 2010, after leaving a tenure-track position at a college in the mountains of North Carolina, I knew I didn't have it in me to go from the unexpectedly cold climate of the Blue Ridge Mountains back north to the cold and icy (and long) winters of New York without at least a year or two of sunshine, so I move to Los Angeles in late summer 2010 "to get warm again." As of this writing, that "year or two" has stretched to nine years! But this summer will be my last in the California sun for a while, as I plan to move back to Rye. Mom will be stepping back from overseeing the farm and downsizing her breeding operation. While Edition Farm will continue, as before when she sold or retired the last of the show horses, she'll now sell most of her broodmares. But I don't see her ever giving up the horses completely. It's my firm belief that the horses are what kept Mom alive after the double blow of Dad and Debby passing, and I believe that if she did get out of the horses completely, she'd be unlikely to live beyond a year. We all need something to live for, and while my siblings and I have families of our own to keep us engaged, Mom's core family has become the horses at Edition Farm. Take that away, and you take away her lifeblood.

VIVI ON MOM

(written in 2009)

My earliest memory of my mom was more of a sense memory than a visual memory. I have early memories of the way she smelled, and how it felt when she held me. I remember how her body felt.

These must have been special moments, as my mother rarely just sat idle! She was always on the move and was busy all the time. I remember, in particular, going over to my grandparents' house on weekends to go swimming in the summertime. I have a real sense memory of putting my head in my mom's lap and listening to her, my grandmother, and my aunt Gladys speak Spanish. That was our family's version of "spelling" in front of the kids, so that stories could be told that weren't necessarily appropriate or necessary for little ears to hear.

I remember that she used to braid my long hair every day. I remember the feeling when she stroked my hair. The memory of Mom's touch is strong for me. She liked to pat my head; I think that was a big thing for my mom.

Because I'm the fifth and youngest child, I think a lot of my early visual memories have to do with my siblings, rather than my parents. I remember all of my siblings coming in after school one day to say hi to me. I was standing in a crib, holding on to the railing, and they were all wearing their school uniforms. And then Mom was standing with them. I don't know if that's a real memory or a dream.

My mom was very quiet. With five kids, it's hard to believe that she barely ever raised her voice, but she really didn't. That's not to say she didn't get frustrated or angry with us, but if she did, she would get quieter. Maybe I remember her touch so strongly for that reason.

The childhood memories that stand out in my mind are also memories of activity. We were all very active. There was constant motion; everybody was involved in sports. We also had the stable and the horses, so I have very early memories of that routine. There was predictability and consistency to my childhood routine, a dependable rhythm in my days, and it was all outside, outside, outside.

As the youngest, I also remember the feeling of always being a little behind. The youngest generally never feels quite strong enough, fast enough, or smart enough to keep up with the older siblings.

The horses hold strong memories for me personally. Horses are big animals, but they're quiet. I feel, in some ways, that there was a very contemplative element to all the activities; being with the horses can be a comfortable kind of solitude. It was very comfortable for me to commune with these silent, special animals. The horse has an incredible capacity to connect and communicate nonverbally, and I felt a deep connection with them.

Several specific stories and memories also stand out. I may not remember these details myself, but they have been woven into the tales and myths of our family.

One time—I must have been about three—we were in Amagansett. We went to the beach with another family, and my dad was driving the Mustang convertible. I watched my dad drive from my position in the back seat, and I was fascinated.

Apparently, my fascination led to experimentation! Later on, I got in the car by myself and thought it would be fun to drive like Dad. I shifted it into neutral; it was parked on a hill, and it started to roll.

And my dad—again, this is not something I remember, but something I've been told—just jumped headfirst into the car! He jumped in through the window, hit his eye or head, and stopped the car from rolling down the hill. It was one of those unbelievable parental adrenaline moments.

Another one of those moments involved my mother. I was young and decided that it would be a smart idea to do a "sailor dive" into the shallow end of our pool. That's a dive in which you hold your hands behind your back, like a dancing sailor. Our pool had a pebbly, rough surface on the bottom. So in I went, hands behind my back, and sure enough, I hit my head on the bottom of the pool.

And so I emerged from the dive with a scraped head, and therefore, I was covered in blood, looking like something out of the movie *Carrie*, I'm sure. I screamed and my mom came running from the stable. She came to the edge of the pool and pulled me out by my shoulders. Now, I'm about nine years old at this point, and I wasn't much shorter than Mom. Yet that parental adrenaline kicked in, and she picked me up, which she hadn't done in a long time. She must have been about my age now, about forty-four.

She not only picked me up, she carried me at a full-tilt run across the entire yard at Five Chimneys. I was scared to death, because clearly, I was way too big for her to be holding me.

My brother Andrew came running out, and she gave me to him. They both got me into a car and to the hospital. So, both parents were able to rise to the occasion in a crisis!

I will never forget those two incidents. Mom and Dad each had a superhero reaction.

But the memories that stand out most clearly in my mind are the times when we were all together, because that was not something that happened all the time. My oldest brother is eight years older than I, and was involved in sports. He was in second grade when I was born, so there were not so many times that I recollect that we were all together.

So, the family gatherings stand out. Like those times at my grandparents' pool, special dinners around the dining room table, special occasions, and holidays. We all had our birthday dinners at Manero's; that was our birthday restaurant. The waiters would come over and sing their special happy birthday song. Those traditions and memories stay with me because they were special.

Church was another occasion for the family group to be to-gether, although when we went with my dad, it was a unique ap-proach: the Harry Malloy "drive-through Communion plan." My mom's more of a rule-follower than my dad; with her, we attended the entire Mass.

Dad, however, would pull into the parking lot, park illegally, and we'd scoot in the side door quietly, just in time to blend into the line, get Communion, come back, say our prayers, and then get a little nudge out the door because we wanted to get to the bakeshop before everybody else.

So, while family was very important, the reality was that with five kids spread over a wide age range, group activities were not easy to find.

My parents believed in letting each of us develop into the per-son that we were going to become. I think they both have a strong sense of faith, and they both have a strong sense of themselves, each of them.

Both parents shared their passions with us. Dad's a passionate golfer, and he clearly has shared that with all of his sons. Mom shared her love of horses with us.

I think that my mom raised me, as a horsewoman, to realize from the beginning the commitment that you had to have to be a true horseperson. I think she exemplified the ideal: the incredible respect for, engagement with, and very subtle understanding of our horses.

She taught me the basics of what it means to be a good horse-woman, in the doing and in the understanding that this is not some-thing to be taken lightly, and that animals are not just worthy and deserving of our respect, but that it's imperative that we respect them. I truly understood what it took to take good care of a horse or an animal, and I've kept that throughout my life.

Debby is cut from the same cloth as my mother. I think she would, and does, spend as much time in the stable, around horses, as she possibly can, because I think she also has a total passion for it. She and my mom are examples of two women who know what they are passionate about and have followed that and been true to that.

In thinking about it, I am still struck by how special it was to have the opportunity to have our horses living with us. And I can't imagine a better model of a horsewoman than my mother . . . or my sister.

Participating in the sport that was my mom's passion had some tricky elements to it, because she wasn't my trainer. She made deci-sions based on what she thought was best in general; she is a much better horsewoman than I, so looking back, I think she made the right decisions.

But it also was kind of tricky, because she couldn't undermine my trainers either. She was very gentle. She would advise, not com-mand.

Both of my parents love to ski, so up we went to Stratton every weekend, a four-hour drive each way. It wasn't really until I got to college that I realized how lucky I was to have had that oppportunity.

One year, when I went back to grade school after Thanksgiving break—we always had Thanksgiving at my grandparents'—I was asked what we had for Thanksgiving at our house. And I said, "Well, we had black beans and rice, suckling pig, and turkey." Everybody looked at me confused!

But I just figured everybody had that. As I've gotten older, I realize how precious these memories and traditions are, and what a treasure it is to have family that passes down cultural traditions. It's interesting how each of my parents interpreted traditions for themselves.

My dad and mom were both schooled by Dominican nuns, a pretty strict order. Yet they approached—"interpreted"—their religious practices very differently. I find it interesting, the way they've interpreted and internalized their traditions for themselves, and what that says about them as individuals. They are both distinct individuals, and yet they came together, married, raised a family of five kids, and have been married for fifty-three years.

It's interesting to see how they made that work, how they complement each other, and how they have worked as a team—especially since they've become empty nesters.

I think my mother's most impressive characteristic is her passion. Her passion and her tenacity, her drive, her faith, her ability to be inspired constantly. She, herself, is inspiring; she describes herself as the eternal student. She is never resting because she's constantly inquiring. There's always more to know.

I think that's incredibly impressive. It would be so easy to rest on your laurels. But my mom has something within her that drives her to keep exploring, keep figuring things out. She does not settle. She's constantly pushing herself to learn more, to be better by her own yardstick, and be true to herself.

Mom considers herself an expert in certain things, but she doesn't do it in a way that's overbearing. More like a gentle instructor, very gentle.

Mom and Dad allowed all of us to become the people that we are. They have said at different times, "It's fascinating for us to see who you've become."

As her daughter, when I was growing up, what made Mom impressive also made it harder for me, as the youngest, to keep up. To have a parent who's so very sure of who she is was, at times, hard to integrate. We also share the same name. I think that had an impact on me.

In my adult life, I have always been very mindful of who I've chosen as my teachers, for whatever it is that I am interested in understanding, knowing more about, learning, or applying in my life. I think that comes from my mom in a certain way. I think that it was very important to me to grow into a sense of myself as my own woman, in charge of my own evolution, development, and learning.

I've stepped out of my mom's shadow as I've gotten older, as I've chosen the course and the path of my life. When we were younger, we had more direction and routines, of course. There was an understood expectation of responsibility. When you're a rider, you must put the horse first, and there are certain things that must be done. We all shared the load, and everyone had chores, and we all contributed. It was definitely a feeling of being part of a whole.

I think it imbued in us a real sense of responsibility for ourselves. My mother generally didn't have to ride us at all in terms of getting stuff done. She set the bar at a certain place and said, "I know you can do this." And we did.

I think that's a big thing for a parent. I now have two young kids. It's hard to muzzle yourself sometimes; hard to let them fall and get up, make their mistakes and learn their lessons.

My parents were authoritative when it was appropriate at a certain age. I think my parents were kind of old-school in that there was a gender split between them regarding their involvement in our activities. Dad spent more time with my brothers, particularly Andrew and Kenneth, because they golfed. Debby, Mark, and I were involved in riding, and so spent more time with my mother.

I think the competitiveness in our family is also interesting, because everybody comes to that from a different place. I think my mom is very comfortable competing, with horses and dogs. She likes ranking herself. Where am I at? Where do I want to be? It's not about beating other people. It's about her own yardstick. She doesn't try to force that on anybody else.

Mom did encourage us to focus. She didn't want us to try to do too many things. "Don't try to do too much, because you will create a conflict." What she was trying to say to me was, "You have a huge commitment with the riding. Don't overextend yourself, because you'll be jack-of-all-trades, master of none."

I think she was worried, because as I got older, I wanted to do other things and still ride, and she was afraid I'd be stretched too thin. We got in fights a lot around that period of time, when I was a teen.

And now, as a mom myself, with a schedule that's crazy, I think about that issue of overscheduling children, and I understand my mother's concern. It's important to decline; it's important to say no, and not jump on every bandwagon.

I find that I have become very consistent, which is very important to me; I want my children to have the same consistency that my parents gave me.

I've always been fascinated by family and by children, and understanding what makes people tick. Maybe because I spent more time with horses growing up, and certainly a lot of time around some people who could have used some additional insight!

I got my master's degree in social work, and I practiced for about six years in a community mental health center with families and children who struggled with behavioral, emotional, or cognitive issues.

My practice left me little time for horses, but after a while, I started to volunteer at a therapeutic horseback riding program. That experience allowed me to return to the horses in a way that integrated my earlier experiences with my clinical training.

Bringing that deeply innate, yet also learned, sense of understanding the horses together with trying to understand the rider's needs, and then letting that relationship happen—I really enjoyed that part of my practice, because it's not about winning. It's not about the competition. It is about everything that leads up to that, starting with your relationship with the horse on a very elemental level. It was a great opportunity to see that in action, with adults, with autistic kids who are nonverbal, or with kids who have a very difficult time in any kind of social interaction. To be able to facilitate that and watch that magic happen . . . well, there's just nothing better.

I think my relationship with my mom is now richer, especially because becoming a mom myself has shifted some perceptions I had about my mom. I now have a sense of what it takes and what it took. We are different in some of our choices and in the way we parent. We're different individuals. My mother did her best to make sure that she imbued the most important values and beliefs in us. I think that is what I truly admire.

I understand that my mom has lived during a time when being a mother—a devoted mother, a full-time parent—and following your dream was incredibly difficult. And she never complained. I think it's huge. I think that she has been true to herself as a mom, and she's been true to herself as a woman, at a time when it just wasn't being done.

My mom knows in her heart what she thinks is right and she goes with it, even if nobody else is doing it. That is incredibly impressive to me. Given the social context in which my mom was raised, got married, and started a family, even more impressive. Even more out of the box.

In some ways, she was two people. She took all of her roles—wife, mother, and horsewoman—very, very much to heart and very seriously. She has her own internal yardstick for achievement. She stayed very true to that. She really is an earnest person. And when she could have complained, and she could have boo-hooed, and she could have reprioritized, she didn't. . . . She just made it happen.

My mom is just so impressive in that way, yet she never toots her own horn. Every once in a while, her big deal is that "My horse won, I'm so excited!" And "Oh, I'm going to get an award." So low-key, yet what's amazing is to realize that in the past five, ten years, she has made herself into an outstanding breeder, from zero; she knew zilch about Thoroughbred racing.

She trained herself, chose her teachers, chose the people that she felt were going to be able to guide her in a way that really felt right, and moved along. Certainly, working with my dad, but she had the vision, like having a new career at fifty!

She trusts her gut so much, and well she should. She takes in new information, but boy, does she have that solid gut, and she goes with it. It's her heart.

As I matured, I turned around one day and started seeing my mom as a separate person, and I think that was a big thing for me. And I think she very, very patiently waited for that. She did. I think what happened for me was I just looked at my mom through a different lens than I had in the past.

I realized that, deep down, she is an amazing woman who has done her best with everything, and she's tried to stay true to herself in the face of a lot of obstacles—social, cultural, timing, number of children—that I don't have to face.

I really started to see her differently. This is who she is. My mom has been true, consistent; what you see is what you get. She was sort of patiently waiting for me to come around, saying, "We're not doing horses anymore, and you're not doing the chores in the barn. You've got your own life to lead." It made a big difference.

I think it was at a certain point when I was just sort of ready to really fully take responsibility for who I was, and for my life and my choices.

Geographical distance has been a reality since college. I think I'm in the right place, in a good place. I think it's been a good move for me, and it continues to be the place where I need to be in terms of living my life, raising my family.

I think it's hard on my mom. I know it is. Not just me, but my sister, Debby, too. I don't think that's what she envisioned. I think she always said, "What happened? Everybody said, 'Have daughters. They'll stay with you. You have sons, they'll go away, but daughters will stay close.'"

So I answer, "Well, you gave us a whole bunch of room, Mom. And we are better people for it!"

HARRY ON VIVIEN

(In 2008 Carol Makovich, a friend of a friend, spoke with Harry about his reflections on life with me.)

CAROL MAKOVICH: Talk to me about Vivien. Tell me about your wife.

HARRY MALLOY: Well, what would you like to know?

CM: Well, you say she's been a wonderful wife and mother.

HM: Yes, definitely.

CM: Do you remember your first impression when you first met her?

CM: First time I ever met her I thought that she was probably the ugliest person I have ever seen. She had just been in a play at Wellesley, a Shakespearean play. She was a date of my friend, who asked me if I would go up there and double-date with him because his date would only go out on a double date. I used to call him Boley (Bolivar). We were both officers in the navy; he was the second division officer.

So, we drove up to Wellesley, Massachusetts. And I met this girl there by the name of Cochran, who was Viv's friend and lived in her dorm.

CM: Do you remember her first name?

HM: Lois? In fact, I just heard today that Lois's husband died last week. I met Lois—to go ahead a little bit—at Viv's fiftieth class reunion at Wellesley a few years ago. Anyway, we went out and that was that.

The first date we went to a bar in the neighborhood. And then we had another date; I wanted to see what this Vivien looked like in a real face. We went to a nice place this time, I think it was John Lombardo's restaurant, which was close to Wellesley.

Anyway, we went out and Boley tried to make a pass at Viv in the back of the car. I told Boley to get out of the car. He got out of the car, and that was that. We drove back to Newport, where our ship was stationed. And then we went north.

We went up to Scotland and Ireland and Spain, all over the place. We were gone for six, eight months, something like that. It was during the Korean War, but we were never over there.

When we came back to Newport, I said to the captain, "Phil, I'm going to go home for a while. I'm a little tired; I'll be back." And I drove home and I get to Larchmont, New York, and I got a call from this friend of mine, Peter Ernst, who was on the *Wasp* at the time. He said, "Listen, Harry, can you get a date? I got this girl that I'm taking out here."

I said, "Sure, I haven't seen you in a year or two, sure." So I called this girl, Ann Harmon. She was a beautiful girl, a lovely lady, and a girl I used to take out quite often.

Ann said that she couldn't make it. Now, there are several stories about this, which I don't have any idea about. But anyway, she said, "There's a girl at Westchester Country Club who was asking about you, Vivien Goodman."

So I said, "Well, I don't remember her."

She said, "You met her at Wellesley College."

And then I said, "Oh, yes," and I don't remember whether I remembered the first face or the second face."

But I gave her a call and I said, "Viv, it's Harry Malloy. Pete Ernst, a good friend of mine from down the block, is going back to the *Wasp*, and they're going somewhere tomorrow and I haven't seen the guy in two years, so he said he'd like to meet us."

I said, "Would you be interested in going out tonight? I know it's late, you know, but I just got back myself." I was still in my uniform. She said yes, and I said, "Okay, I'll pick you up." And I didn't know where she lived—she lived in Rye.

I found my way up to where she lived, and Sylvia, who worked for the Goodmans, answered the door. I walked into the living room, sort of like we have here, and I walked into this den and the whole family was there. I said, "Uh-oh." There's got to be a problem.

Anyway, we went out that night and we had a good time. She was a lovely woman and she was very pretty, very beautiful. And I asked her that night to go sailing with me the next day. I used to do a lot of sailing for many years, and I really loved it.

We were racing that week down at Manhasset Bay Yacht Club. It was an annual race. This fellow, Paul Ryan, and I had an International, and we were going to race it. So I told Viv, "Well, this isn't exactly sailing, it's racing, and I'll tell you what to do and where to go and what to move, you know."

Viv said yes. So I picked her up around seven in the morning because we had to drive all the way to Larchmont. We had breakfast or coffee or something at the club there. Paul came over and we went out—I think my brother was a crew on it, and one of Paul's relatives was also a crew, because it was a thirty-five-foot boat and you need a lot of crew.

Viv was sitting down below. And I asked her, "Do you enjoy sailing?" And she said that she did. Well, I really felt sorry for her because there are no heads on boats like that, and to sit down below, it really wasn't very comfortable. Especially when you're racing; you're just moving around and, you know, it's difficult. Anyway, that was the last time that Viv ever went racing on a sailboat with me or anyone else.

It was strange. But that was the first time I really got to know Viv, and we started going out after that.

CM: In spite of the boat race?

HM: Yes. That was a crazy race. You've got to be the first boat out of the harbor going toward the lighthouse to win, because everybody inside the harbor is jammed up.

CM: Was it love at first sight?

HM: Um, I don't know. That's a very good question. I'd been out with a lot of ladies, you know. I don't know, what is love at first sight? I have no idea. It could have been, because I mean, you know, it just grew.

CM: And what was it that made you start to think: This could be my wife?

HM: Ooh, that's a good question. If I had to tie back in my mind somewhere, I could probably tell you if I wanted to, but I don't know what it was. I mean, I was getting older. I was twenty-six when I got out of the navy.

I know that I definitely thought she was just, you know, really something, the most special thing I'd ever seen and ever been associated with. And she was really a nice person. She was just a wonderful gal.

I just remember one day I asked her to marry me. I told her that I wanted to speak to her father, and she said, "What?"

I said, "Well, I want to speak to your father, because I'm in love with you and I want to marry you. I'm serious."

I guess she said something to her mother, who said something to her father. I remember her father, Andy, used to have a little office off of his bedroom, which was a really nice little place. But Viv's younger brother, Eddie, was running around, up and down.

I went upstairs and Andy said, "Eddie, get out of here!"

So I asked him for his daughter's hand in marriage and he said, "Absolutely." It was very nice. And that was the beginning, and then from there on, you probably know the rest.

CM: Well, I know quite a bit.

HM: I'm sure you do.

CM; But I'm interested in your viewpoint. How long did you know Vivien when you married?

HM: That's a good question. . . . Maybe a year, something like that. I think we got engaged around June or July.

CM: You had a chance to get to know each other a little then.

HM: Yes, we got married in January, so we knew each other over a year.

CM: Looking back at the first few years of marriage, is there any particular story or memory that's close to your heart or brings a smile to your face?

HM: Well, after the wedding we went to Nassau on our honeymoon, thanks to our friend, a golfer named Tommy Goodwin. Tommy was a very good player; he was a New York State champion at twenty-five years old, and twenty-five years later he was the New York State champion again.

Tommy was married to a girl from Nassau and her family lived in Nassau. They have quite a club there, a famous old club, the Bahamas Country Club, which was right on the water. You looked across to Paradise Island and there was nothing on it.

There was one house on Paradise Island, and I think it belonged to a very wealthy family. But you couldn't get over there; there was no bridge. You had to take a boat if you were invited. Anyway, we went out there and I think we made our first child on Nassau, because Andrew was born in October of 1957 and we were married in January. So, that was pretty good.

CM: It really was.

HM: We had a great life, it was terrific. We lived in an apartment down on the corner of Larchmont and New Rochelle for a couple of years. Then, Vivien was going to have another baby, and I said that we're going to have to move because we didn't have enough room.

Her folks lived up in Rye and they had lived there for a long time. We went up there and looked around and found a very nice house in a place called Indian Village. There are five streets named after Indian tribes. Ours was 26 Mohawk Street.

It was a nice area. The houses were built about 1928. It was really one of the first group of homes ever built in the East. But they were lovely places, and everybody lives on a quarter of an acre—they were nice.

Anyway, we thought it was plenty of room there. Now we have two children, and I don't know, I think it must have been the Catholic religion, now we're going to have another baby. And 1963 comes around, we'd owned the house for maybe four years, five years, something like that. And I sold the house for double what I had paid for it.

I happened to run into somebody who told me that they had a house for sale, a big house. It was twenty-eight rooms, and when I say "rooms" I'm talking about twelve-foot ceilings, big windows; it was huge, with ten acres of property.

We went up, we looked at it, it was beautiful. As a matter of fact, the fellow's grandfather, who we bought it from, lives right around the corner here, on Hunt Lane in Waccabuc. I used to be able to hit a golf ball there from here.

Anyway, we bought this place and all of our kids grew up there and that's where our interest in horses started. Well, Viv rode horses all of her life, but I did it twice. I got thrown off both times, both on the same day. My wife said, "Honey, get back on."

And I said, "Honey, I don't know whether you've ever played baseball, but there is a saying in baseball, three strikes and you're out, and I've got two against me now. That's it. I'm walking back." And I did. I smacked the horse on the you-know-what, and walked back. That was fun, though.

CM: So horseback riding wasn't for you. When did you start playing golf?

HM: That's a long story. A friend of mine asked me if I liked to play golf, and I said, "I don't. I played once in the navy, at the Newport Country Club, and I shot 188."

He said, "You're kidding. Come on, we'll go up and play Saxon Woods Golf Course." And Saxon Woods is very close to Larchmont.

We got there at six in the morning, we teed up at eleven o'clock. As a matter of fact, a guy I graduated from high school with, who was with us, was the assistant pro, and he couldn't do any better than eleven o'clock.

We got in at seven o'clock at night. And I said, "Thirteen hours, this is not my game." So, I don't know whether it was on Thursday or Friday, but the three of us were on leave from the service. I was down at the Larchmont Yacht Club that weekend, talking to Corney Shields, an older man who was a really great sailor.

Corney was a member of Winged Foot Golf Club. I told him that I had never been there, but I'd like to join, and asked him if he would sponsor me. He said, "Sure."

So I asked him, "Well, what do I do?"

Corney said, "Nothing. I'll take care of it."

And believe it or not, within two weeks I get a phone call from the club, telling me that I was a member. Ninety-five dollars a year because I was a junior member.

You know, that was the deal. Holy Moses. And that's where I started to play golf, and that's where I brought Viv up, and she started to learn and she was very good also. But then she started to have babies, so she hadn't played in, well, she hadn't played in a long time.

And then she got interested in the riding bit again with the kids. So, I don't think she really started to play golf again seriously until we came up to Waccabuc. We moved here about twenty years ago now. Now she's very good again, and me, I can't even walk for Christ's sake.

CM: When did you and Vivien get interested in skiing? I know it was a big part of your family life.

HM: Well, in 1957 or '58, we went up to Manchester, Vermont, and skied Bromley Mountain. We enjoyed it; it was fun. We took the kids up in '61 or '62, and we were skiing with a guy who was on the ski patrol at Bromley. And I said, "Darn it, aren't there any other mountains around this area?" He told us that they'd just opened one up about twelve miles away.

So the next morning, we drove up a five-mile dirt road to

Stratton Mountain. There were three trails and two lifts. And we went into the original base lodge. They had a big porch out in front and we walked out, looked up at the Suntanner trail, and there was one single chairlift going up. Over on the left-hand side there was another trail, a very short, flat trail for the kids.

Then we went into the Bear's Den, the bar in the lodge. I used to drink martinis in those days. I ordered a martini and I said to Viv, "Honey, I like this place. It is really nice." As it turns out, a guy from Greenwich, Connecticut, whose son went to school with our kids at Whitby, was building condominiums there.

And there was nothing there at that time. I mean, there were three trails and two lifts. Now, I hate to even . . . we went up there two or three years ago, and I couldn't believe it. I mean, the place was a zoo.

CM: I've been to Stratton, I know what you're talking about.

HM: Now they have almost one hundred trails and ten or eleven lifts and a gondola and the whole nine yards.

Anyway, we wanted a place there. I had made some investments with a friend from Winged Foot Golf Club. So, I made a killing, I don't know how. I don't even know how real it was, but I kept getting checks, so I said, that's fine, that's wonderful. Putting it in the bank. I went up and I bought one of the condominiums from Tom Cholnoky, who was the builder.

It was in the first group on Birch Hill Road. You could actually see Stratton Mountain from Birch Hill. I had told Tom that I wanted an end unit, but I got one right in the middle. I told him that I would sell it to a good friend, Joe Kelnberger. Joe and I were roommates at Villanova and he loves to ski. So, I sold it to him and bought the end unit on Moose Maple Road the next year.

And believe it or not, we still own it and the kids use it and the grandchildren use it, and they love it. But that mountain has gotten so popular.

CM: There must have been a lot going on during those years with the children. What words would you use to describe Vivien as a young wife and mother?

HM: Wonderful. She was the best. You don't get any better than that. That's the only thing I can say. I mean, she was just wonderful with the kids, and I was in New York City working most of the time, and she was great. She was just marvelous. We didn't have any help—well, a woman came in once in a while.

But she was terrific. Plus, we're sitting in that huge home. I mean, I'm not kidding. That home must have been twelve thousand square feet: There were three stories. I liked it.

I used to mow the lawn with a tractor. And God forbid it should rain one day, because it would take me four days to mow the back lawn and the front lawn. In fact, our land was right where Purchase Street meets the Hutchinson River Parkway.

We owned all the way out on the dirt road right next to the parkway; we had ten acres all together. It was beautiful. As a matter of fact, Maria Cuomo and her husband, Kenneth Cole, own it now.

One day Maria and I were in at the same dentist. She asked me why we had named the house Five Chimneys. I told her, "Because it had five chimneys." And she said that it didn't have five chimneys now. And I said, "Well, it did when we were there."

Originally, I sold the house to a Hollywood producer, not to Maria and her husband. Anyway, I said, "Maria, can I come back and take a look?" So I drove in there and sure enough, the fifth chimney that had been over the kitchen area was gone. I couldn't believe it. I said, "I can't believe that they'd take that down."

We had planted a forest of white pines in the back—it was beautiful. You couldn't see any other houses. The producer had cut down all the trees; all the screening was gone, and you could see the houses behind us.

CM: Too bad for them.

HM: It's just awful. But those things happen.

CM: Does Vivien still surprise you after fifty years of marriage?

HM: Yes, yes. As a matter of fact, she scares me. She doesn't surprise me.

CM: In what way?

HM: She has really come into her own. I think she should have been president of the United States. She's gotten very political. And don't get me wrong, not political in the way that, you know, politics . . . she's involved in boards and things like that, and she's good at it, she really is.

Since our children have grown up and gone away, she's really gotten involved in a lot of things, particularly with the horses. We bought a small farm up in Dutchess County, which I'm sure she's told you about.

CM: I've seen it.

HM: That was my fault actually, because we had a horse up in Wallkill. . . . For the life of me, I don't even remember the name of the horse. It was January and we went up to see the horse where it was stabled.

He was just a baby horse. It was cold—January's cold—there was snow on the ground. And we drove into this, Jesus Christ, this place, it looked like a real dump. So we got out and we walked over. There's a guy standing in the barn. I said, "Could you tell us where our horse is?"

He said, "He's right here in the stall."

So I asked him, "When do you take her out?"

"Oh, we're not taking her out," he said.

I said, "Well, aren't baby horses supposed to be outside?"

He told me it was too icy. I said, "It's not that icy, I just walked in here. If I could walk in here anybody can walk in here."

After we looked at the horse, we got into the car, and while we were driving home, I said, "Honey, we should get a farm." That was probably the worst thing I've ever said. The worst—what is it?— one, two, three, four, five words: "We should get a farm."

So Viv's driving around looking at farms, and she said, "Oh, I found a great spot. Let's go see it." So we drove up, and here's this beautiful piece of property. And a very old house; it was 150 years old at the time, I think. There were two barns and a Dutch wind-mill. She said, "Honey, this is perfect."

The farm's name was Clay Haven. The owner, Henry Clay, had died; then his wife, Annette, died two years before the farm was put up for sale. There was a training track in the middle of the front field. Clay raised trotters; he was in the harness-racing business. His brother, Lucius Clay, the commander in chief of U.S. forces in Europe after World War II, was in charge of the Berlin airlift.

Anyway, I found out that the farm was in a trust and the trustee was Citibank. And as it turns out, I had just played golf at West-chester Country Club the Saturday before I found this out, with George Ross, an executive at Citibank. George was a golfer, and a golf nut. I liked him—he was a nice guy.

Then I talked to the lawyer who was a trustee of the farm at Citibank. After we finished our conversation, I got on the phone right away with George. I said, "George, I'm really interested in the Clay farm. I'd like you to help me out. You know, you're this guy's boss. So, tell him I'm serious, and I don't want to be taken to the cleaners."

George, I guess, spoke to the guy, and next time I got on the phone with him he said, "Oh, you know Mr. Ross?"

I said, "Yes, I do. Let me ask you a question: I know that the house is on the market for seven hundred. What is the best offer you've had so far?" He told me six-ninety. "Is that a good offer?" I asked.

He said, "Yes."

I said, "What is the next best offer you have?" He told me six-ten.

I said, "Is that a good offer?"

He said, "No."

I said, "Okay. I'm going to offer you six-fifty and I want you to come down, and we'll meet somewhere in the middle, wherever you want to meet me."

So, he said, "How about six-thirty-five?"

I said, "Done." It was all done on the phone in five minutes. And that's how Edition Farm began. Edition Farm was named after Viv's first horse, First Edition. And that's how that farm that you've seen began. We've put a couple of shekels into it.

CM: It's a showplace now.

HM: Yes. Viv has done a great job there, she really has. At one point we sold it, believe it or not; we sold it for about four years. The man who bought it was really a nice guy. He was with Salomon Brothers, a brokerage firm in New York.

Anyway, he put a half a million bucks into the place, mostly fixing the farmhouse. But unfortunately, he tore down some things, and I was not too excited about that. But as it turns out, it worked out all right. I bought it back from him five years later for the same price that I sold it to him for, and he had already put half a million bucks into it. It's a nice place and is worth a couple of shekels now.

CM: When you look back on your marriage, not a lot of people make it to fifty years—that's a wonderful accomplishment. What is it about your relationship with Vivien that has made this fifty-year relationship so successful?

HM: I guess because I love her so much, she can do nothing wrong. And we've had some arguments and so on and so forth. But whenever we've had an argument or anything like that, each one of us in his own way goes back and thinks about it: Is this the way it's supposed to be?

And because fifty years is a long time, and to go back over every year, we've had some tough times, and we've had some wonderful times. We've had more wonderful times than we've had bad times. It's a very long period.

And we've got wonderful children. We've had wonderful luck with everything. She's very lucky and I know I'm very lucky. And you know, even in Las Vegas, we walked away with more money than we went in with last time. That's not bad, but four days in Las Vegas is about all that I can take.

Anyway, now I think it's just the fact that Viv's a wonderful person and she's a really intelligent woman. As dumb as I am, she's intelligent. She seems to have, within the past twenty years, suddenly come into her own.

She never stops, that's the problem. I'm serious. Boy, I'll tell you—she's walking, she's playing with the dogs. She's got these dogs, I mean, this dog would have had a UDX [Utility Dog Excellent, an obedience title], which is pretty good. I mean, even *I* don't know what that means.

CM: I'm sure you do, but I have no idea. Now, when you look at your children, do any of them in particular remind you of Vivien, or are there characteristics you see in your children that you think are of Vivien?

HM: Yes. Debby is a Vivien. In fact, she's almost a little more than a Vivien. She's married to my son-in-law, who is older than I am, but he's a pretty successful guy in the equestrian world. But Debby is a tough Vivien.

Kenneth, well, there's a picture of Vivien at age four, and a picture of Kenneth at age four, and these two could be absolute twins: They looked exactly alike.

But all of our children are different. Andrew should've been a model or a movie actor. He's a beautiful kid, and a bright guy. He's a very good financial guy. Debby rides. She is one of the great riders. Kenneth, an athlete, is a terrific golfer. I mean, two handicap, zero.

One of Kenneth's boys, who just graduated from Brown, was the captain of the Brown golf team. Brought them up to third place in the Ivy League. He's got a younger brother, a junior at Iona, who's played number-one man on the golf team since he was a freshman. Kenneth's a great father, terrific. He's got four children, great kids.

I think Vivi is probably the smartest one in our whole family. She's married to a lawyer; they met at the University of Michigan. She got her master's degree in social work, and she does equine therapy with children.

CM: Therapeutic riding?

HM: Yes, and she's terrific at it. And then she and her husband,

Rich, have two children, a boy and a girl. Owen is a really bright kid. I've got to tell you, his father's bright, but this kid is, I don't know, there's an extra gear in there somewhere. And his sister couldn't be sweeter, she is a Vivien, Julia.

And then there's Mark. Mark teaches photography at Appalachian State University. He's the assistant director of photography, and he's married to Heather, who used to be at school with him when he taught at New England College in Henniker, New Hampshire. I don't know whether you've ever heard of Henniker. It's the only Henniker in the world.

Mark really knows what's going on, too, he's a great guy. But all of our kids are terrific, I mean, they're just great. And fortunately, most of them take after their mother, because she's a bright woman.

Anyway, that's about our kids, and then of course, we've got grandchildren. We've got one, two, three, four, five, six, seven, eight, nine—we have nine grandchildren. And Andrew has been married three times and adopted Lily, a Chinese girl. He lives in Colorado. I hope I'm not forgetting anybody.

CM: Are there any particular events or anniversaries that you recall being a very special moment for you?

HM: Yes, our fiftieth. We went down to Palm Beach to the Breakers, and we renewed our vows over in the church across the street. We took all the kids with us and stayed for four or five days. We had a marvelous time, but the weather was horrible. I still can't believe it. It was forty degrees, and at the price you're paying down there . . .

CM: Are there any smaller moments that you recall, even just a family moment that you recall, as particularly touching or memorable?

HM: Yes. There's got to be a lot. I'm just trying to think. I guess, it's sort of funny, but it was one of our children. The night Andrew was born, we were having dinner at my parents' house in Larchmont, and Vivien had a bag in the car all the time.

And I remember Viv said, "We've got to go."

I said, "What?"

She said, "We've got to go. I'm ready." Jesus, we ran outside, jumped in the car. My mother didn't know what was going on. Well, she did. It took me about fifteen minutes to get to New Rochelle Hospital.

I stopped at the door, tooted the horn, and some security guard came out because it was now eight, nine o'clock. So I said, "She's ready, she's ready!" And he told us to come on in. I said, "I can't come in. I'm going to park the car, you take her out.

So some nurse heard this and she put Viv in a wheelchair and I checked her in. And bang, she had Andrew, just like that.

When Mark was born, Andy, Viv's father, and I went to the hospital. We were at the hospital together and we were just sitting there waiting, waiting. It's like two in the morning. So I said—we used to call him Popi—"Do you think she's all right?"

"Oh, she's all right," he said. Bang, boom. There was a baby, beautiful.

"Listen, Popi, come on, let's go get a drink," I said. So we went into Ray Konopka's bar on the corner across from Iona and New Rochelle High School. I told Mr. Konopka, "I'm a friend of your son Ray, and we just had a baby and I'd like some champagne." It was two o'clock in the morning, and he was just about to close.

CM: Wouldn't be Beechmont Tavern, would it?

HM: Yes, Beechmont Tavern, that's right. So we're drinking champagne and I don't know how long Andy and I were there. But I said, "Listen, I've got to go play golf, I've got a match this morning at ten o'clock." He told me to go ahead. Now he's had a couple drinks but got home all right. I played golf the next day, not very well, but I played.

Anyway, in our marriage, very few days have been bad, and there have been a lot of days. How many days are in fifty-two years? Are you that good of a mathematician?

CM: More than fifteen thousand?

HM: Probably right. That's a lot of days. Holy Moses. With the same person. No, Viv's marvelous. She couldn't be better. You know,

I just wish that everybody could have the same type of life that I've had, and then probably we wouldn't have all the problems we've got in the world today. And that's it.

CM: That's lovely. Any more memories? How did you and Vivien get into racing?

HM: Viv and the children were in a lot of shows—jumpers, hunters—getting better and better, and winning more blue ribbons and trophies. I was sitting in our small den, and I looked up and all around the ceiling were blue ribbons. Even some red-white-and-blue ribbons, which I guess are bigger than just blues.

And I'm looking at them, and I went into the kitchen where Viv was and I brought her into the den. I said, "Honey, look at these beautiful blue ribbons, all of them, marvelous. How much do you think each one of them costs?"

"Oh, fifty dollars, forty dollars," she replied.

I said, "No. How much do you think it costs to win each one of these?"

"Fifty dollars?" she said.

I said, "How about one thousand each?"

She said, "What?"

I said, "Let me ask you a question. Can't we buy a horse that can run around the track in a minute and make us ten thousand dollars, because we haven't gotten any money from these things?" And that basically is how we got started in the racing business.

CM: That's funny.

HM: That's how we got started. And it's still Edition Farm. That's a true story, not that the rest of them aren't true.

In Memoriam

HARRY AND DEBBY

Harry and Vivien, photographed by Hella Hammid, in their barn at Five Chimneys, Purchase, New York, 1975.

HENRY LAWRENCE MALLOY

January 26, 1931 – October 22, 2010

HENRY LAWRENCE MALLOY, OF WACCABUC, NEW YORK, PASSED away on October 22, 2010, after a courageous battle with cancer. Born in New York City on January 26, 1931, the son of Henry Thomas Malloy and Ellen Neville Malloy. He graduated from Mamaroneck High School, class of 1948, attended Colby College, and graduated from Villanova College with a BS in Economics, class of 1953. Mr. Malloy enlisted in the U.S. Navy from 1953 to 1955 attaining the rank of Lieutenant. His employment career spanned from Hearst Publishing, BBD&O advertising agency, Bergdorf Goodman as head of customer service and then on to Republic Hogg Robinson, currently known as Wells Fargo Insurance, where he retired as Vice President in P&C insurance. He was also a former member of Westchester Country Club in Rye, New York, and an active member of Waccabuc Country Club in Waccabuc, New York, Shinnecock Hills Golf Club in Southampton, New York, and Stratton Mountain Country Club in Stratton, Vermont, and The Turf and Field Club. He married the former Vivien Goodman on January 12, 1957. He is survived by his wife Vivien Malloy; five children: Andrew of Castle Rock, Colorado, Debby Winkler of

Warendorf, Germany, Kenneth of Rye, New York, Mark of Los Angeles, California, and Vivi Hanson of Chicago, Illinois; grandchildren: Courtney, Conor, Caitlin, Maggie, Kenny Jr., Shane, Owen and Julia, step granddaughter Bailey, step grandson Jack, and Lily; one brother, John N. Malloy, of Harrison, New York. Henry, known to all his friends as Harry, enjoyed golf above all the other activities that he shared with so many family and friends. He fell in love with Stratton Mountain in 1968 and spent weekends and holidays there skiing with his family. As owner of New York's Edition Farm, he enjoyed his time at the races rooting for his Thoroughbreds. There will be many friends that will miss his great sense of humor and camaraderie they shared with him over the years. Contributions can be made to the charity of one's choice in honor of Henry L. Malloy. The family will receive friends at the Graham Funeral Home, Rye, New York, on Monday from 4 p.m. to 8 p.m. A mass of Christian Burial will be held at the Church of the Resurrection on Tuesday at 10 a.m.

Published in The New York Times *on October 24, 2010.*

DEBBY MALLOY WINKLER

April 3, 1959 – February 21, 2011

DEBBY MALLOY WINKLER, DEVOTED WIFE OF HANS GÜNTER Winkler and daughter of the late Henry L. Malloy and Vivien G. Malloy, died February 21, 2011, following a tragic fall from her horse at her home in Warendorf, Germany.

Born on April 3, 1959, in New Rochelle, New York, Debby was the second of five children. She was the granddaughter of Andrew and Nena Goodman and great-granddaughter of Edwin Goodman, founder of Bergdorf Goodman.

For the first twelve years of her life, Debby shared two passions: Alpine ski racing and horseback riding. At age thirteen, after finishing third in the Eastern Nationals for her division, she reached the pinnacle of junior ski racing when she was selected to the U.S. Ski Team development squad.

At that point, Debby knew that if she wanted to compete at a world class level, she would have to commit to a single sport: she chose her greatest passion, horseback riding. Explaining her decision to her mother in a way that was "classic Debby," she said, "Mom, I can't talk to my skis."

Her successful riding career began in the show rings, pony clubs, and hunting fields of the United States. From an early age, Debby had a gift with horses. She instinctively connected with and understood them, committing herself completely to their care and training. Never one to delegate responsibility for these precious animals, Debby worked tirelessly to bring the talent she knew each horse possessed to its highest potential. As many in the horse world who were lucky enough to know her realized, she made it look easy. She was the penultimate horsewoman.

By the age of fifteen, Debby was considered one of the top junior riders in the country. Trained first by Judy Richter and later by George Morris, she showed at the highest level of competition, including The National Horse Show at Madison Square Garden, The Pennsylvania National Horse Show, and The Washington International. Among her victories as a junior were the 1977 American Jumping Derby in Newport, R.I., aboard Frogs Have Wings, and the Rothmans Grand Prix in Quebec City, Canada, on Plain Jane.

By the age of eighteen she was competing internationally. In France, she trained under Nelson Pessoa. Her next stop was New Zealand and then on to Australia. In 1985, she took the opportunity to return to the States to ride for Gaelic Stables in Virginia. It was there that she met Hans Günter Winkler, who was conducting a clinic in Morven Park. After the clinic, Hans offered Debby the opportunity to ride his horses in Germany. Accepting his offer fulfilled her dream of returning to Europe to compete on an international level. This set the stage for the rest of Debby's life.

Once in Warendorf, Debby established herself as one of the premier equestrians on the European show jumping circuit. In her new home, many people were instantly taken with her kind heart, quick wit, and unrelenting tenacity to be the best rider she could be.

After Debby and Hans married in 1994, they established a formidable team as co-owners of a string of show jumpers. Hans, the most medaled Olympian in equestrian show jumping history, and Debby, his protégé, wife, and love, trained and showed many horses over their twenty-five years together. Debby's successes on the European circuit included victories in Versailles, Hamburg, Rome, Donaueschingen, Bad Oeynhausen, and Spangenberg, amongst others.

Debby was a devoted wife, daughter, sister, aunt, and cousin, who will be missed terribly by her loving family. Despite the miles that separated her from her family in the States, Debby was committed to maintaining close relationships with all and was faithful and frequent in her correspondence. Those lucky enough to have known her will always remember her boundless energy, how she could light up the room with her warmth and humor.

She cared not only through words, but deeds, and was a devoted lifelong friend to many. We will miss her gift for storytelling and her ability to make us laugh.

She lived each day to its fullest, and loved every living thing on this earth.

There was a funeral service in Warendorf on March 1, 2011, and a memorial service in Waccabuc, N.Y., on April 3, 2011, which would have been her fifty-second birthday.

(written by Vivien Malloy Hanson)

Debby's close friend HRH Princess Haya Bint Al Hussein, former president of the International Federation of Equestrian Sports, spoke about Debby in an interview with Horse Talk *magazine, February 26, 2011. Below is an excerpt.*

THERE IS A COMFORT IN KNOWING THAT HORSEMEN AND WOMEN who move on from our world, straight from the saddle, have done so on the terms they would have wished for. And yet I cannot find the

Debby in her top hat and shadbelly, with her sandwich case (the judge could look inside and make sure there was a fresh, edible sandwich, or take points off), on Something Else, at the Junior Hunter Classic, Ox Ridge Horse Show, June 1974.

words to justly pay tribute to Debby. She was so quiet in her ways, so kind and accepting, so humble and gentle that one would have thought she would live forever.

Many of us get into this sport in pursuit of personal greatness and sporting ambition. The race of people like Debby who get into it, and stay with it, for the love of the horse in its absolute purist form, are rare. Rarer still are the ones who strive to conquer the philosophy of the sport and the art form. That was Debby. In her, horse sport has lost one of the greatest human beings and horse-women it ever had.

My heart goes out to Debby's beloved husband, and to the Malloy family, for a wife and a daughter who quietly touched so many people in the most profound way, with eternal elegance and dignity. Rest in peace, Debby. We know, beyond all doubt, that every horse in heaven is waiting for you.

Vivi's eulogy at the memorial service at our home in Waccabuc, on April 3, 2011 (Debby's fifty-second birthday):

As I look out on so many familiar faces dear to Debby, I know that the whole of her family—not only her relatives but also her dear friends— are here to honor her and to celebrate her life. She would have loved this.

In February, just after Debby's death, a dear friend of the family sent beautiful flowers to my mother. On the card it read: Debby is a shining star! In the days that followed, as I tried to grasp what had happened, this phrase kept coming back to me. During these past weeks, as I've struggled to accept that she is gone from our side, I have come to understand why that phrase stuck with me. As I re-flected on my memories of Debby, I realized that, in many ways, to me, her little sister, Debby was like a star.

From my earliest memories, my big sister seemed special. Ex-traordinary. Set apart. She was authentic—for better or worse, you always knew where you stood with Debby, and she was incapable of guile. To me, she lived each day with certainty. She seemed to hold within her much more than the mundane details of everyday life. I always remember her in deliberate motion, and perhaps like many younger siblings, I felt that I was constantly trying to catch up.

Debby never acted "by committee." She acted decisively. "Lead, follow, or get out of the way" was a favorite quote of hers. An early decisive act occurred while Debby attended Whitby School. When an unfortunate kindergarten classmate of hers had the audacity to claim that her daddy was better than our daddy, Debby took it upon herself to champion her hero, our dad, by pushing the little upstart into the sandbox. She walked away and didn't think twice—no one was better than my dad. It was a story she shared with us last fall as we gathered by my father's side, still firm in her resolve that she was right.

Though she was truly in her element among horses, she was a natural leader among the children in our family. A tribute to her leadership was her ability to somehow convince the entire Malloy

Gelding, 8, Wins Jump

Special to The New York Times

DEVON, Pa., May 28—JJust about five years ago, Henry L. Malloy and his family built a small shed on their property in Purchase, N.Y.

"The idea," said his 18-year-old daughter, Debbie, after she rode Frogs Have Wings to victory today in the junior jumper class at the Devon Horse Show, "was to have a shelter for a pretty scrawny little pony that we had bought for about $50."

The shed has expanded into Edition Farms. The shed, in fact, is no more. Now there is a barn in its place, and the Malloys have seven horses of their own plus a couple of boarders on hand.

Malloy, an insurance broker with Penn General, does not ride, and, according to his daughter, sometimes appears distressed at all the equestrian activity on his 10 acres.

Happy When She Wins

"My father is very pleased when I win," said Miss Malloy, a graduate of the Rye Country Day School, who is scheduled to enter Lafayette University for the spring semester next year. "He doesn't know too much about hunters and I think he wonders if it's all worth it when I lose."

Miss Malloy has three brothers and two sisters. One brother and one sister also ride in shows. Her mother, Vivian, is a former equestrienne who piloted a horse named First Edition in her days in the ring.

As for Frogs Have Wings, he's an 8-year-old chestnut gelding who bounced into contention for the junior jumper championship with his victory. With one class remaining, Frogs Have Wings has 5 points to 8 for Hillary Kuhne's Honkey Dory, who is leading.

Debby on Frogs Have Wings in their winning jump, 1977, covered by *The New York Times* (with a couple of small errors).

family, her dear Malloy cousins included, to celebrate a wedding between Special Edition, the most patient pony on earth, and our cousin Chris Malloy. Debby officiated. I was the flower girl, and we all wore matching Edition Farm sweatshirts.

But Debby didn't lead or teach in a heavy-handed way. In fact, one of the most essential things I learned from Debby was something she never told me. She didn't have to tell me what a true horsewoman is, because I saw it and understood it in her. She was the real thing. I knew that my love of horses was on a different level from hers, and, in many ways that insight helped me to find my true path. Like navigating by the light of a star, Debby helped to guide me toward my true talent.

Debby began the adventure of her life early. She made the difficult and monumental decision to leave home before she was twenty, an act that left me in awe of her courage. As sisters with so much distance between us, it was hard to connect as we made our way through life. We chose different paths, and for many years, we let our different choices define us as sisters.

Last fall, when our dad called us home, the precious days we spent together were a blessing. We couldn't have known then the profound gift he gave us—to bring us together—just Mom, Dad and the children, the way it all began. We spent hours telling the countless stories that made up our life together. Debby was particularly moved by those days, suspended and rarefied, and she rarely left Dad's side.

As happens when all the details of life fall away and you are united in a single purpose, we all realized what is true and lasting. Perhaps that was the real blessing. During the days and weeks after my father's death, I came to treasure my sister, Debby, in a way that I had not before. I understood, finally, that though to me she seemed to live her life with an inner road map she rarely questioned, she was acutely aware of "the road not taken" and, like me, though she lived far from home, what grounded her were the friends and loved ones she had found early in her life.

Despite her unforgiving schedule, Debby found a way to stay connected to us all. In the weeks after our father died, as the stories and memories came pouring out of all of us, it was Debby who began collecting them. Her emails came fast and furious, bursting with energy and love. Debby channeled her grief into creating something precious and lasting, encouraging us all to add to the list of "Dadisms," pick our favorite memory, tell our favorite Dad story. She wrote of how lucky we were to have had such an amazing dad, and many times without her knowing it, her words would replace my sorrow with laughter and gratitude. She focused, as she always had, on what keeps on, not what ends. During those difficult days, she shined light onto the darkness in my heart.

So back to the phrase that has stayed with me: Debby is a shining star!

After Dad died it was Debby who had told all of us to be on the lookout for signs—signs that would let us know he was still with us, watching over us. Though not superstitious in a fearful way, Debby was Irish, and as such, she never took for granted the power of a good luck charm or the meaning of a sign.

So, with her voice in my ear, I kept watch. Two days after her death, I stopped to listen to a melancholy jazz tune that happened to be playing. The melody was familiar, but it took me a minute to recognize "Have Yourself a Merry Little Christmas." I registered that it was an odd thing to hear on a February night and walked outside, the lyrics continuing in my head. Then I came to the line, "Hang a shining star upon the highest bough," and I looked up at the overcast night sky. There were only two stars in the sky, right next to each other, over my head.

As Debby shared at Dad's funeral, his parents came and took him home. So, I believe, our father came and took Debby home with him, and they are watching over us together.

As I grieve for the loss of her loving, laughing smile and the hugs that made up for all the months apart, I think of her now like a star. Though she is far away, the memory of her love, energy, and laughter can lighten our hearts. Though she is gone from our side, she is keeping watch over our shoulder, brilliant, strong, and constant. And though she has left this life, her husband, Hans, her loving family, and her family of friends, her life ended when she was doing what she loved above all else.

So Debby, I won't say goodbye, instead I'll say what we told each other all those times we parted after getting together: I'll see you. Because on the next starry night, I'll walk outside, look up to find the brightest star, and there you'll be.

I'd like to end by reading a quote at Debby's request.

"…I bade you farewell, wished you a journey full of blessings.
Every hour you exist, when you go to sleep and when you awake
Keep in mind the troth between us. I am waiting for you.
Come safely back, come safely back."

ACKNOWLEDGMENTS

FIRST, TO MY DAUGHTER VIVI, WHO GAVE ME HER TIME, HER WISE counsel, her patient and learned ear. She was my original editor. "Mom, do you really want to say that?" was her mantra. I shed many tears of memory as we soldiered on with our work for four or five days at a time, after she dropped the children at school and before she had to pick them up. Vivi is so intelligent, so well-read, so soft-spoken. She urged me to read other biographies and I did, lots of them. I think my favorite was Robert Gottlieb's, editor at Simon & Schuster and Alfred A. Knopf. He talked about the ways in which his authors were different and how many were difficult. How one would storm out of his office and slam the door after a disagreement over a semicolon. I was not that insistent on grammar—only content. "Hey," Vivi would say, "After all, it is your book and your life." Thank you, Vivi. You understood that only I knew the true story—I was there.

To Thea, my niece. Vivi said that we should give even the rough first draft to Thea, a published author, a professor of creative writing, and part of the family story—as well as someone who would understand it was a work in progress. Vivi and I read every word of your critique and your compliments and encouragement. We did everything you said and hope you like the result.

To Carol Makovitch. I spoke my story into your little tape recorder, and you transcribed my words. There were many tears and giggles, and it was, at times, rough going. You divided my life into chapters, and I got a sense of what the book would finally look like. You interviewed Harry and Debby before their deaths, and I am so, so thankful you were able to do that. The original text was conversational. Then came the hard part: getting the text into narrative, written form. Thank you for setting me out on the path that is now coming to an end—publication. You are a gem, and I thank my friend Kathy Landman for introducing us. Networking in life brings forth wonderful connections, as happened to us.

To Carolyn Viola John. We worked together on the text to polish it grammatically and factually. Then we catalogued all the photos, placing them in the correct chapters. You helped me refine the chapters and their titles. I often got sidetracked as we spoke of travel and books, and you brought me back to the task at hand. You were strict with facts and grammar, and we spent time looking things up. I learned a lot of Cuban and United States history in our sessions. Thank you for all the hard work.

To Mark. You are a dear and talented son, and the photo work reflects all your effort. I am blessed to have you in my life and proud as punch that you are my son/photo editor supreme.

To Trisha Thompson and Fred Levine of Small Batch Books. Thank you for taking on this task of getting my book to bed, as they say. Again, networking in life is amazing—my sister Minkie's husband was in publishing for years and knew a man who had just published his memoir. He recommended I call him to find out who his publisher was, and it was, indeed, you, Small Batch Books. I am glad we found each other, and I hope you've enjoyed the process as much as I have.

Of course, there have been so many family and friends who kept asking, "When will this book be finished?" And so, I knew I had to persevere, even when life got in the way. I have always loved to write, so that part was easy. It was the putting aside other things that I found difficult to do—my family, my farm, my friends, my doggies, and, of course, the horses. . . .

My editors—all of them—would ask, "What will your Wellesley classmates say if _____?" Fill in the blank—if my historical facts were erroneous, if my references to books or plays were incorrect, and, God forgive, as an English major, if my grammar was sloppy. That definitely made me sit up, pay strict attention, and be very careful. I want my class of '54 to be proud of me too!

Finally, I hope that someday Cuba will be free again. I hope that it will come back to all its natural and architectural glory. The spirit of the Cubans will never be snuffed out—their warmth, their humor, their music, their love of family. I am proud I was born there. Even though I left so soon, I feel that Cuban, as well as Spanish and Italian, blood runs in my veins. What a combination, what a miracle life is!

God bless us all,
Vivien